Market Cities

How City Leaders Use Smart Policy and the
Power of the Market for Economic Development

STUART C. STROTHER

NA

NorthAmerican
Business Press
Atlanta - Seattle - South Florida - Toronto

North American Business Press, Inc
Atlanta, Georgia
Seattle, Washington
South Florida
Toronto, Canada

Market Cities: How City Leaders Use Smart Policy and the Power
of the Market for Economic Development
ISBN: 9780991607136
© 2014 All Rights Reserved.

Along with trade books for various business disciplines, the North American
Business Press also publishes a variety of academic-peer reviewed journals.

Library of Congress Control Number: 2014959548
Library of Congress
Cataloging in Publication Division
101 Independence Ave., SE
Washington, DC 20540-4320
Printed in the United States of America
First Edition

TABLE OF CONTENTS

LIST OF GUEST CASES

CHAPTER 1

Introduction

The City of Louisville, Kentucky was a city in decline. Families and individuals had been leaving the city since the 1950s, many of them moving from the urban core to nearby unincorporated suburbs; a migration made possible by the newly constructed freeways of Eisenhower's Federal-Aid Highway Act of 1956. During the time from 1960 to 2000, the city had lost 34% of its population dropping from 390,639 to just 256,231.

Spacious and cheap new homes were springing up in the suburbs, thanks to ready financing made available by the Federal Housing Administration which provided mortgage insurance and liquid funds to local mortgage banks. Grass was greener in the suburbs and urban residents, especially whites were chasing the American Dream in the 'burbs.

Businesses were also closing their doors in the "Falls City," a nickname based on Louisville's location on the Ohio River. A two-mile fossilized reef called the "Falls of the Ohio" was the only stretch of the 900-plus mile riverway that was not navigable. The need for porters to carry cargo from one side of the falls to the other was the reason the City of Louisville was founded. After the Civil War, Louisville grew to be a major industrial supplier in the efforts to rebuild the South. The Louisville and Nashville Railroad rapidly expanded to be the primary carrier for all of the South which further developed the city as a major transportation hub.

Louisville thrived during our nation's Gilded Age as a strong manufacturing economy was established to produce important goods such as aircraft, tires, vehicles, appliances, chemicals, steel pipe, concrete and ships. The city's "sin industries" were robust including the production of tobacco and alcohol, especially cigarettes and bourbon. The manufacturing in Louisville only grew stronger during the times of the two World Wars as factories operated at high capacity to meet wartime needs.

By the 1950s, however, many businesses were closing, with much of the manu-facturing being moved to cheaper locations in the deep South, or offshore. Many companies producing services, instead of tangible goods, found it cost-effective to close their urban operations and reopen in the suburbs where land was plenti-ful, new construction was cheap, taxes were lower, and the workforce was more educated. In addition to these "pull" factors; the crime, congestion, density and pollution associated with city life also "pushed" businesses and individuals out-ward. By the 1990s city leaders began earnestly worrying about whether Louisville's economy would ever recover. How can the economy be developed?

This is the central question this book seeks to answer: How can a city develop its economy? Like the Louisvillians, city leaders across the U.S. face similar chal-lenges. Productive citizens and businesses alike may be leaving the city for other locations in the U.S. or abroad. As businesses close, workers are laid off. The money previously spent by the business or the workers is no longer spent and multiplied in the local economy. To develop an economy, cities must have businesses, thus a major focus of economic development policy is to attract, retain and develop businesses in the city.

This book is a study of the theory, practice, and impact of economic development policy and practice in US cities. The inquiry presented in this book is guided by the age-old questions, "To what extent can government influence markets?" and "Should government step back and let free market forces grow the economy?"

For centuries scholars like Adam Smith and John Maynard Keynes have argued about the place of government in capitalist economies. Their theories, and the theories of others, have led to a vast array of economic development policies, practices, and programs employed at every level of government in the U.S. This book explores the theoretical perspectives driving economic development policy, then examines current economic development practices, and finally, empirically evaluates the impact of the practices.

Throughout the book, the wisdom of government intervention is analyzed, ques-tioned, praised where successful and criticized where unsuccessful.

The Problem of Resource Scarcity

City governments face the classic economic problem of resource scarcity, and they experience the dilemma of having to choose how to allocate these scarce resources among numerous competing interests. In the name of economic development, local governments assign public resources and employ various strategies and tactics. The efforts of economic development officials focus both on supply-side economics (attracting, retaining, or expanding local firms) and demand-side economics (redistributive policies, human capital development, and even "equity" policies).

It is thought that these efforts result in positive growth in the local economy as measured by jobs, firms, tax revenue, and incomes (see for example, Ahlbrandt and DeAngeliz, 1987; Bowman, 1988; Bartik, 1991, Eisenschitz, 1993; Eisinger, 1988; Reese and Fasenfest, 1997; and Schwarz and Volgy, 1992).

Some of the literature indicates, however, that certain economic development efforts yield no results, or possibly even negative results (see for example, Schmenner, 1982; Feiock, 1991; Lynch, 1995; Green, Fleischmann, and Kwong, 1996; Dewar, 1998; Hinkley and Hsu, 2000). If economic development practices are ineffective, public resources have been wasted.

Public funds earmarked for economic development could have potentially been put to better use elsewhere. Libertarian economists argue that these resources should never have been made "public" (transferred from private hands to government through taxes) but instead should have been left in the hands of entrepreneurs and individuals.

What is "economic development?"
The phrase "economic development" takes on different meaning in different bodies of scholarly literature. At the macroeconomic level, "economic development" typically refers to national government intervention in markets resulting in an outward shift in the production possibilities curve, or, simply put, economic growth.

At the international level, "development economics" refers to activities of wealthier nations providing aid to "developing" countries.

A third definition of "economic development" concerns subnational governments. Bartik (1994) offers a definition as state and local government programs "that assist individual businesses with tax or financial subsidies, or special public services, in order to increase local jobs or improve local businesses' competitiveness" (p. 847).

"Local" economic development refers to public and private sector actors on the local level, but the phrase more often describes the activities of community-based organizations rather than local governments. Separate distinct bodies of literature exist that represent the macroeconomic, international, subnational, and local perspectives of economic development. This book focuses on the economic development policies and programs of subnational city governments in the U.S.

Much of the economic development literature focuses on the efforts of local government officials. The expectation is that those from the public sector can stimulate growth in the private sector. This assumption runs throughout the theoretical economic development literature. The empirical literature, however, routinely finds the private sector grows and improves as a result of market forces rather than government intervention. That is, businesses and individuals thrive with less government intervention in the economy. Of course, governments thrive with more government intervention, whether or not the overall economy improves.

Rowing or Steering?

The metaphor of rowing or steering a canoe illustrates the dilemma of government actors managing an economy. In a fast running river, efforts at rowing are ineffective in moving the canoe and rowing certainly cannot change the current. Instead, the paddler should just learn to be at harmony with the current and just steer the canoe. Similarly, in economics, government bureaucrats have proven effete in answering the basic economic questions of who produces? and who consumes? In this book, we take the approach that solving market problems (such as an absence of employers, or a labor force skills mismatch) requires market-based solutions.

In many cities, such as Louisville, city leaders understand the power of the free market and apply market-based solutions to economic problems. While it may seem oxymoronic to expect government officials to act like free market agents, the reality is that market-based solutions, even government policies, consistently and empirically are associated with economic growth. (See Chapter 12 of this book for a relevant literature review and an empirical analysis). Of course, in many cities private actors such as business leaders, chambers of commerce and others are actively involved in economic development practice.

Where market principles are applied, whether by public or private agents, we are calling these places Market Cities. It is the aim of this book to provide an objective survey of economic development policies and practices, but also to provide the reader with example after example of how Market Cities have improved their local economy through the power of free enterprise.

Background

Part One of this book covers background and theory. Chapter 2 chronicles the history of federal, state and local government economic development intervention in U.S. cities. Distinct eras of federal government urban polices are described. The "retrenchment" of the federal government from urban affairs and structural changes in the U.S. economy are offered as partial explanations of why state and local governments have become more active in economic development policy and practice in recent decades. In other words, federal government intervention in local economies was not successful, therefore "retrenchment" was essentially a free-market decision. The label "decentralization" could also be applied as state and local governments expanded their efforts at managing the economy. But cities are not all equal in terms of their ability to affect local economic matters.

Local governance structures are established under state statutes or local charters. A coherent government structure should produce clear assignment of responsibility, good policy making processes, and effective implementation of policies. Local government is also enhanced by members of a governing board that work well together. In general, a strong mayor or council-manager form of government is best equipped to implement economic growth policies, such as using incentives to attract businesses or initiating capital improvements which might improve a city's business climate and therefore its economic prospects.

Economic Development Theories

No single theory fully explains economic development policies, but numerous economic, political, and locational theories inform the economic development policies and practices in U.S. cities.

A key assumption of economics is that people make rational decisions, which means they always seek to improve their own welfare. In a local economy, government, private firms, households and individuals all benefit from overall economic growth of the local market. In theory then, all of these stakeholders desire increased output in the basic resources: land, labor, and capital. The classic economic dilemma, however, suggests that resources are scarce. We never quite have enough of what we want. Not enough resources, money, jobs, firms, etc.

Public and private sector leaders respond to the economic dilemma with numerous programs and policies commonly dubbed "economic development" activities. The goal of these programs is to increase output resulting in economic growth and higher living standards for all in the region. Numerous theories exist about the best way to increase output. In Chapter 3 of this book, the theories of classical, neoclassical, and Keynesian economics are described with an emphasis on the way these theories influence economic development policy.

Conservatism, neo-conservatism, and liberalism are the political perspectives most relevant to economic development. Conservatives, neo-conservatives and liberals both agree that political and social life should be built on the following principles: 1) individual equality, 2) prosperity replacing poverty, and 3) democratic rule (Weinberger, 2001 p 39). They agree these are worthwhile ends, but the means to accomplish these ends are disputed. The general ideas and principles of these political philosophies are described in Chapter 4 of this book with an explanation of how these theories influence economic development practice.

Many location theories also influence economic development policy, including central place theory, the theory of market areas, the theory of agglomeration, and growth pole theory. These theories attempt to explain the location decisions of individuals and businesses within a geographic area. Spatially-based economic development programs such as enterprise zones and tax increment finance districts give evidence that economic development policymakers are somewhat influenced by location theories. Chapter 7 explains place-based theories of development.

Economic Development Practice

Numerous economic development practices are utilized in U.S. cities. An immense body of literature exists in the scholarly, trade, and popular presses disclosing the latest economic development methods, programs and practices. The literature consistently cites three objectives of economic development practice: 1) attracting new businesses, 2) retaining existing businesses and 3) developing new businesses. The percentage of time the typical economic development agency spends in these three categories is shown in Figure 1.1. Developing new businesses gets most of the attention (38%) with retention (29%) and attraction (25%) receiving less attention.

Figure 1.1 Percent Time Spent on Various Economic Development Activities (source: ICMA)

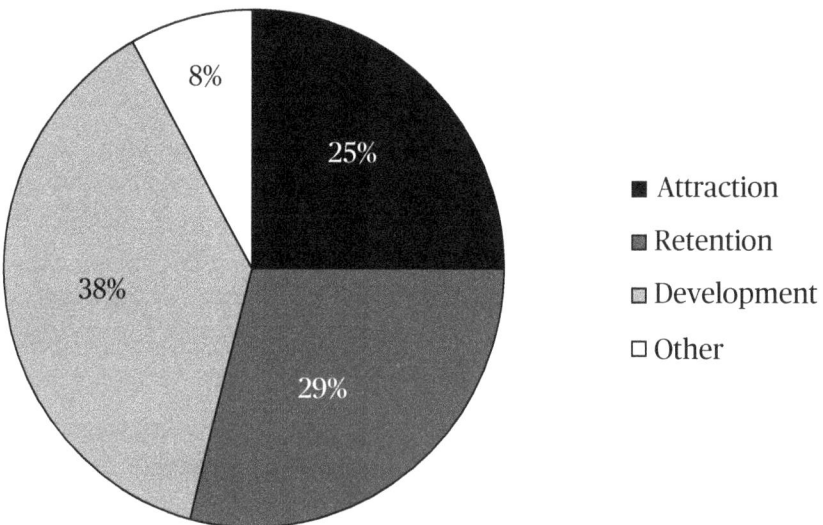

Part Two of this book includes Chapter 5, 6 and 7 which fall under the heading of business attraction incentives. Chapter 5 describes marketing techniques cities use to make businesses aware of their city. Most cities have dedicated part of their websites to the economic development function, which is a relatively low cost technique, whereas other cities employ expansive (and expensive) marketing campaigns including taking out full-page ads in publications such as the Wall Street Journal or The Economist.

Chapter 6 describes fiscal incentives cities use to grow their economy. In some instances, new businesses are given rate reductions on expenses such as property taxes, permits, or utility rates. In other instances, businesses are given very generous incentive packages including free land and tax waivers. Many criticize city leaders who give away public resources to private firms, but other argue the "incentive wars" are necessary, because every other city in the U.S. is offering the same incentives. To not offer them puts the city at a competitive disadvantage.

Chapter 7 details various location-based economic development techniques. On the local level, city leaders have been known to implement programs such as free land, land write-down, or tax-increment financing. A number of federal programs also exist, including Enterprise Zones.

Part Three of the book communicates business retention and development techniques. Chapter 8 describes common business retention practices including publicity for local firms, ombudsman programs and export assistance. The idea is that local leaders can assist local businesses with their business functions, such that if they succeed and are profitable, the business will remain in the city. A business that stays will continue to spend money in the local economy, and hire local workers who will also contribute to the local economy. These business retention practices are often carried out in the private sector, especially by the local chamber of commerce. In this way, private organizations are hard at work using free market principles to assist local businesses.

Chapter 9 illustrates business development techniques. Hearing the word "business" many think of large corporations, but the reality is that most companies are small- or medium-sized enterprises. Research shows these small businesses are responsible for most job creation. City leaders would therefore do well to facilitate the development of new private enterprises in their locale. Chapter 9 lists many of these techniques such as business development centers, business incubators and executive-on-loan programs.

Chapter 10 digresses from the market-based local economic development policies which dominate this book. Such policies, rooted in neoclassical economic views, suggest improving the local economy by supporting private firms. When businesses succeed, employees directly share in the success of the business through wages earned. Other citizens benefit indirectly as the wages and business expenses are multiplied throughout the local economy. In this chapter we diverge from such neoclassical economic thinking and put on a Keynesian economic hat, which looks a bit like the liberal political hat. In other words, this chapter introduces local economic development strategies and policies which focus more on the individual than the private firm. Human capital policies are those that focus on increasing the skills, training and education of the workers, whereas so-called "equity" policies intend to bring the poor into full economic participation, especially by helping them get jobs. The federal Welfare-to-Work program is one such example.

Chapter 11, covering public-private partnerships, is guest written with Professor Steven G. Koven, a leading economic development scholar from the University of Louisville. A public-private partnership is a formal complementary relationship between two or more public and private entities to achieve a common objective in which all parties derive some benefit. They have been on the rise in recent years as a means of "power-sharing" between public and private organizations. These partnerships also represent an opportunity for the public sector to shift risk to the private sector.

When public-private partnerships are tendered for the purpose of economic development, the overall objective of the partnership is usually to increase the number of jobs or the number of employers in a region, or to revitalize the physical assets of an urban area. The chapter describes the rise of partnerships in recent years, methods of partnership for economic development, and different partnership models especially for infrastructure projects.

Economic Development Impact

When the number of firms increases, economic growth is thought to be more likely to occur. In addition to attraction, retention and development techniques, city governments also use certain location techniques, human capital development techniques, "equity" techniques, fiscal tools, and public private partnerships. These are all described in this book, and the prevalence of these various economic development practices is also reported. The source for the statistical data regarding is the Economic Development survey conducted by the International City/County Management Association.

Local governments invest millions of dollars in economic development programs, yet few empirical studies exist that examine the impact of these programs. Much of the current literature of urban economic development is theoretical and anecdotal rather than empirical. Certain studies investigate impacts of indirect policy measures such as tax rates and general government expenditures, but few studies empirically analyze the specific impact of economic development policies. The scant empirical research generally contends that government economic development efforts are only modestly correlated with economic growth. A common theme throughout the literature, as Dewar (1998) points out, is that government development programs rarely "develop" as much as was hoped.

The empirical study reported in the final Chapter 12 of this book seeks to determine whether the economic development practices employed by local governments in U.S. cities are correlated with measures of economic growth in U.S. cities. The major hypothesis states, "The level of public sector economic development activity in U.S. cities is positively correlated with local economic growth." It is thought that cities that are more proactive in their economic development activity will have more economic growth, all other things being equal. This hypothesis is addressed using inferential statistical analysis and a quantitative data set built from multiple sources.

The study uses cities as the unit of analysis and analyzes economic growth from one period to another. Because economic development policy is designed to have wide impacts on a local economy, this study considers changes in the number of firms, jobs, and income as evidence of economic growth. The source of the economic growth data is the U.S. Census Bureau's County and City Data Book. A large set of U.S. cities (n = 412) is used to represent all U.S. cities with populations over 25,000 (N = 1,070).

Survey data are used as independent variable measures of economic development activity. Some of the economic development variables are economic development staff size per capita, per capita government spending on economic development, the number of economic development initiatives (for attraction, retention, development and "equity"), the use of incentives, and the use of innovative loan programs. Certain control variables that represent factors that affect city economies are also used. Perhaps economic growth is explained by control variables rather than economic development policy variables.

The study discovers only modest evidence that local government economic development programs are correlated with economic growth in American cities. Despite this discouraging news, the results of this study do have certain applications to real-life local economic development policy decisions, which are detailed in the chapter. Mainly the results indicate that market-based policies and programs (i.e. assisting businesses to become successful) have the most statistically reliable results. It is the Market Cities which are likely to experience economic growth.

Contemporary Context

The context in which we live and work has dramatically changed over the last few decades. Thanks to reduced trade barriers and rapid technological change, economic activity has greatly expanded beyond national borders into what we now call a globalized economy. Workers are increasingly more willing and able to choose jobs in cities, states, or even nations, far away from their place of origin. Similarly, reduced trade barriers have allowed firms to sell their products in faraway markets, and to produce their products in faraway places. Indeed the globalization of markets, production, and culture is having dramatic effects on our lives and work.

In response to the increased mobility of individuals and firms, city leaders across the world endeavor to retain and attract these individuals and firms. In the post-World War Two economy, cities competed with each other to attract new industrial firms. New businesses provided good-paying manufacturing jobs that created stable local economies. This "smoke-stack" chasing later gave way to urban development policies that fostered the creation of new businesses. Local governments and chambers of commerce assisted entrepreneurs in founding new enterprises. In the 1980s, we learned from Birch (1987) that these small businesses were responsible for most of the job creation in America. In the 1990s, researchers such as Richard Florida (2002, 2007) identified individuals as the drivers of economic growth. City leaders took note and determined to make their cities attractive places not only for companies, but also for individuals.

With the internet and telecom boom of the 1990s, high tech businesses became the focus of economic development officials especially as many heavy industries declined due to automation and global outsourcing. Such business trends facilitated a major population migration from northern industrial Rust Belt cities, to Sun Belt cities in the southwest. Meanwhile, as Detroit declined, foreign automakers such as Toyota, Hyundai and Mercedes built factories in a new cheap-labor, non-union Auto Belt stretching from Ohio to Alabama.

The Great Recession of 2007-2009 resulted in many business failures (and, of course, many government failures also, which receive little press) and the highest unemployment rates we've seen since the Great Depression. At the same time, city governments are facing even greater resource scarcity, resulting in a time of great economic turbulence. Within this dynamic context, I offer this book, which details economic development background, theoretical foundations, policies, and empirical evaluation. Before we start, let's find out what happened in Louisville.

Back to Louisville

Up until World War Two, Louisville was one of the nation's most prosperous cities. One third of the workforce held high-paying manufacturing jobs making important products such as GE appliances, Ford trucks, Reynolds aluminum, Jim Beam bourbon whiskey and Marlboro cigarettes. The transportation and finance sectors were as advanced as any other city's. But these mature industries do not readily innovate nor adapt well to changing economic conditions.

Socially, the city was also experiencing much turbulence. White flight saw the city lose over 100,000 white residents to the suburbs and nearby unincorporated areas. The urban core, meanwhile, still had not been rebuilt since the pressures of the Great Depression and two World Wars, which all took a toll on infrastructure such as roads, bridges and schools. The failed Urban Renewal policies of the 1960s resulted in the bulldozing of the city's key black business district. This and other instances of racism sowed the seeds for an inner city riot in 1968 and violent protests by blue collar whites in 1975. Educationally, Kentucky lags behind the rest of the nation, and many uneducated people from the rural counties were also moving to Louisville.

The national economic crises of the 1970s and 1980s were particularly hard on Louisville. The city essentially de-industrialized as the number of manufacturing jobs dropped from 29% in 1969 to just 11% in 2005. Important national brands such as International Harvester, Seagram's, American Standard, and even the venerable L&N Railroad were all closing their operations in the city. Over 30,000 jobs were lost.

In the 1980s, however, a group of small but vocal young business entrepreneurs were challenging the old ways of doing government and commerce. The entrepreneurs along with a non-establishment mayor (politics are very parochial in Kentucky), set a recovery in motion that focused on three goals: 1) support and expand existing economic opportunities for which the city is already prepared, 2) restore functional civic relationships, and 3) prepare for new economic opportunities (Bennett and Gatz, 2008). These goals were largely achieved as the city elected an entrepreneurial mayor, investment was made into public education, and the research capacities of the University of Louisville were greatly enhanced.

A group of business leaders created their own business attraction campaign initially called Project 2000 which supplanted the disjointed and ineffective development efforts of the city government and the local chamber of commerce. The group raised millions of dollars and was successful in recruiting a number of smaller businesses, especially back-office service jobs. Meanwhile the national trend of corporate consolidation resulted in many branch locations of national companies closing their doors in Louisville. The group kept the faith, however, and eventually had three great successes.

United Parcel Service had moved from Chicago to Louisville in 1981, and by the mid-1990s was thinking of moving again because it had to expand its operations. In 1997 it was announced that UPS was considering closing their headquarters operation in Louisville, Kentucky and relocating to another U.S. city. Due to their difficulty in staffing their late night package handling positions in Louisville, UPS began looking for another city that could meet their midnight labor demands. Facing the immediate threat of losing the city's major employer, government and private sector leaders in Louisville developed a plan to retain UPS and help it expand. Typical economic development financial initiatives were engaged to prevent the departure of UPS, but in the end, the creation of the innovative Metropolitan College program became the key component in retaining UPS. This case study is further described in Chapter 11 of this book.

The second major success of the Project 2000 group, and its affiliates, was the turnaround of the labor climate. Formerly dubbed "Strike City" in the 1980s, Louisville was infamous for its clashes between labor and management, especially at the manufacturing sites. Manufacturers such as GE and Ford were tempted to move production elsewhere. City leaders, both public, private and at the University of Louisville, changed the labor climate with a number of initiatives which helped the two sides to better get along. In the end major manufacturers were retained in the city.

The third major success is with healthcare. By the 1950s and 1960s much of Louisville's downtown was crumbling. Businesses had moved out and the large shipping centers along the waterfront were no longer active. City leaders wisely set aside part of the city adjacent to the CBD and designated it a health sciences center. With additional investment into the medical and dental schools of the University, and private investment in hospitals and health insurance, the Louisville health sciences industry grew to include 10% of all jobs in the city. Entrepreneurs built many successful related businesses, most notably Humana and Kindred Healthcare, which today are two Fortune 500 companies.

Louisville has a bright past as an industrially prosperous and relevant U.S. city, but the Falls City city fell into economic decline in the 1960s, 1970s, and 1980s. But in the 1990s a group of business leaders eagerly and intentionally worked to re-develop the economy. Following free-market principles, but still partnering with local and state government officials the team spurred an economic renaissance. The aim of this book is to encourage readers to similarly follow market principles to develop urban economies into what we might call Market Cities.

CHAPTER 2

HISTORICAL BACKGROUND OF LOCAL ECONOMIC DEVELOPMENT

This chapter chronicles the historic intervention of federal, state, and local governments in the economies of U.S. cities. The U.S. system of federalism is currently characterized by major decision-making at the federal level, while implementation is carried out at the state and local levels. Koven and Lyons observe, "The national level of government often supplies the funding and defines the rules, but it relies upon the state and local levels to implement the policy" (2003, p. 4). After a brief explanation of three different public policy models, this chapter describes the historic involvement of federal, state and local governments in local economic affairs.

Models of Public Policy

Public policies that drive government intervention in economic markets take on three forms: allocational, redistributive, and developmental (Peterson, 1991). Through allocational policies, public funds are spent on public goods such as parks, sanitation, and police and fire protection. Redistributive policies spend public funds on private individuals through programs such as welfare and subsidized housing. Developmental policies are designed to attract private sector development and investment, so public funds are spent on projects such as airport expansion, convention centers and waterfronts. Table 2.1 illustrates these three policy types.

Table 2.1 Public Policy Models

Policy Type	Examples	Public Investment and Return
Allocational	parks, sanitation, police and fire protection	$1 tax = $1 return to average taxpayer
Redistributive	welfare, subsidized housing	$1 tax = less than $1 return to average taxpayer
Developmental	convention centers, education, waterfront development	$1 investment = greater than $1 return to average taxpayer

Based on Peterson, 1991.

During the late 1960s and 1970s, government involvement in urban economies was largely driven by redistributive policies, such as transfer payments (Nathan, 1977; and Peterson, 1991). But recent years have seen a shift in public policy away from redistributive policy (as evidenced by welfare reform) toward developmental policy. Another notable change is the "retrenchment" of the federal government out of urban affairs, and the increasing role of state and local government involvement in local economies.

Federal Government Intervention in Local Economic Development

The history of federal involvement in local economic affairs can be understood by grouping the events into five major eras: dual federalism, cooperative federalism, suburban development, The War on Poverty, and new federalism (Kleinberg, 1995). Table 2.2 illustrates the different eras of federal involvement in local economic affairs.

Table 2.2 Major Eras of Federal Involvement in Local Economic Affairs

Era	Time Frame	Key Characteristics
Dual Federalism	1776-1933	limited federal influence states viewed as independent sovereigns

Cooperative Federalism	1933-1945	FDR responds to Great Depression with New Deal
		federal government cooperates with local governments to deliver services
		massive federal government "safety net" programs:
		    social security
		    welfare
		    unemployment
		    FDIC
		    public housing
		    job programs

Suburban Development	1945-1964	guaranteed home loans for veterans Ike develops U.S. highway network suburban sprawl urban decay Urban Renewal (a.k.a. "Negro Removal")
War on Poverty	1964-1969	LBJ declares war on poverty massive redistributive federal programs Community Action Programs Model Cities
New Federalism	1969-present	federal retrenchment decentralization federal spending cuts block grants (UDAG) replace categorical grants

Dual Federalism

Dual federalism has its roots in colonial times, when states were viewed as independent sovereigns, and the national government only regulated a few issues. Under this system, "all powers not explicitly designated as federal were reserved to the states" (Kleinberg, 1995, p. 95). Federal influence on states was limited. Although the nation was rapidly urbanizing, there was "no substantial federal involvement until the 1930s" (Kleinberg, 1995, p. 95). The only exception is, perhaps, the federal government's land grant program in which cities could secure federal land for public schools, railroads, and other similar public building projects.

Cooperative Federalism

National, state, and local governments cooperated to meet the new economic challenges posed by the Great Depression. The federal government bailed out many municipal governments that otherwise would have been bankrupt (Kleinberg, 1995). At this time FDR launched the New Deal, which was a moment of vast federal expansion into urban affairs. The Great Depression and resulting poverty represented a challenge to urban areas.

The New Deal provided a huge "hand up" for urban dwellers through programs such as social security, welfare, unemployment, FDIC, public housing, numerous job programs such as Works Progress Administration, and an aggressive Public Works Administration (PWA) program that began massive construction projects. Many of these programs were administered through categorical grants from the federal government to states and localities.

As is usually the case with those who control the money, the national government also influenced the development, design, and implementation of many urban policies and programs. For some programs such as public housing the federal government provided funds and direction, but left the administration of the program up to lower level jurisdictions. This intergovernmental relationship is a prime example of "cooperative federalism."

The New Deal is characterized as a mixture of redistributive policies. The organizational milestones of the New Deal are the creation of the "big four" agencies that are "the core of the urban policy system," PWA, WPA, USHA (United States Housing Authority), and the FHA (Federal Housing Authority).

Suburban Development

After World War Two the nation's attention again turned to domestic issues, and the American urban landscape dramatically changed because of housing and transportation. The two most important national urban policies that define this era are found in the Federal Housing Authority (FHA), and Eisenhower's 1956 Highway Defense Act.

Although the FHA was created in 1934 as part of the New Deal, the significant impact of the FHA was not felt until immediately after World War II, and throughout the 1950s. The FHA guaranteed mortgages for homebuyers, and supplied funds to banks, which induced banks to once again invest in home mortgages. Banks were previously less willing to invest in mortgages after millions of homeowners defaulted on their loans during the Great Depression. Guaranteed VA loans for veterans contributed to rising rates of home ownership because veterans were only required to pay a down payment of as little as 3%. By contrast, buying a home in Western Europe often requires a 30% down payment. Today over 67% of Americans own their own homes. These policies were initially intended to spur an economic recovery in the construction industry, but the unintended consequence was the birth of the suburbs (Kleinberg, 1995). But suburban sprawl would not be possible without new roads, and more automobiles.

Cities used to "cluster develop" along rail lines, which guaranteed density, but the 1956 Highway Defense Act enacted under Eisenhower's administration allowed for "fluid development." People could now build anywhere. The Highway Act established the Highway Trust Fund, which received funds from a federal gasoline tax. If states and cities came up with the first 10%, the Trust Fund would supply the remaining 90% of the cost of building new roads and highways. The interstate highway network that resulted gave city dwellers ready access to new suburban developments. The middle class out-migration to the suburbs left a vacuum behind them that "clearly contributed to the decline of central cities" (Kleinberg, 1995, p. 130). Thus urban development from the late 1940s through the 1960s is characterized by both suburban development, and urban decay.

The War on Poverty

Poverty was "rediscovered" in the 1960s and LBJ declared a War on Poverty in 1964. The "War" reflected a shift from previous programs in which the federal government cooperated with locals to provide services, to a top-down hierarchical organization. This period saw a massive effort to redistribute wealth via federal social programs through CAPs (community action programs). These programs were basically a duplication of existing efforts. CAPs ran such programs as Head Start, College Bound, health, rehab, manpower training, neighborhood conservation, and Model Cities. CAPs were, in a sense, designed to empower the poor as communities, not just as individuals. But in 1964, and for the next four years, massive urban riots occurred across the country and LBJ lost faith in the Poverty War. The War on Poverty had been dubbed "creative federalism," but the programs and the coinciding riots perhaps only served to "create" a significant conservative opposition to liberal social policies. Also created at this time were civic-business-labor organizations such as the Urban Coalition and the National Alliance of Business, who focused their activity on "providing job opportunities to the urban disadvantaged" (Colman, 1989, p. 174).

Urban Renewal policies (also known as "slum clearance" or "negro removal"), in effect since the late 1950s, were also having a negative impact on cities. These policies, from Washington DC, mandated that cities should deal with "blight," and that cities had the permission to clear blighted land. In fact, the federal government would pay two-thirds of all clearance and development costs. This resulted in cities buying land, clearing land, rebuilding land, and then selling it to developers who started new development. Corrupt city officials manipulated the system and made money by declaring a neighborhood "blighted" based on the appearance of the physical environment. As a result of these "windshield assessments," entire communities were destroyed with no regard for the people who lived there. Jane Jacobs argues that the people make up a community, not the environment, but nonetheless, vibrant neighborhoods such as Cabrini Green in Chicago, Brownsville in New York, and Pruit Igoe in St. Louis were razed, later to be replaced with sterile public housing projects. The official name for this was Urban Renewal, but many called it "negro removal" because the federal bulldozers displaced thousands of African-Americans from their homes.

New Federalism

In response to rising poverty and the urban policy failures noted above, federal urban policies were reorganized under the Nixon administration. From the Nixon era to Clinton era "the federal government began a systematic disengagement from efforts to revitalize cities" (Cummings and Killmer, 1997, p. 308). President Carter admitted that, "A unified and coherent national urban policy designed to solve the problems of nation's communities and those that live in them is not possible" (Cummings and Killmer, 1997, p. 308). The big-government urban policies pushed by the liberal left had lost their credibility.

A significant organizational change associated with New Federalism is that the federal government, in many ways, "washed their hands" of urban problems. Instead of micromanaging the 100-plus categorical grants, they consolidated them into six large block grants. This change marked a new trend of decentralized implementation, which was believed would stimulate greater participation by local citizens.

A disadvantage of decentralization is that local administrators of grants can target the money toward developmental objectives favored by business rather than needed social services.

The final phase of New Federalism, sometimes called Federal Retrenchment, is characterized by deep spending cuts that might totally defund the grants and turn the responsibility over to the states, which often proved inept at addressing urban problems. At this point, Kleinberg suggests, "cities must expect to proceed with relatively little help from higher levels of government" (1997, p. 253). This local self-reliance is evidenced by a new wave of "local" economic development efforts, and the initiation of new public-private partnerships between local government and the private sector.

Current Federal Economic Development Programs

The current economic development efforts of the federal government are administered by the Economic Development Administration (EDA), which is part of the Department of Commerce in the executive branch. The EDA was established by the Public Works and Economic Development Act of 1965, and is designed to "generate jobs, help retain existing jobs, and stimulate industrial, technological, and commercial growth in economically-distressed areas of the United States" (Economic Development Administration [EDA], 2002, p. ii). Putting a positive spin on federal retrenchment from urban affairs, the EDA admits, "Distressed communities must be empowered to develop and implement their own economic development and revitalization strategies" (EDA, 2002, p. ii). David Sampson, Assistant Secretary of Commerce for Economic Development, cites wealth creation and poverty alleviation as the end goals of economic development activity. He explains "it is not the public sector that creates wealth and minimizes poverty, but the private sector," therefore the role of government in general, and the EDA specifically, is "to foster a positive environment where the private sector will risk capital investment to produce goods and services and increase productivity" resulting in high skill/high wage jobs (EDA, 2002, p. iii). Therefore the EDA no longer has a "processor of grants philosophy" but an "investment philosophy." This philosophy is at the root of the EDA's eight major investment programs listed below:

Public Works Program

Through the Public Works Program distressed communities receive grants to upgrade physical infrastructure necessary for attraction of new businesses, and retention and expansion of existing businesses. Sustainable development is encouraged by upgrading or redeveloping existing infrastructure, including brownfield reclamation projects. Projects eligible for this program include water and sewer facilities, roads, rail spurs, ports, and training facilities.

Economic Adjustment Program

The Economic Adjustment Program provides support to states and localities whose economies are structurally declining. Communities that have lost major employers, had a military bases close, or suffered a natural disasters participate in this program. Grants are given to support strategic planning or project implementation, and revolving loan funds are also used.

Research and National Technical Assistance Program

This program has two objectives: 1) develop a comprehensive body of information about economic development practices through research and evaluation grants, and 2) disseminate the information to economic development practitioners through newsletters, web sites, and conferences.

Partnership Planning Grants and Short Term Planning Grants

These two programs provide grant funding to local and regional economic development planning agencies, including a focus on Indian tribes, for the purpose of preparing, implementing and maintaining a Comprehensive Economic Development Strategy (CEDS). Long-term grants are renewable each year, while short term grants are limited to twelve months.

Technical Assistance Program

Grants provided under this program are designed to fund feasibility studies of possible new projects such as industrial parks and business incubators. Potential projects are analyzed according to their economic, financial, and social impacts.

University Center Program

This program makes university resources available to economic development practitioners. The university centers provide technical assistance, perform feasibility studies and conduct impact analyses. Technical assistance might involve engineering, management, or marketing expertise.

Trade Adjustment Assistance Program

This program, authorized by the Trade Act of 1974, helps firms that have been negatively impacted by increased imports of cheaper foreign goods that have eaten into their market share. Bureaucrats at twelve nationwide Trade Adjustment Assistance Centers help businesses apply for EDA assistance, which, if granted, normally pays 50% of a firm's cost to restructure.

It is evident in these eight programs that the federal government has chosen to offer assistance to communities in need. These grants invest federal money in distressed areas with the intent of spurring development. In the case of the Trade Adjustment Assistance Program, efforts are made to increase the global competitiveness of specific firms.

National Urban Policy

Some argue in favor of an integrated national urban policy, while others see benefits in the decentralization of governance to lesser governments. The federal government has been involved in urban affairs since FDR's New Deal, but rarely has there been a clear policy that articulates the roles of different levels of government in forming and implementing urban policies and programs (Vogel, 1997, p. 410). Numerous obstacles such as institutional barriers and political barriers preclude the issuance of an actual policy; presidents have tended to focus on more pressing domestic issues such as healthcare, education, and recently homeland security. In light of the global trends of decentralization it seems unnecessary to have a national urban policy. Taxpayers do not appreciate bigger government, and local city leaders would not readily give up their autonomy. It seems unlikely that a national urban policy will be anything more than it has been since the Nixon era–an expression of the point of view of the administration, rather than specific policy directives.

In general, there is consensus that if a national urban policy was politically practical, then the policy should include housing, labor laws, health, public transportation, roads, welfare, crime control, education, land use, and economic development. Without being officially named "urban policies," housing, labor, welfare, and roads are heavily regulated by the federal government. Of the other categories, cities could benefit from a national urban policy on land use and economic development. Tighter federal regulation could perhaps prevent localities from creating more urban sprawl, but more importantly the federal government could help the competitive position of the U.S. in the global marketplace by implementing national economic development practices. The zero-sum game, where foreign firms put U.S. cities in bidding wars against them might be managed better on the national level.

There is currently no consensus on what the federal role should be in urban affairs. Most urban theorists would agree which issues comprise "urban affairs," but the extent to which the federal government should be involved in such affairs it seems there are two major camps. The liberal camp is in favor of more government involvement and control over local urban affairs. Regarding urban policy, the liberals had national influence from the 1930s up to 1968, but it seems that more conservative views gained favor since the New Federalism of the Nixon era. Conservatives prefer smaller government, less federal involvement in local affairs, and decentralization of power. National security is one exception to this generalization, but the absence of any serious national urban policy is evidence enough that decentralization is the order for the day.

State Intervention in Local Economic Development

Beginning with Mississippi's Balance Agriculture with Industry Program in 1936, states aggressively attempt to attract new businesses into their borders, and prevent existing businesses from defecting. Numerous incentives are offered to attract, retain or create jobs, and thereby protect a city's tax base. These incentives include tax-abatements, grants, loans, tax-exempt bonds, equity financing, exemptions or credits, regulatory relief, customized training, and infrastructure development (Blakely 2002; Bland 1989; Butler 1981; Eisinger 1988; Hamlin and Lyons 1996; Luke et al., 1988; Matz and Ledebur 1986; Mikesell 1995; Sbragia 1996). Many states create complex programs designed to attract, retain, or expand individual firms. All the states have an official economic development agency, and an economic development plan that prioritizes job retention and creation. State governors typically work closely with the economic development agency.

From a fiscal perspective, economic development programs are not a major focus of the states. Most of the states' expenditures are for infrastructure and social services–the top five expenditure areas are education, welfare, health, hospitals, and highways. These are typically not classified as "economic development" programs, but they do contribute to the overall "business climate" of a region (Colman, 1989). Fisher (1997) alleges that a state's investment in public safety is a strong determinant of economic growth. States also directly contribute funds to local governments. States also indirectly influence economic development is by restricting local governments' ability to tax, spend, and borrow.

The degree to which states have been involved in the private sector has largely depended upon the industrial composition in each state. Natural resources, such as gold in California and oil in Texas, often drive state economic development policy (Colman, 1989). During the Dual Federalism era of American history, the U.S. states were more active than the federal government in economic regulation and economic development. State governments actively tried to increase overall production in their regions through investment in public works and investment in major industries such as railroads (Koven and Lyons, 2003). During the era of "big government," beginning with FDR's massive New Deal, the federal government became more involved in urban affairs. But since the federal retrenchment, associated with new Federalism and Nixon's withdrawal from urban affairs, states became more responsible for economic development in their cities and within their borders. State involvement in local economic development is often described as three different "waves" of activity, which are described below and illustrated in Table 2.3.

First Wave

The "first wave" of economic development was aimed at the attraction of new firms into a state, or local economy (Blakely & Bradshaw, 1999). First wave attraction techniques, often called "smokestack chasing," include the use of grants, loans, tax-exempt bonds, equity financing, tax abatements, exemptions or credits, regulatory relief, and infrastructure development. An example of first wave efforts include the luring of old industrial firms to the South and West (Blakely & Bradshaw, 1999).

Second Wave

The "second wave" began in the 1980s (Blakely & Bradshaw, 1999). The goals of "second wave" economic development efforts are retention and expansion of existing businesses. Second wave strategies also include "indirect firm-level assistance, such as creating new businesses, increasing investment capital, developing incubators or providing technical assistance to help local businesses grow or expand" (Blakely & Bradshaw, 1999). Clarke and Gaile (1992) state that second wave strategies are consistent with a strong investment and entrepreneurial approach. This approach includes the use of revolving loan funds, below-market loans, enterprise zones, and tax increment financing. Ross and Friedman (1990) identify second wave strategies as efforts to accelerate technology transfer, expand work-force training programs and increase capital for small to medium size business.

Third Wave

Rather than simply offering direct payments to firms, in third wave economic development practices, states seek to create a fertile business climate that will of itself be attractive to businesses (Fosler, 1992). Consensus is lacking in terms of the exact parameters of "Third Wave" development. It has been recognized, however, that such development can shift the focus from the state-led activity onto local development "by creating the context for economic growth through public-private partnerships, networks that leverage capital and human resources to increase the global competitiveness of a group of strategically linked firms" (Bradshaw & Blakely, 1999). Literature also describes third wave economic development strategies as oriented to building "institutional and human capacity to create a competitive environment" (Fitzgerald & Leigh, 2002, p. 45). Another key characteristic of the "third wave" is an emphasis on developing specific industrial clusters, rather than general smokestack chasing (Porter, 2000). Equitable job opportunities for the poor is another element of this new "third wave" (Fitzgerald & Leigh, 2002).

First and second wave economic development efforts have been primarily led by the states, but third wave strategies shift the focus onto localities. First wave strategies were "place-based" in the sense of attracting firms to places while second wave strategies were "firm-based" since they relied upon retention and expansion of existing businesses. First and second wave techniques are now "giving way to the third wave" primarily because businesses have greater mobility and their location choices have become less predictable (Blakely & Bradshaw, 1999). This is clearly true for large multinational corporations such as United Parcel Service. The Post-Fordism "techno-economic paradigm" described by Ruigrok and van Tulder (1995), also contributes to mobility. Free trade, globalization, and cheap labor are significant factors that have motivated domestic and international relocation choices for firms (Hill, 2002). Therefore states can no longer count on a single industry or firm to generate economic activity. According to Fosler, "states are now more concerned with the overall performance of the state economy" (1992, p. 5). The third wave does not replace earlier techniques, but more importantly uses first and second wave techniques within a larger strategic context.

Using data from a national survey of state development agencies, Eisinger (1995) notes three seemingly contradictory trends in the 1990s: 1) states are losing interest in economic development, 2) states are regressing from entrepreneurial policy, favoring industrial recruitment strategies instead, and 3) "third wave" policies are being embraced. Eisinger suggests that these changes are not driven by research, but program survival driven by political pressure.

Numerous empirical studies have examined the effectiveness of direct state economic development activity. Other studies have examined the general business climate of states as a predictor of economic growth. These studies are discussed in the summary of empirical literature of economic development in Chapter Five.

Table 2.3. Three Waves of State Economic Development Policy

	Policy Objectives	Key Actors	Focus	Typical Tools
First Wave, up to 1980s	business attraction	states	place-based strategies	free (or low cost) land, grants, loans, tax-exempt bonds, equity financing, tax abatements, tax exemptions, tax credits, regulatory relief, and infrastructure development
Second Wave, 1980s	business attraction, business retention, expansion of existing firms	states	place-based strategies, firm-based strategies	*all the above, and* incubators, increasing investment capital, individual firm level assistance, technical assistance to local firms, export assistance to local firms, revolving loan funds, below-market loans, enterprise zones, tax increment financing
Third Wave, 1990s onward	business attraction, business retention, expansion of existing firms	states, cities, private organizations	place-based strategies, firm-based strategies	*all the above, and* create a fertile business climate, public-private partnerships, human capital development, cluster strategies, equity strategies

Based on Blakely & Bradshaw, 1999.

Local Government Economic Development

Like the states' economic development activities, cities also followed the "waves" of economic development practices. Economic development practitioners in U.S. cities have actively sought to attract and retain businesses (first wave); expand existing firms (second wave); and participate in creative new programs and partnerships to boost the economy and create a pro-growth business climate (third wave). Over the past three decades, public and private city leaders have implemented numerous programs and policies in the name of economic development "to create jobs and enhance their tax base" (Feiock, 1991, p. 643). To summarize the economic development activity of local government in U.S. cities, this section first explains why locals have become more directly involved in economic development activity; and second, this section identifies specific local actors who are getting involved in the economic development process.

Increased Local Economic Development Activity

Over the past three decades, "local development activity has intensified dramatically" in response to numerous economic and political changes (Feiock, 1991, p. 643). Three major changes that have driven local city leaders, public and private, to become more involved in economic development activities are the urban crises of the 1970s, federal retrenchment, and structural change in the macro economy.

1970s Urban Crises

The urban crises of the 1970s are typically characterized by stories of concentrated poverty; welfare dependency; crime; high unemployment; derisory housing; inadequate public transportation; disrepaired streets and highways; pollution; urban sprawl; spatial mismatches of jobs and workers; and fiscal crises experienced by local governments. While these problems have always existed to some extent, it is in the 1970s that they worsened and compounded. A recession developed in 1974, resulting in fewer jobs in the private sector and fiscal stress faced by states and localities. In some cases, funds earmarked for the poor were diverted to other uses. Local governments used funds provided through Comprehensive Employment and Training Block Grants to "fund existing public service positions" rather than training the poor (Kleinberg, 1995, p. 196). In the 1991 book, *America's Ailing Cities*, Ladd and Yinger explain that cities have an increasing lack of ability to raise revenue to meet service demands because they have low revenue-raising capacity and high service costs. They argue that local economic development techniques such as industrial revenue bonds and enterprise zones do not work, and that the crisis can only be resolved with more federal support and state support, including taking on delivery of basic services.

The problems of the urban crises of the 1970s exacerbated and manifested in what Rusk called "America's real urban problem," which is the "racial and economic segregation that has created an underclass in many of America's major urban areas" (1995, p. 1). William Julius Wilson, in his book *The Truly Disadvantaged: The Inner City, the Underclass, and Public Policy*, explains that the rise of the urban underclass (defined as "the most disadvantaged segments of the black urban community," including the long-term unemployed, the unemployable, the poor, the

welfare-dependent, and street criminals (p. 8) is not caused by racial discrimina-
tion, but is a result of complex demographic and economic changes including the
mechanization of agriculture in the South, the migration of blacks to Northern cities,
the spatial mismatch caused by jobs moving to the suburbs, and overall industrial
restructuring from manufacturing to services. The convergence of these multiple
"urban crises" of the 1970s got the attention of city leaders and is one cause of
increased economic development activity by local city leaders.

Federal Retrenchment

Another reason why the economic development activity of local city leaders has
increased in recent years is the federal government's withdrawal from urban affairs,
often called "retrenchment." In the U.S. political system of federalism, municipalities are the lowest-order governments and have "little capacity to directly
intervene in a new globally based economic structure" (Blakely and Bradshaw,
2003, p. 24). According to Dillon's Rule of 1872, lower-tier governments, such as
cities and counties, are subservient to state and federal governments. So cities
have typically assumed a reactive posture to higher-order governments (federal
and state), rather than a proactive posture.

The urban policies of the Nixon and Reagan administrations drove local government officials to be more involved in economic development. The premise of the
Community Development Block Grant (CDBG) program was to "decentralize"
decision-making power from the federal level to the local level. It was thought
that locals could more effectively use the funds, and the Nixon administration was
eager to distance itself from direct involvement in urban problems. After Nixon
took office in 1969, the federal government "quickly acted to minimize the role of
citizen participation" in Federal urban programs such as Model Cities (Kleinberg,
1995, p. 206), which put CDBG funds squarely in the hands of local government.
The position of the Reagan administration was that "urban development was best
left to the processes of the market and of social voluntarism" (Kleinberg, 1995, p.
226). So Reagan's "nonurban urban policy" provided a strong impetus for local
city leaders to take economic development matters firmly in their own hands.

Economic Restructuring

A third reason that local government leaders have become more involved in economic development is in response to structural changes in the global economy.
According to Robert Reich (1991), U.S. Secretary of Labor during President Clinton's
first term, the economic problems in U.S. cities, such as unemployment, have their
basis in the competitive position of the city in the national and world economies.

The recent structural change in the world economy has it roots in both industry and politics.

In the past thirty years, the industrial mix of the U.S. economy has changed from being dominated by manufacturing to services. According to Fitzgerald and Leigh, "manufacturing jobs are important to a local economy because they pay higher wages overall than service industries for people with comparable skills" (2003, p. 103). But many cities have lost much of their manufacturing base as firms have moved to the suburbs and many "Rust Belt" cities have seen many of their manufacturing firms move to the "Sun Belt" (Rusk, 1995; Fitzgerald and Leigh, 2003). With national borders becoming increasingly more open, many U.S. firms have moved their production facilities to other countries. After NAFTA many U.S. firms opened shop in *maquiladoras* across the border in Mexico, but the latest shift in manufacturing jobs has been to Asia. White collar service jobs are also being moved offshore to places such as India where there is no language barrier. "U.S. companies are expected to send 3.3 million jobs overseas in the next 12 years" declares *Time* magazine (August 4, 2003, p. 36). City leaders have noticed this new expanded mobility of firms and actively seek to retain businesses who consider leaving. Savitch and Kantor (2002) suggest that, in the face of global restructuring, deliberate planning by city leaders combined with national urban policies can help cities engage the international marketplace.

Besides globalization, Wyly, Glickman, and Lahr (1998) suggest other macro trends that affect national growth (technological change, demographic trends, and selective flows of people, jobs, and wealth) are also magnifying inequality in opportunities for individuals and communities. According to Wyly, Glickman, and Lahr (1998) these processes are creating numerous problems such as income inequality, social polarization, uneven urban growth, inner city neighborhood decay, housing unaffordability, and fiscal shortfalls faced by large cities.

Politicians like Bill Clinton who embrace free trade have opened U.S. borders through agreements like NAFTA that reduce trade barriers such as tariffs and quotas. U.S. participation in multi-national institutions such as the International Monetary Fund (IMF) and the World Trade Organization (WTO) has contributed to "greater interdependence with the rest of the world" (Litan, 2000, p. 35). This interdependence is characterized by the "globalization" of production and the globalization of markets. Because of trade deregulation and advances in transportation and telecommunications, firms can now produce their goods virtually anywhere, and sell those goods in any market. But globalization has its pros and cons. In simple terms, U.S. consumers benefit from cheap imports, U.S. firms and labor benefit by having access to new foreign markets, but U.S. labor also suffers by not being able to compete with cheap foreign labor. Bernstein observes, "It's a paradox that while globalization brings big gains at the macroeconomic level, those pluses are often eclipsed in the public eye by all the personal stories of pain felt by the losers" (2000, p.39). A major effect of globalization is that the economies of U.S. cities are suddenly more dynamic and volatile–capital and labor are more mobile than ever, making it difficult for city leaders to keep up with the changes. According to Blakely and Bradshaw, "American communities can no longer depend, if they ever could, on a participating local business base that will pledge long-term loyalty to a community or to its workers" (2003, p. 25).

These structural economic changes bringing about global interdependence are compelling sub-national governments, including cities and counties, to be more active in local economic development. In fact many U.S. state and local economic development agencies do not limit their economic development efforts to local actions only; many interact directly with foreign firms and governments (Fry, 1998).

Local Economic Development Actors

Government officials and agencies, business elites, and community-based organizations all participate in the efforts to develop and expand a city's economy. In the *Economic Development 1999* survey, the International City/County Management Association (ICMA) found that of 1,042 municipalities that responded, 92.6% of the municipalities had city governments actively involved in economic development; 48.3% had county governments involved; 76.5% had chambers of commerce involved; 54.9% had private business involved and 15% had ad hoc citizen groups involved. These groups can be broken down into three main actors: government, business, and community-based organizations (ICMA, 1999).

Government

City government leaders have two primary objectives: 1) make their city competitive in the world economy, and 2) ensure the social needs of the region's citizens are satisfied (Savitch and Vogel, 1996). While these two objectives remain the same among all cities, each city has its own economic complexities which yield different modes of political response from city government.

One such response is for city leaders to focus economic development activity on specific niches. Blakely (2002) suggests that each city should know its own unique resources and challenges, and city leaders should favor economic development techniques that develop human capital and develop high tech industries. Blakely explains this "local" economic development is crucial because cities cannot count on help from federal, state, or even metropolitan governments. Eisinger agrees that cities are "increasingly cut off from federal aid and program initiatives," and as this federal devolution continues, city mayors must "focus more and more on making the most of the resources they control" (1998, p. 309). Eisinger suggests that in these tough times, mayors have abandoned their former moral crusades (racial, economic, social) and are now concentrating on employing public management techniques to make the most of their scarce resources.

Another economic development response by government officials is to form a metropolitan government that can represent the entire region, especially for the purpose of business attraction. In the 1996 book, *Shaping Suburbia: How Political Institutions Organize Urban Development*, Lewis suggests that political institutions influence the location decisions of firms and developers. Therefore centralized metropolitan government should manage land-use planning, control traffic congestion, downtown decay, and sprawl. Lewis avers that fragmented metropolises are more likely to have sprawl, weak downtowns, and spatial mismatches of jobs and housing. Some, such as Tiebout, encourage a multiplicity of decentralized governments. Others note the limits of structural analysis. Careley explains "distribution of authority and legal powers as reflected in a city government's formal structure is not equivalent to the distribution of actual influence..." therefore "... no simple change of governmental structure, such as adding a metropolitan area-wide layer, was magically going to eliminate these (urban) problems" (1977, p. 122). Nonetheless, the ability to attract new firms to a region remains one of the key arguments in favor of metropolitan government.

Business Elites

Non-governmental private sector actors often involve themselves in economic development policy and practice. Most notably in the literature is the case of the "urban regime" in Atlanta described by Stone (1989). In an urban regime, business leaders and elected officials cooperate to exploit institutional resources for sustained decision-making that benefits both sides. For example, in Atlanta white business leaders pushed for relaxed restrictions on business development, and black businesses benefited from the contracts they were awarded by the white developers as a result of the relaxed restrictions. A fraternal bond is formed as the elites cooperate across institutional sectors and community life. According to Stone regimes are capable of development, but less capable of addressing social problems.

Others have built upon Stone's regime theory, such as Flores (1999) who delineated four distinct types of urban regime: machine city, reform city, entrepreneurial city, and international city; and Imbroscio (1998) who offered three other urban regime types: community-based, petty bourgeois, and local statist. The regime characteristics are largely based on who dominates the business sector, government operations, and the electoral structure (Reese and Rosenfeld, 2002).

Labor unions represent another private sector entity involved in local economic development. Their actions tend to influence elections (Fitzgerald and Leigh, 2002), and their progressive policies might include city minimum wage laws that exceed state minimums, requirements for employers to provide benefits such as health insurance or pay higher wages, and workers' rights to form unions (Meyerson, 2001). A city whose politics are dominated by labor unions would more likely invest resources in human services, and be less ideologically committed to offering incentives to businesses such as tax breaks for new firms.

Community-Based Organizations

A third type of actor in urban economic development is the community-based organization (CBO). Many religious and civic groups are considered CBOs, including churches, neighborhood associations, philanthropic organizations, charities, political groups, religious parachurch organizations, fraternal organizations, clubs, and youth groups. While individual CBOs are often concerned with a single issue such as affordable housing or education, CBOs have been involved in just about every aspect of economic development policy. CBOs are not only involved in the local government political process, but they are also "assuming functions formerly undertaken by local governments" such as helping the poor and elderly (Van Dusen Wishard, 1999, p. 94).

Community Development Corporations (CDC), a broad category of CBOs, sprang out of the 1960s War on Poverty. CDCs differ significantly from business-led development efforts because they operate in low-income communities, and they encourage grassroots community involvement in the economic development process (Kleinberg, 1995). The National Congress for Community Economic Development 2003 Community Revitalization Policy Agenda boasts that CDCs have generated 247,000 jobs, created 550,000 units of affordable housing, developed or rehabilitated over 71 million square feet of commercial space, and secured over $1.9 billion in small business loans over the past thirty years (Pitcoff & Widrow, 1998).

Due to federal retrenchment from urban affairs, overall restructuring of the U.S. economy, and the urban crises of the 1970s, the past thirty years have seen a myriad of local actors get involved in economic development planning, policy, and practice. These diverse local actors include local government, business elites, and community-based organizations.

Chapter Summary

For most of the twentieth century, government intervention for the purpose of economic development in U.S. cities was characterized by massive federal government programs. After the federal government discontinued many of these programs, state and local governments took economic development matters into their own hands. Their efforts have followed three "waves," (1) business attraction, (2) business expansion, and (3) entrepreneurial programs. Certain major decision-making still occurs at the federal level, while implementation is carried out by various public and private actors at the state and local levels. The next chapter describes various theories of economic development that inform and influence economic development policies, programs, and practices.

Guest Case: Redevelopment as an Economic Development Tool in the State of California

By: Brian Sprague and John Sprague, Assistant City Manager, City of Roseville and CEO, Roseville Community Development Corporation

Redevelopment was created by the California State Legislature in 1945 through the Community Redevelopment Act, for the purpose of providing California cities and counties with an economic development tool to address "blighting" conditions within their communities. As originally enacted, Redevelopment provided local jurisdictions authority to establish Redevelopment Agencies. In 1951 California voters amended the State Constitution, Article XVI, Section 16, allowing Redevelopment Agencies to use Tax Increment funding as a financing tool to carry out Redevelopment Plans in adopted Redevelopment Project Areas. In response, the California Legislature passed the California Community Redevelopment Law (CCRL), enabling Redevelopment Agencies to use Tax Increment, codified in Section 22670 of the California Health and Safety Code.

Over Redevelopment's 67 years of operation the CCRL has been modified numerous times by the legislature and voters. However, in 2011 the California State Legislature passed and Governor Brown signed AB 1X-26 which in combination with a State Supreme Court decision in December, 2011 eliminated all California Redevelopment Agencies effective February 1, 2012.

Redevelopment In California:

As of February 1, 2012 a total of 425 Redevelopment Agencies had been established by California's cities and counties under the provisions of the CCRL. Each of these agencies had adopted one or more Redevelopment Plan Areas and created an estimated $29.4 billion in outstanding bond debt.

Redevelopment Agencies used the funding raised through issuing bonds to finance a wide array of public/private development projects focused on eliminating "blight" in their Redevelopment Plan Areas. Project examples include, infrastructure upsizing, land acquisition/assembly, construction financing for commercial and residential development and rehabilitation funding of existing structures.

In order to secure Tax Increment revenue to fund redevelopment projects CCRL required the Redevelopment Agency adopt a Redevelopment Plan Area. The Plan Area established the physical boundaries encompassing commercial, industrial and residential areas within the community with "Blighting" influences needing to be addressed. Upon adoption of the Redevelopment Plan Area the County Assessor's

Office and Auditor/Controller's Offices will 1) identify the Tax Rate Areas located in the Plan Area. Tax Rate Areas identify the Taxing Entities in the Project Area which currently receive a portion of the property tax revenues currently generated in the area, and 2) determine the base year Assessed Valuation (AV) for all real property in the Plan Area. Section 33670 of the California State Health and Safety Code (H&SC) authorizes the allocation of property taxes among the various local agencies and community redevelopment agencies. The "frozen base assessed valuation" is the value of

property at the time of the adoption of a redevelopment project plan. The "incremental assessed valuation" is the cumulative increase in the value of property within a project area above the frozen base assessed valuation. Tax increment revenues are produced by applying general and debt service tax rates to the incremental assessed valuation. By 2009 the frozen base assessed valuation was at $162 billion, and the incremental assessed valuation was at $553 billion for total assessed valuation of $716 billion.

Tax Increment Funding represents a policy decision by the State and its voters to shift the incremental growth in property tax revenues generated in Redevelopment Plan Areas from the existing Taxing Agencies to the Redevelopment Agency for the purpose of financing projects that alleviate or remove "Blight". Property taxes outside Redevelopment Project Areas are distributed to Taxing Agencies in the State of California as follows: 30% to the county, 15% to the city, 45% to school districts, and 10% to fire districts.

In practice Tax Increment Funding essentially caps the amount of property tax revenue the existing Taxing Entities receive to the amount received at the time the Redevelopment Plan Area was adopted.

Redevelopment coupled with Tax Increment Funding and the ongoing, consistent revenue stream it represented provided California cities and counties with the ability to invest in significant public and private projects in areas which could not attract private investment. The State's policy decision to eliminate Redevelopment Agencies has removed the ability of cities and counties to access Tax Increment Funding. Although Tax Increment Funding is no longer available the public policy issues associated with "Blighted" neighborhoods and commercial areas remain and are growing, particularly in the current economic environment. Stimulating new investment and economic growth in California's cities and counties remains a top policy priority requiring identification of new funding models for redevelopment and economic development.

CHAPTER 3

THEORIES OF ECONOMIC DEVELOPMENT

"The ideas of economists and political philosophers, both when they are right and when they are wrong, are more powerful than is commonly understood. Indeed the world is ruled by little else. Practical men, who believe themselves to be quite exempt from any intellectual influence, are usually the slaves of some defunct economist. Madmen in authority, who hear voices in the air, are distilling their frenzy from some academic scribbler of a few years back." (Keynes, 1936, p. 383).

The quote above by John Maynard Keynes illustrates the concept that we make decisions based on the ideas of others, whether we admit it or not. In the economic development context, city leaders make policy decisions based on their best ideas to improve the local economy. Keynes would argue, however, that a policy decision is actually influenced by "some academic scribbler of a few years back" and that leaders making economic decisions are "slaves of some defunct economist." Ironically, it is Keynes' own work that has since become some of the most influential economic theory. Whether slaves or not, economic development policy decisions certainly have some basis in the theoretical leanings of the policy maker.

This chapter provides the economic theoretical foundation of this book. Classical and contemporary economic and political theoretical sources are drawn upon. The chapter begins with a discussion of the "economic problem" of resource scarcity, and discusses three economic perspectives relevant to economic development: classical economics, neoclassical economics, and Keynesian economics. Next, the chapter discusses three distinct political perspectives that influence economic development practice: conservative, neoconservative, and liberal. Many of the contemporary theories of economic development described in this chapter have both economic and political implications. The chapter is therefore organized such that the various contemporary theories relevant to economic development are included in the economic and political sections according to the most salient characteristics of the theory.

Economic Theory

A key assumption of economics is that people make rational decisions, which means they always seek to improve their own welfare. In a local economy, government, private firms, households and individuals all benefit from overall economic growth of the local market. In theory then, all of these stakeholders desire increased output in the basic resources: land, labor, and capital. The classic economic dilemma, however, suggests that resources are scarce. We never quite have enough of what we want. Not enough resources, money, jobs, firms, etc. Public and private sector leaders respond to the economic dilemma with numerous programs and policies commonly dubbed "economic development" activities. The goal of these programs is to increase output resulting in economic growth and higher living standards for all in the region. Numerous ideas exist about the best way to increase output.

Capital resources are mobile, and many local economies suffer when resources leave, such as when an employer closes a manufacturing facility and reopens in another city. Over the past few decades American cities have been losing manufacturing jobs to cheap overseas labor, but within the past five years, service jobs have also started to shift overseas. Low telecommunications costs have paved the way for U.S. call centers to relocate to such places as Bangalore or New Delhi. From 2003 to 2005, "U.S. companies are expected to send 3.3 million jobs overseas...primarily to India" (Thottam, 2003, p. 36). As national labor forces are blended into a single world labor force, the price of labor is a key variable in determining future economic prospects of cities. More than ever, U.S. city leaders are actively employing a variety of economic development strategies to attract and retain firms, whose capital is increasingly more and more mobile.

Like capital, the labor resource is also mobile. Certain regions experience "brain drain" where workers with the highest skills leave the area, making it difficult for local firms to meet staffing needs. City leaders routinely report a lack of skilled labor is a barrier to economic development in their city.

Economic markets in cities, suburbs, towns, counties and regions have much in common with the "macro" national economy where goods and services are exchanged. Some goods and resources are privately owned such as land, cars, homes, and businesses. Other goods and resources are publicly owned such as parks, highways, airports and schools. Likewise, enterprises are either private (U.P.S., Coca-Cola, Joe's Car Wash), or public (U.S. Postal Service, the U.S. Army, kindergartens). Local economies therefore experience competition between government, private firms, and individuals all competing for a scarce amount of resources, goods and services.

Every economy faces "the economic problem" that resources are scarce and people can only get a fraction of the goods and services that they want. The way resources are allocated determines how efficient a market will be. Market participants must decide what to produce, how to produce it, and for whom to produce it, sometimes called the "Three Economic Questions." Of the three basic economic systems, traditional, market, and command, U.S. cities most closely follow the market system. The presence of government regulation, however, illustrates it is not a pure market system–there are elements of the command system at work also.

In a pure system of capitalism, decisions about resource use are determined by buyers and sellers through competition in a free market. Resources are privately owned and private enterprises produce all goods and services. In a command system, resources are publicly owned, and government authorities dictate how resources will be used. The system of pure capitalism and the command system represent extreme opposite ends of the spectrum of economic systems. Most nations in the world today have adopted various forms of capitalism, while a few communist, socialist, or totalitarian nations have adopted command economies.

U.S. cities have elements of both command and market economic systems. Local governments influence where private firms can locate through zoning laws. Local governments charge firms taxes to pay for police and fire protection, both of which are monopoly services. This is an example of the command philosophy because private firms are required to pay for the service, even if they never use it, or even if they already provide that service for themselves, such as employing private security guards to protect a business's property in lieu of the police. On the other hand, U.S. local governments do not dictate what goods or services businesses should produce, and local governments can reduce or waive taxes as an economic development strategy; both examples of the free market system. Thus, both command and market principles are at work in local economies. The extent to which a local government favors the command or the market philosophy largely depends on the economic paradigm held by government officials. The evident trend in the U.S. seems to be more market and less command as evidenced by the recent deregulation of major industries such as airlines, telecommunications, and utilities.

While the U.S. national economy and U.S. local economies mostly follow the capitalistic market system, an argument can be made that the economic thinking of mercantilism is seeing a resurgence. In mercantilism, nations limit their imports and encourage exports so that cash will accumulate in the nation. The contemporary "protectionism" movement at the national level could be seen as a form of new mercantilism. The economic base theory used to analyze urban economies also has elements of new mercantilism in that cities try to keep resources from leaving the local market.

The economic theories currently influencing economic development practices in U.S. local economies are grouped according to three major schools of economic thought: Classical economics, neoclassical economics, and Keynesian economics. These three foundational schools of economic thought are described in the next section with an emphasis on how they inform and influence contemporary theories of economic development. Table 3.1 compares these three major economic theories.

Table 3.1 Comparison of Major Economic Theories

Theory	Goals	Key Scholar	Key Characteristics	Solutions to Market Failure
Classical	economic prosperity full employment increased production	Adam Smith	focus on supply (supply creates demand) free markets limited government intervention in markets	market failures are short-term the "invisible hand" of competition supply and demand deregulation reduced corporate taxes government action to spur production
		David Ricardo	labor theory of value adversarial class relations comparative advantage	
		Joseph Schumpeter	creative destruction innovation drives growth	

		Menger, Jevons, Walrus	focus on demand theory of marginal utility	market failures are short-term the "invisible hand" of competition supply and demand deregulation reduced corporate taxes government action to spur consumption
Neoclassical	economic prosperity full employment increased profits	Alfred Marshall	demand determines equilibrium	
Keynesian	economic prosperity full employment increased spending	John M. Keynes	government intervention in markets Keynesian multiplier	market failures might be long-term regulation counter-cyclical fiscal policies deficit budgets

Classical Economic Theory

Classical economics is a school of thought that values a free market economic system with limited government involvement. The goals of economic prosperity and full employment are thought to be achievable through the market forces of supply and demand, dubbed "the invisible hand" by Adam Smith. The focus is on production–it is thought that supply creates its own demand (known as "Say's Law"). Recessions and inflation are thought to cure themselves. Whatever "leakages" occur (savings and taxes), will reenter the market as "injections" (investments and government spending). Therefore government intervention is unnecessary.

This section discusses the roots of classical economics with a focus on two of the most influential economists in the Classical school, Adam Smith and David Ricardo.

Mercantilism

The classical economic school of thought has its roots in the mercantilism system and the Physiocrat movement. By the 16th century the mercantilism system had taken root in many nations. Mercantilism is a system where government policies limit imports and encourage exports, which would allow the accumulation of gold and silver.

Adam Smith

The 18th century, with its Enlightenment, Industrial Revolution, and American Revolution, was a century of discovery and new ideas. During this time the Physiocrats appeared, who believed in the laws of nature, and that all wealth sprung from the land. Consequently, only "husbandmen," such as farmers, miners, trappers, etc, were the only true producers; and tradesmen, craftsmen and industrialists were not productive. The Physiocrats argued that government should not interfere in economic affairs. Their mantra was *laissez faire et laissez passer*, literally "let make, and let pass," meaning "don't interfere, for the world will take care of itself." The Physiocrats set the stage for the father of modern economics, Adam Smith.

In his 1776 book, *The Wealth of Nations*, Smith makes his argument for a new economic system based on free markets and limited government intervention. These two arguments are the pillars of classical economics. Smith claimed that government intervention created inefficiency, and he argued that mercantilist policies should be stopped. Government should no longer subsidize private firms; government should no longer grant monopolies to private firms; trade restrictions should be removed; products should not be regulated; and minimum wage laws should be repealed. Smith's core belief was that competition would act as an "invisible hand" to create proper pricing in the market. Free market competition would result in economic growth that would benefit all members of society. Capitalists would have greater profits, and labor would experience higher wages.

From an international trade perspective Smith argued that free trade will lead to economic growth because of absolute advantage. Absolute advantage is the "situation in which one country is more efficient at producing a product than any other country" (Hill, 2002, p. 129). In Smith's day, the English were the best at producing textiles because of their advanced manufacturing processes, and the French were the best at producing wine because of their climate, soil and expertise. Countries should specialize in products where they have an absolute advantage then trade for other goods. Through free trade, the English and the French can both enjoy a glass of fine wine while wearing fancy duds.

In Smith's analysis, an economy has unlimited upward growth potential. Smith's optimistic outlook appears to be shared by economic development officials in the U.S. who also expect increased economic growth each year. Although they share Smith's positive outlook, often their numerous policies and actions contradict Smith's ideal of a free market without government intervention.

David Ricardo

David Ricardo, was a contemporary of Adam Smith's and another Classical economist. He believed that "economic freedom led to maximum profits, that profits were the source of investment capital, and that a competitive economy would lead to profit-maximizing investments" (Fusfeld, 1999, p. 41). Ricardo was therefore a staunch supporter of pro-business policies because he believed that free markets lead to economic growth. Ricardo extended Smith's original work three ways: by offering the labor theory of value; by describing adversarial class relations; and by explaining the law of comparative advantage.

The labor theory of value suggests that the market price of a good is ultimately determined by the amount of labor time embodied in the production of the good. Thus goods that are more labor-intensive to produce have higher prices. The value of a good is then measured by the number of man-hours or "person-years." According to Ricardo's Iron Law of Wages, the wages of workers naturally trend to a minimum level that allows workers to only meet their basic subsistence needs. Wages are expected not to rise above this "iron" limit. This idea is attractive to factory owners because labor remains dependent on the firm, yet labor remains economically powerless.

Unlike Smith, who believed in unlimited economic growth potential, Ricardo believed that economies generally move toward a standstill, because natural resources are limited, and because capitalists will exploit workers. Ricardo's ideas about labor and the propensity for adversarial class relations influenced Karl Marx in his pessimistic views about the opportunity for workers to benefit from capitalism. Ricardo himself admits that a free market untouched by government intervention is not perfect, but is nonetheless the best economic system.

In the context of an imperfect market system, Ricardo's law of comparative advantage emerged which built upon Smith's theory of absolute advantage. The theory of comparative advantage suggests that a country should specialize in the production of goods that it produces most efficiently and to buy from other countries goods that it produces less efficiently. For example, U.S. firms in the 1970s had an absolute advantage in producing computer hard drives–we could make them more efficiently than foreign firms. But if we continued to invest our land, labor and capital resources into making computer hard drives in the U.S. today, we would have less of those resources to invest in another good where the U.S. has absolute advantage over foreign countries: aerospace products. Although U.S. firms can probably still produce goods such as computer hard drives more efficiently than foreign firms (absolute advantage), the opportunity to invest those resources in another, perhaps more profitable, venture are lost. Because the "opportunity cost" of making computer hard drives in the U.S. is so great, we can choose to import them, and invest our resources producing other goods such as aerospace products. Following the theory of comparative advantage, countries specialize their production, and import what they do not produce. It is thought that such specialization and trade lead to greater economic benefits for all countries.

Other economists who contribute to the classical school include Thomas Malthus, Leon Walras, and Alfred Marshall. Malthus deviated from Smith's optimistic opinion of economic growth, and instead predicted "perpetual misery" caused by food shortages. Population will grow geometrically, while food output will only grow arithmetically. Malthus worried about deaths caused by not eating enough, but in fact, these days deaths are caused by eating too much: obesity is now one of the top causes of death in the developed world. Walras and Marshall contributed to classical economics by suggesting that mathematics, such as Cournot's supply and demand curves, would add precision to economics.

Contemporary Theories of Economic Development Rooted in Classical Economics

Classical economic thought is still widely influential in current economic development practices. Many cities have very limited official economic development activity, preferring instead to allow market forces to determine their economic fortune which evinces the presence of *laissez-faire* policy. Of the 1,042 cities and municipalities that responded to the ICMA survey, 45.7% report that they have no written economic development plan. Coupled with the fact that 2,266 cities and municipalities ignored the survey altogether (31.5% response rate), we might speculate that these cities ignored the survey because they had no economic development "officials" to complete the survey. In these cities it could be that local government officials agree with Smith that the "invisible hand" of competition will bring prosperity, not government intervention.

The cities that did respond to the ICMA survey report that most of their economic development efforts favor supply-side economic policies designed to increase the attraction, retention and expansion of businesses which is a characteristic of classical economics. In general terms then, cities and municipalities exhibit classical economic theory that either have no official economic development activity, or have only what Koven and Lyons (2003) call "top-down" activity that focuses on the supply-side.

Certain theories of economic development have their roots in classical economics, including Schumpeter's theory of economic development, Tiebout's public choice theory, economic base theory, product cycle theory, and Friedman's monetarist theory.

Schumpeter's Theory of Economic Development

Schumpeter's theory of economic development (1934) is characterized by the phrase "creative destruction," which refers to the process of new technology replacing old technology. Through innovation, entrepreneurs create new products, services, institutions, processes and markets. These new creations have a destructive impact on the old. The inventions of word processors and mobile telephones, for example, have wreaked destruction on the typewriter and payphone industries. The Brother company was a medium-sized manufacturer in the city of Bartlett, Tennessee. When the market for Brother typewriters evaporated, 227 Bartlett workers lost their jobs ("Manufacturing Jobs Disappearing," 2001). Schumpeter would argue that this job loss is a painful yet necessary process towards growth in the overall economy. According to Schumpeter capitalism is grounded in principles of adaptation to change, the possibility of bankruptcy, and responsiveness to market demand. Although Brother laid off 227 workers, today the company is manufacturing fax machines and printers and continues to be a major employer in Bartlett.

Unlike Adam Smith, who thought competition drives economic growth, Schumpeter alleged that innovation is responsible for economic growth. So the Shumpeter theory of economic development views business cycles as a necessary component of growth. From an urban economic development perspective, Schumpeter's theory influences government officials to encourage innovation within its polity. Technology business incubators can be used to aid the development of new high tech firms, and partnerships between researchers and businesses can also encourage innovation. If Schumpeter's "creative destruction" is an accurate portrayal of a market economy, then economic development officials would do well to ensure that their polities experiences the "creative" rather than the "destructive."

Tiebout's Public Choice Theory

Political science often assumes that people (especially elected officials) generally act in the public interest, while economics assumes that people act in their own interest. Public choice economics is "the application of economics to political science" (Mueller, 1989, p. 1). One of the seminal works in public choice theory is Tiebout's (1956) "Pure Theory of Local Expenditures" wherein Tiebout argued that people "vote with their feet":

"The consumer-voter may be viewed as picking that community which best satisfies his preference pattern for public goods... at the local level various governments have their revenue and expenditure patterns more or less set. Given these revenue and expenditure patterns, the consumer-voter moves to that community whose local government best satisfies his set of preferences." (p. 418).

If a person (or firm) is dissatisfied with the municipality he resides in, he can simply move to a more advantageous locale. This illustrates the economic principle of rationality–individuals (and firms) make decisions based on their own interests. City government officials, noticing the rationality and mobility of individuals and firms, must compete to attract and retain residents and firms. They do this through their revenue and expenditure policies. Through expenditures, cities provide a "basket" of public goods, such as infrastructure, parks, schools, colleges, utilities, beaches, police, and transportation. To pay for these expenditures, cities charge its residents and firms taxes. Tiebout observed that consumer-voters have certain preferences for services, and they do not mind paying reasonable taxes so long as their preferences for public goods are met. When the allocation of municipal resources is unsatisfactory, or the tax burden is too costly, consumer-voters will move on to other communities. A government's objective is to ascertain the consumer-voters' wants for public goods and tax him or her accordingly.

In Tiebout's model, revenue and expenditure patterns are "more or less set," but in reality, city leaders have discretion to change revenue and expenditure policies. The model also assumes that consumer-voters are fully mobile and have full knowledge about different municipalities. While these were constraining elements of the 1956 model, full mobility and full knowledge are no longer simple theoretical constraints, but quite realistic in the New Economy.

So, the public choice theory articulated by Tiebout is relevant to urban economic development policy in that it illustrates competition between municipalities for firms and individuals. When local government recognizes the preferences of the businesses in its area, and provides a "basket" of public goods that satisfies those preferences, those businesses are less likely to move away. Also, by providing a desirable bundle of public goods, new firms might be attracted to move into the area.

Economic Base Theory

In a sort of "new mercantilism," economic base theory suggests that economic growth occurs only through exports, therefore cities should encourage exports and limit imports. Just as mercantilism advocated accumulating gold and silver through exportation, the economic base theory suggests a city can accumulate wealth from other cities when its firms sell goods and services to residents of other cities. Orlando, Florida and Ocean City, New Jersey are two cities whose economies are almost totally export-based–tourism is the primary industry in these two cities.

The multiplier effect is the most essential component of the economic base model. The export of goods starts a chain reaction where money is both reinvested in the means of production and paid to labor through wages. Thus a multiplier effect is at work in this model, where each dollar of export income generates more than a dollar in economic activity.

Local government officials who buy into economic base theory place high value on developing the "basic sector," which includes firms that rely on external markets more than the local market. General Motors, for example, sells some cars to Detroit residents, but most of its sales are in external markets. Determining which industries are basic is often done with shift-share analysis using employment proportions, or firm income as the unit of analysis.

Not only should exports be encouraged, but imports should be limited. In economic base theory, imports are viewed as "leakages," so import substitution is advocated. Local governments and local firms are encouraged to "buy local," to keep the dollars within the local economy.

Product Cycle Theory

Product cycle theory is typically considered a component of the economic base theory. This theory contends that a product has three distinct stages (see Figure 3.1).

Figure 3.1. The Product Life-Cycle

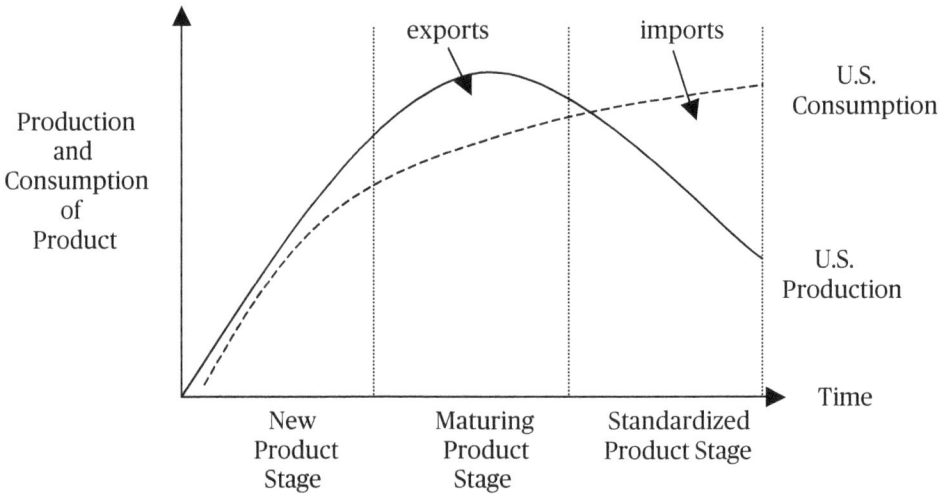

Source: Vernon, 1966.

In the first stage, new products are created and utilized in the same region. This occurs in wealthy regions because they possess the resources necessary to create new products, and they have consumers wealthy enough to purchase the products (Vernon, 1966). Personal computers illustrate the product cycle. During the "new product phase" of the 1970s and 1980s, the Apple II, Radio Shack TRS-80, Atari 800, Commodore 64, and the IBM 5150 PC, were all invented, produced and consumed in the U.S..

In the second stage, the "maturing product stage," the region produces more of the good than it consumes in order to meet new demand from consumers in other regions. Thus the product is exported as was the case of personal computers during the 1980s.

In the final stage, the product is standardized. Today only two personal computer standards are available: the Macintosh and the IBM PC. Standardization allows for mass production (rather than batch-production) resulting in lower costs and prices (Sievert and Dodge, 2001, p. 92). With lower prices, profits are also often lower, so firms seek new innovative products and shift the production of mature standardized products to less wealthy areas. This is the case with personal computers as the U.S. now imports more computers than it exports.

The relevance of product cycle theory to economic development is that city leaders should be aware of the product cycles for goods produced in their locales, and innovation should be encouraged because it contributes to economic growth. The first color television sets were built in 1954 at an RCA factory in Bloomington, Indiana (Browning, 1993). Bloomington possessed relatively cheap labor and was centrally located in reference to the national market for televisions. Bloomington developed economically largely because of major innovative employers such as RCA and GE. But televisions are now in the latter phase of the product cycle. RCA has since been sold to Thomson Consumer Electronics, a French company, that has closed U.S. factories and moved the production to China where labor is cheaper ("Thomson Will Cut 820 Jobs," 2003).

Friedman's Monetarist Theory

Nobel laureate Milton Friedman claims the three societal goals of political freedom, economic efficiency, and shared economic power are "best realized by relying, as far as possible, on a market mechanism within a 'competitive order' to organize the utilization of economic resources" (1948, p. 246). In Friedman's view, the market system most efficiently allocates resources; and government intervention only aggravates economic problems. Friedman's "monetarist" theory suggests that government should only try to influence business cycles by controlling inflation and recession by managing the money supply rather than through more government spending.

Inflation occurs when the overall price level of an economy increases. Inflation has numerous compounding negative effects including decreased purchasing power, redistribution of wealth, a reduction in productive work, a reduction in the savings rate, and an increase in interest rates. The most common type of inflation, called "demand-pull" inflation, occurs when the supply of money in circulation increases– more money is available to buy the same amount of goods, so prices rise, similar to the effect of bidding at an auction. Increased demand for goods "pulls" prices up.

To prevent demand-pull inflation, the federal government, through the Federal Reserve Bank, tries to control the supply of money. The Fed controls money supply in many ways, but most notably through interest rates. When interest rates are raised, banks are less likely to borrow from the Fed, and therefore less likely to loan money to firms and individuals. Thus higher interest rates limit the total amount of credit available in the economy, so the supply of money climbs at a slower rate, therefore limiting inflation.

Another fiscal tool used by the Fed to reduce inflation is to sell more securities such as Treasury bills and Treasury bonds. The cash that investors pay for these debt obligations reduces the amount of money in circulation, which also reduces inflation.

Recession is when "total spending or aggregate demand falls below the amount needed to bring about full employment and potential GDP" (Sievert and Dodge, 2001, p. 342). A drop in spending is caused when individuals and firms pay more of their money towards taxes and savings combined with decreases in government spending and/or investment spending. Thus recession is the opposite problem of inflation–not enough money is in circulation. Fiscal policies that combat recession are those policies that encourage more money to circulate. The Fed lowers interest rates, thus making more money available through credit, and the Fed buys back its Treasury securities–replacing debt obligations with cash.

Today the federal government attempts to control the money supply by adjusting interest rates just as Milton Friedman suggested–a stable money supply creates an environment for investment and growth. This focus on monetary policy rather than fiscal policy is what separates Friedman from Keynes. In the post-September 11 recession, Friedman was quick to criticize governments for intervening in the distressed airline industry, and for returning taxes to stimulate the economy (Ashtead, 2001). Friedman's influence is apparent in the last thirty years in the movements toward downsizing government, reducing taxes, and the greater use of market mechanisms to provision and provide public goods and services. Local government officials who ascribe to Friedman's theory are likely to ignore specific urban problems in hopes that the mechanics of the market system will eventually solve those problems.

Neoclassical Economics

Neoclassical theories of economics largely follow the same logic and arguments of classical economics. The economic problem is again seen as the study of allocation of resources that are scarce, and competition in the market economy is still seen as the best path to economic growth. Neoclassical economics is not as neatly defined as classical economics, and is largely seen as an improvement upon, rather than a departure from, the classical economic school of thought. Some of the major emphases of neoclassical economists include marginal utility, equilibrium, profit maximization, and microeconomics. This section briefly explains these emphases and describes how neoclassical thought is influencing economic development practice.

The theory of marginal utility, developed in the 1870s, states that the value of a good or service is largely determined by the amount of utility it provides to the consumer. "Marginal" utility refers to the additional satisfaction received from consuming one more unit of the good or service. This marks a significant change from the view of the classical economists that the value of a good or service was determined by the amount of labor resources devoted to its production. In his 1890 textbook, *Principles of Economics*, Alfred Marshall explains that this shift in emphasis from supply to demand infers that consumers, rather than producers, exert more influence on determining equilibrium in the marketplace. Economic development officials ascribing to this view would then be likely to implement programs that help local firms benefiting from a high demand for their products. This logic is at the root of economic development programs that target the expansion of local businesses. If consumers (demand-side) are seen to have more control over the labor market than amount of labor to produce the good (supply-side), which appears to be true in market economies, then economic development officials are likely to implement programs that aid employers deemed likely to produce products in high demand.

Equilibrium is the stated goal of neoclassical economists. When equilibrium is not present in a regional economy, shortages or surpluses of resources occur. Market forces are expected to move the economy back into equilibrium. For example, if wages are too high, firms hire less workers, resulting in a labor surplus, usually dubbed, "unemployment." High unemployment is just one of many situations that lower labor costs–ultimately equilibrium is achieved.

Unlike classical economics that values increased output, neoclassical economics emphasizes increased profits. In classical economics, a firm increases production output through increased resource inputs, especially labor. In neoclassical economics, firms attempt to find their optimum scale of plant, where profits are highest, which might not be at the maximum production point. Workers also make decisions according to profit maximization; weighing income, benefits, time off, etc., against the personal costs of working a job. The individual maximization decisions of firms and workers are thought to move the market into equilibrium. Therefore the macroeconomy is explained by the aggregate economic decisions of microeconomic actors such as firms and workers. This emphasis on microeconomics is evident in current economic development practices that target certain industrial clusters, individual firms (such as the efforts to attract new auto plants), or practices that target certain types of individuals (such as skills training for unskilled workers).

Contemporary Theories of Economic Development Rooted in Neoclassical Economics

Some of the contemporary theories of economic development that seem to have their roots in neoclassical economics include Porter's clustering theory, Birch's small business theory, and Peterson's City Limits theory.

Porter's Clustering Theory of Economic Development

Michael Porter, a Harvard professor, is another economic theorist whose ideas have proved relevant to urban economic development. Much of Porter's work is characterized by a call for corporations to abandon short-term goals, and focus on long-term strategic planning to increase competitive advantages. These same concepts apply to the private sector also. Porter (2000) suggests nations, regions, and cities can increase their competitiveness in economic markets by investing in their core industries, or "clusters." Inner cities, for example, can experience economic growth by exploiting certain competitive advantages such as labor supply, proximity to interstates and other infrastructure, rather than solely relying on redistributive social programs.

Birch's Small Business Theory of Economic Development

David Birch, an MIT physicist, radically influenced economic thought with his 1987 book, *Job Creation in America: How Our Smallest Companies Put the Most People to Work*. As the subtitle suggests, Birch found that small businesses create 82% of all new jobs. Birch's empirical findings shifted attention to firms of all size, large and small, while before the 1980s much macroeconomic thought, and therefore policy, solely concentrated on large companies. Congress and local economic development officials then spawned many new policies that favored and encouraged entreprenuership (Case, 1989). In a study similar to Birch's, University of Minnesota researcher, Paul Reynolds, found that 42% of the net new jobs in Minnesota were added by new businesses (Reynolds, 1999).

Peterson's City Limits Theory

Peterson's (1981) City Limits thesis posits that the limited resources available to local governments prevent them from addressing all of the needs in their locality. City governments never have enough tax revenue to pay for all the services that citizens demand. Because of these "city limits," government leaders must choose which of the numerous distributional, allocational and redistributive policies and programs to implement.

Peterson recommends that suburbs should favor developmental policies. "Because of their limited size, (suburbs) can modulate their local policies to suit the particular preferences of a relatively small number of residents" (1981, p. 104). Using zoning laws, suburbs can control how their land is used, keeping out undesirable firms and individuals, "thereby minimizing interresident variability in the benefit/tax ratio...all residents pay roughly the same amounts for the services" (1981, p. 104). Peterson concludes that "redistribution is kept to a minimum" in suburbs (1981, p. 104).

Regarding central cities, Peterson observes, they "cannot escape from engaging in a considerable degree of redistribution" (1981, p. 104). A central city has traditionally been able to "exploit the great wealth their location generated to provide a level of public services that far outstripped the outlying communities" (1981, p. 105). But due to advances in transportation and communication systems, people and firms are now more free to choose where to live and do business.

Today Tiebout's public choice model is more reality than theory. Since World War II, central cities have been losing both firms and residents to the suburbs. Suburbs compete more evenly with central cities for firms and residents. "The luxury of redistribution which was once possible is becoming increasingly difficult to sustain" (1981, p. 106), therefore, central cites should focus attention on the economic base. Somebody else (i.e. state and federal governments) should worry about social issues such as housing and poverty.

Keynesian Economics

In his influential 1936 book, *The General Theory of Employment, Interest, and Money*, John Maynard Keynes argues that government should intervene when markets fail. Keynes' argument laid the foundation for increased government intervention in economic markets, and government intervention in many other parts of society.

The neoclassical economists before Keynes believed that market equilibrium is produced by supply and demand alone. So-called "market failures" were only short term and required no government intervention. Market-driven adjustments in prices and interest rates were thought to eliminate disequilibrium in markets. For example, in response to high unemployment (such as during the Great Depression), neoclassicals suggest reducing labor prices, which reduces prices of manufactured goods, which increases buying, which should lead to economic recovery.

Keynes argues that these causes do not always have the desired effects; therefore market equilibrium is not automatic. So Keynes suggested "counter-cyclical" fiscal policies. When a nation's economy was in recession, government could pump money into the economy through deficit spending. During prosperous times, government can suppress inflation through increasing taxes or cutting government spending. The Works Progress Administration and the Public Works Administration, both part of FDR's New Deal, are examples of Keynesian ideas put into practice. These programs, which provided numerous jobs in massive public construction projects, illustrated that government spending can have positive impacts on the overall economy.

Keynes observed that production increases are affected more by increases in public spending, rather than increases in private consumption. This phenomenon, dubbed the "Keynesian multiplier," led to the conclusion that increased government spending might exponentially increase production. This idea appears to have been widely accepted as local government capital investment has dramatically increased throughout the twentieth century. Keynes' ideas are also the basic foundation of liberal politics that favor higher taxes and government spending.

Many American city leaders espouse the virtues of free market capitalism, which if it truly was the primary model, we would see very little government intervention in the marketplace. The fact that state and local governments have established official mechanisms to promote economic development suggests that the Keynesian approach is alive and well in local markets across the country. But neoclassical economic theory has not lost its influence. The coupling of free market capitalism with limited government intervention, often called the "Neoclassical-Keynesian Synthesis," characterizes the current U.S. economy, and is the dominant school of thought in mainstream economics.

Contemporary Theories of Economic Development Rooted in Keynesian Economics

Equity planning theory, the new markets theory, and the labor force theory of development are three contemporary theories of economic development that seems to have their roots in Keynesian economics.

Equity Planning Theory

Many of the theories of economic development policies noted above can be labeled "pro-growth," or "corporatist." The corporatist label refers to a system of governance wherein government and business maintain a close relationship that benefits both parties (Schmitter, 1974). An opposite perspective is referred to as "progressive," or, in the urban scene, "equity planning." Both camps share the same objective–economic growth, but they see different paths to that end. The pro-growth camp takes a supply-side economic approach to growth; the economy is stimulated by investing public funds into private firms. The "equity" camp favors economic growth through demand-side redistributive policy (Goetz, 1994). The two groups battle each other in local political arenas. Since the mid-1980s, growth machines have declined in many U.S. cities and the equity planners have gained more traction. This reflects a shift toward more progressive policies that "redistribute public and private resources to the poor and working class" rather than directly to firms (Metzger, 1996, p. 112). In response to the urban societal problems of the 1970s, many suggested government funds should be invested in education and programs that result in increased family support.

New Markets Theory

The new markets theory considers "ghettos and declining rural areas as economic opportunity zones" for retail investment (Blakely & Bradshaw, 2002, p. 61). While many retailers focus on a "big-box" suburban strategy, the $85 billion inner-city retail market is often overlooked. Boston Consulting Group research found that more than 25 percent of inner-city retail demand is unmet. Retail firms might experience burdensome operating costs due to crime and vandalism, but the BCG claims the rewards outweigh the risks: "High volume and preferences for certain high-margin goods translate into attractive bottom-line results" (BCG, 1998, p. 2). Areas that are typically underserved include grocery, apparel, pharmacy, and fast food. The influence of the new markets theory drives city economic development officials to try to attract retail back into central cities so that the vast purchasing power of city residents is kept in the city.

Labor Force Theory of Development

The labor force theory of development, "stresses the importance of an educated, skilled, and dependable workforce for attracting and growing businesses" (Koven & Lyons, 2003, p. 189). An educated workforce contributes to a "good business climate," making a city more attractive to firms looking for new locations (Fitzgerald & Leigh, 2002, p. 194). Development of a city's labor force can also be instrumental not only for business attraction, but also for business retention. The case of Metropolitan College in Louisville illustrates how economic development officials developed a unique part of their labor force (third-shift package handlers) to retain United Parcel Service, the largest employer in the state (Koven & Strother, 2002).

The Workforce Investment Act of 1998 consolidated the more than 160 federal government job-training programs under one system. Previous research indicated the federal job-training system was inefficient (Fitzgerald & McGregor, 1993), perhaps because institutions of education and employment training, such as schools and community colleges, are structurally separate from official economic development entities. Local economic development officials typically work with developers and businesspeople, rather than poor individuals in need of skills training (Fitzgerald & Leigh, 2002). Effective labor force development therefore requires effective linkage between development and education and includes not only a focus on training, but also on placement, retention, advancement, and mentoring (Kodrzycki, 1997).

Chapter Summary

Various classical and contemporary economic and political theories inform the economic development policies and practices in U.S. cities. From a broad perspective, it appears that no single theory fully explains economic development, yet neoclassical economic theory (with its focus on reduced taxes for business, and limited government action to spur production), conservative political theory (with its focus on business development and public-private negotiation to manage development), and various location theories seem to yield the most influence on contemporary economic development practice in American cities. Neoclassical economic theory also closely aligns with what we are calling Market Cities principles, meaning city leaders, whether public or private, favor policies and practices (or the lack thereof) that favor free market principles rather than government interventionist policies.

Guest Case: How Natural Disasters Can Result in Urban Revitalization and Economic Recovery

By: Thomas D. Cairns, Azusa Pacific University

Anyone who has ever experienced a hurricane, tornado, flooding, mud slide or earthquake knows the damage it causes. The loss of human life and property is tragic but in every dark cloud there is a silver lining for those communities that survive.

Cities such as Tuscaloosa, in West Central Alabama are an example of how a natural disaster can result in an opportunity for a community to not just rebuild but revitalize. In April of 2011, a mile wide tornado left a path of destruction 6 miles long through the heart of the city. In 6 minutes over 12% of the city was destroyed along with over 5,000 homes, 53 dead, and 1,200 injured and 7,000 left homeless. However, in just two months following this disaster Tuscaloosa would be named the "most liveable city in America" by the U.S. Conference of Mayors.

The loss of human life is not to be diminished as loved ones are irreplaceable and care needs to be taken to comfort those who suffer. Recovery efforts start the moment the storm passes. The assembling and distribution of food, clothing and shelter to storm victims. There are rescue and cleanup operations. Financial aid from federal, state and local governments is being determined along with charitable donations from corporations and private citizens. These monies can total into the millions of dollars and is used to assist in the recovery and rebuilding efforts. In most instances, the monies are used to replace what has been lost i.e., homes, schools, hospitals, etc. However, the city of Tuscaloosa chose to take a different approach than simply replacing buildings that were destroyed to strategically assess how the money should be invested to not only rebuild but revitalize the city.

The Mayor and City Council proactively created a Tuscaloosa Forward Strategic Rebuilding Plan. The plan included a vision for the future and required the cooperation and support of the city government, business and community. The plan addressed everything critical to moving the city forward such as infrastructure, energy, transportation, natural resources, zoning and quality of life. The plan was full of progressive ideas for the future and would be used to guide the overall recovery efforts to assure objectives were achieved. The Council formally presented the plan across the community through townhall meetings. The Council proactively sought and received the input and feedback from over 3,000 people who attended the townhalls and 70,000 hits on the plan's website.

Once the plan was finalized the Council had a blueprint for assuring physical and economic recovery. The plan would take months to complete. In the meantime the Council had to address the immediate aftermath of the storm. The Council had provided for immediate financial relief by setting aside a reserve of $10 million dollars. That allowed the city to address the loss of low-income housing that had been completely destroyed in the storm. The city was able to create new high-density housing that met the demand and was a showcase for urban housing in the future. The high-density housing enabled the city to rezone some residential areas to mixed use and that encouraged commercial development. It was a win-win.

The city of Tuscaloosa received a commitment of $60 million dollars from the federal government. However, implementation of the plan has been slow because it took almost 15 months after the storm before the first federal funds of approximately $17 million were received. The Council was able to prioritize their investments because they had a plan and stretch remaining funds through interest free loans. All these efforts have produced $170 million dollars of economic activity in the city with construction, restaurants, banks, retails shops, etc.

The success of the city's efforts can be attributed to their approaching the recovery with an eye on the present and future. This took leadership, vision, time, community support and resources. Not everything has gone according to plan and delays have drawn criticism but the Mayor and Council have not sacrificed the long term for the short term. The experience of Tuscaloosa represents a model for how other cities faced with recovering from a natural disaster can rebuild and renew for the future.

CHAPTER 4

POLITICAL THEORIES RELEVANT TO ECONOMIC DEVELOPMENT

Conservatism, neo-conservatism, and liberalism are the political perspectives most relevant to economic development in the U.S. All three agree that political and social life should be built on the following principles: 1) individual equality, 2) prosperity replacing poverty, and 3) democratic rule (Weinberger, 2001, p. 39). They agree these are worthwhile ends, but the means to accomplish these ends are disputed. This chapter explains the general ideas of these three political philosophies, and how they influence economic development practice. Table 4.1 offers a comparison of these three major political perspectives.

Conservatism

The conservative political philosophy is characterized by a preference for limited government, and a resistance toward rapid change. Traditional norms are valued and should be "conserved" while radical changes are to be avoided. In general terms, the word, "conservative" describes an attitude that values the way things are, and resists the "liberal," "radical," or "progressive" philosophies and movements.

Reacting to the radical new utopian ideas associated with modernism and the Enlightenment towards the end of the eighteenth century, English political philosopher, Edmund Burke, articulated conservative thought. Burke argued it would be disastrous to try to remake society's established order–an order based in religion, tradition, and aristocracy–into a new society based on the abstract principles of individual rights and equality.

Paradoxically, conservatives today agree that, "Change is inevitable, that democracy is inevitable, that democracy is good, and that all human beings are born as moral equals" (Weinberger, 2001, p 38). So, conservative thought today is mainly characterized by the general idea that radical societal change should be avoided. Conservatism's general ideas, politics, and influences on economic development practices are described below.

Typical of most political philosophies, conservatism values individual equality, prosperity, and democratic rule. Conservatives believe individual equality is achieved when all members of society have "equality of opportunity," and they admit this does not guarantee "equality of outcome." A conservative might be content if an economic development program, such as job skills training, is made available to society's poor, even if the poor choose not to participate in the program. Similarly, conservatives might "judge inequalities in mature democratic societies to be legitimate and not the result of rigid, and thus unfair advantages" (Weinberger, 2001, p 40).

The leisure/labor trade-off in the economic literature is relevant here; if a person chooses more leisure, we shoult not be upset that he has less wealth than someone who chose labor.

Since conservatives like Russell Kirk (1978) reject utopian ideals, societal inequalities are tolerable–at least in the short term. Prosperity is a long term prospect. Since conservatives value individual responsibility, the assumption is made that irresponsible people might live in poverty. It is this notion of individual responsibility that drives conservatives to oppose the welfare state, transfer payments, and big government. Conservatives would rather, as the proverb states, "teach a man to fish and feed a man for life" than "give a man a fish and feed him for a day." Most conservatives, like the Catholic theologian, Michael Novak (1982), are opposed to centralized economic and political planning and prefer to let free market capitalism solve societal problems. In fact, many conservatives consider government to be the cause of many societal problems. Conservative ideas about politics and government are characterized by the idea of limited government, largely in response to the liberal "big government" redistributive social programs that have prevailed in the twentieth century.

Table 4.1. Comparison of Major Political Theories

Theory	Goals	Key Scholars	Key Characteristics
Conservative	equality of opportunity prosperity replacing poverty democracy	Edmund Burke Russell Kirk Michael Novak	traditional societal order should be conserved focus on big business social inequalities are tolerable individual responsibility and morality "irresponsibility" drives poverty prosperity is a long-term prospect opposition to centralized economic and political planning free market capitalism deficit government spending
Neo-Conservative	equality of opportunity prosperity replacing poverty democracy	Irving Kristol	balanced budget spending democratic capitalism to be exported abroad focus on small business development public-private negotiation to manage development equity social programs in moderation

Theory	Goals	Key Scholars	Key Characteristics
Classical Liberal	democracy liberty checks and balances freedom individual rights	Montesquieu John Locke	plurality in government toleration social justice intervention equity economic development techniques
Modern Liberal	equality of outcome social justice government intervention	John Stuart Mill Herbert Croly Woodrow Wilson	equity justice communal ends protection of the weak

In the U.S. the Republican Party is the home of conservative ideology. Conservatism appeals more to rural and suburban-dwellers, and less to central city residents and members of the "chattering classes" (intellectuals, journalists, educators, and public administrators) (Weinberger, 2001, p. 41). Regarding certain social issues, contemporary political conservatism favors traditional values of personal responsibility, support for moral values, and opposition to programs that reward broad classifications of people such as affirmative action. Regarding certain economic issues, conservatism favors limited taxes, limited regulation of business, reduced size of government, and opposition to the welfare state. The influence of these conservative ideals can be seen more in the economic development practices that favor business attraction and retention, and less in economic development practices dubbed "community development."

Neo-Conservative

A neoconservative is "a liberal who has been mugged by reality," says the "godfather" of neoconservatives, Irving Kristol. Early neo-conservatives were socialist-leaning liberals. But they began to despise the anti-Americanism of the 1960s liberal counterculture, and so began to break away from liberalism. Not fully liberal, and not fully conservative, the neo-conservative political philosophy could be described as a synthesis of the two. Neo-conservatism's general ideas, politics, and influences on economic development practices are described in this section.

Like conservatives, neo-conservatives believe individual equality is achieved through "equality of opportunity" rather than the "equality of outcome" favored by liberals. They supported the civil rights movement, but grew disillusioned with massive social programs such as Johnson's Great Society. In his 1999 book, *Neo-Conservatism: The Autobiography of an Idea,* Kristol describes U.S. welfare programs as "the best of intentions, the worst of results." Unlike liberals who favor massive social welfare programs, and unlike conservatives who largely prefer free-markets and supply-side economics to alleviate social problems, neo-conservatives prefer social welfare programs on a small-scale.

Regarding the pursuit of prosperity, neo-conservatives believe that economic growth is driven by the supply side of the economy. Therefore, cutting tax rates is a reasonable policy to "stimulate steady economic growth" (Kristol, 2003, p. 23). But unlike conservatives, they think government should be "far less risk averse" and that government should avoid "reckless" budget deficits and be "more sensible about the fundamentals of economic reckoning" (Kristol, 2003, p. 24). So neo-conservatives are content to tighten their belts today in order to achieve a more affluent tomorrow. However, they recognize that society's "egalitarian illusions and demagogic appeals" drive politicians to spend tomorrow's money today (Kristol, 2003, p. 24).

Regarding democratic rule, neo-conservatives "are comfortable in modern America" (Kristol, 2003, p. 24), but would like to see democratic capitalism implemented across the globe. Neo-conservatives appear more vocal regarding foreign policy issues, rather than domestic issues. They have historically been opposed to communism and are hawkish admirers of Teddy Roosevelt's "big stick" interventionist foreign policy. In some circles, "neocon" is a derogatory term reserved for those who favor American hegemony across the globe.

Neo-conservatives are more likely to prefer "developmental" policies designed to attract new businesses or retain existing businesses, rather than "equity" redistributive programs. But they recognize that "development alone is not reducing poverty and unemployment," and that government should use market mechanisms to plan, design, and implement programs. "Public-private negotiation" is seen as a way to manage development in a way that balances the needs of both firms and individuals (Frieden, 1989, p. 85-86).

Politically, neo-conservatives have been ostracized from the Democratic Party and have only been allowed into the Republic Party as "parasites," according to staunch conservative Pat Buchanan. Buchanan (2003) says they are influential only because they attach themselves to powerful hosts such as Ronald Reagan. But not everyone agrees. Kristol argues that the moderate views of neo-conservatives have converted the Republican Party "into a new kind of conservative politics suitable to governing a modern democracy" (2003, p. 23). Regarding urban economic development, Siegel (1997) embodies the neo-conservative view that most urban problems have been caused by the policies of liberal politicians.

Liberalism

The political philosophy that is currently labeled "classical liberalism" values the personal liberty of the individual as the end goal. In general terms, liberalism is a reaction to political oppression and official abuse. Individual freedom is therefore more important than the state. Liberalism's foundation was laid by the French philosopher, Montesquieu (1748), who articulated the ideas of constitutionalism and the separation of powers to avoid official corruption and abuse. James Madison, in *The Federalist Papers* (1780s), argued that civil liberties would be protected in a pluralistic civil society (instead of an aristocratic society), and the government should be representative in its composition, and limited in its power and scope. Locke's, *The Second Treatise of Government* (1689), a warning against powerful government, also informs classical liberalism. Because personal liberty is paramount, liberalism is characterized by the ideals of plurality, toleration, justice, and intervention. Liberalism's general ideas, politics, and influences on economic development practices are described below.

Classical liberalism also values work, private property, checks and balances, and rule of law. In the late nineteenth century, John Locke's classical liberalism had evolved into reform liberalism. Reform liberals "are noted by their desire to use governmental power to remedy the inequalities of the marketplace" (Koven, 1988, p. 66). Reform liberalism focused on issues of equity and assistance for the "little people." Reform liberals found that to achieve greater equality, "redistribution of social resources and opportunities may be necessary," although liberals disagree about the "degree of equality necessary for realizing full liberties" (Rosenblum, 2001, p 116). Prosperity is society's objective, but consensus lacks in the liberal camp on how to define prosperity, and how to achieve it. Regarding democratic rule, liberalism values plurality, toleration, justice, and intervention. This is evident as liberals were the driving force behind women's suffrage, the civil rights movement, and affirmative action. Powerless minority groups should be protected in a democracy, and "not at a disadvantage in the public distribution of social goods" (Rosenblum, 2001, p 118).

Therefore modern liberals favor "equity" economic development programs and practices that benefit the poor and minorities. Business incentives should be avoided, and city leaders should invest instead in targeted disadvantaged areas (Kleniewski, 1989). In their 1992 book, *Separate Societies*, Goldsmith and Blakely argue that government economic development policies and programs should be implemented that redistribute public and private resources from larger society to the forgotten and isolated urban poor.

Liberal political ideology is mostly at home in the Democratic Party in the U.S. Liberalism appeals to the poor, blue-collar workers, central city residents, and the "intelligentsia." Liberals support affirmative action, environmental protection, regulation of business, and most government social programs including welfare, healthcare, unemployment benefits and retirement programs.

Because classical and reform liberals see poverty and inequality as an affront on personal liberty, they are more likely to follow the Keynesian economic school of thought, which advocates government intervention in the marketplace. This intervention is demand-side focused—people should be pulled out of poverty into "liberty." Because liberalism focuses on personal liberty, economic development is viewed from the perspective of microeconomics. Thus, social programs that use redistributive transfer payments to help individuals are preferred over programs designed to help private firms. Liberals also fear that big business leads to exploitation of common people and big government is needed to balance the power of big business.

Location Theories of Economic Development

Central place theory, the theory of market areas, and the theory of agglomeration illuminate economic development in cities because these two theories attempt to explain the location decisions of individuals and businesses.

Central Place Theory

Central place theory suggests that cities emerged as places where society's needs for defense, worship and trade were met (Maki & Lichty, 2000). Central place theory assumes transportation is a major factor in economic decision making, therefore as the agrarian economy changed to an industrial economy people began to locate in cities for proximity to industrial work, and entertainment. Agricultural surplus is another explanation for cities as central places; as farmers produce more goods than they can consume, they travel to urban centers to sell their surplus goods. Central place theory is a "purely market explanation for the emergence and location of cities" (Maki & Lichty, 2000, p. 85). People from the hinterlands gathered in a central place, and cities were born.

Theory of the Market Area

The theory of the market area simply suggests that firms want to locate near their customers. The market area is the region in which a firm sells its product. Alonso observes, "Since the median of the distribution of customers will tend to be in large cities, this is one of the reasons why big cities tend to grow bigger" (1972, p. 18). Firms achieve profits through economies of scale, so firms seek to enlarge their market area or simply locate in the middle of the market area (Lösch, 1964). This creates an increased demand for land which in turn drives up the price of real estate in the city center. Paradoxically the customer base in an urban economy exerts a centripetal force pulling firms inward, while higher rents exert centrifugal force pushing firms outward.

Similar to the theory of the market area, a "theory of the resource area" could be explained. Firms whose natural resources are expensive to transport will probably locate near those resources (Maki & Lichty, 2000). This explains why oil companies are headquartered in Texas, and limestone companies are headquartered in Indiana. Booze offers a good example. Wineries prefer to locate near their suppliers due to the cost and weight of their inputs. It takes three pounds of grapes to make a bottle of wine that only weighs one and a half pounds, so wineries choose to locate near vineyards and ship the lighter finished product out to their customers. Breweries on the other hand locate near their customers. Their lightweight inputs (hops, malt, and yeast) are distributed to breweries then mixed with the heaviest input, water. The finished product is heavier than the inputs so it is more economical for breweries to be dispersed in cities around the country.

Agglomeration Theory

The theory of agglomeration suggests that similar firms tend to locate near each other to benefit from shared technology, and to be nearer to suppliers and specialized labor (Marshall, 1920). For example, firms in the garment industry have tended to agglomerate in New York City to be near the pool of labor that specializes in garment-making. Houston, Texas is home to many chemical companies whose leaders understand the value of locating near their needed natural resources (oil), but also in proximity to other firms in their industry.

Growth Pole Theory

Unlike the concept of equilibrium that suggests growth flows to less costly areas, the growth pole theory suggests that geographic "poles" exist that attract growth (Perroux, 1983). Many cities in Silicon Valley, for example, are growth poles that have attracted numerous high-tech firms. West Louisville's "Rubbertown" neighborhood could also be considered a "growth pole" as it has attracted over a dozen chemical, rubber, and tire factories over the past century.

Chapter Summary

Various classical and contemporary economic and political theories inform the economic development policies and practices in U.S. cities. From a broad perspective, it appears that no single theory fully explains economic development, yet neoclassical economic theory (with its focus on reduced taxes for business, and limited government action to spur production), conservative political theory (with its focus on business development and public-private negotiation to manage development), and various location theories seem to yield the most influence on contemporary economic development practice in American cities. Conservative political theory is most closely aligned with Market Cities principles as conservatives expect businesses and individuals to work hard and prosper with no need for government assistance.

Guest Case: Wal-Mart, Not-Smart

By: Fritz Huber

Economic development constitutes the heart of thriving, healthy communities and the economies that support them. It increases the tax base, which helps serves to improve and maintain local infrastructure such as roads, parks, libraries, and emergency medical services. It also advances job development, providing better wages, benefits, and opportunities for residents. In addition, it improves business retention, which in the long run contributes to the municipal economy by enabling businesses to continue to operate locally. Economic development also fosters economic diversification, which helps to expand the local economy and reduces a community's vulnerability to fluctuations in a single business sector. It empowers the local economy to be increasingly more self-sufficient, and lastly, it increases the quality of life in the developing community. The increase in local tax dollars and job creation raise the economic tide for the entire community, including the overall standard of living of the residents.

Although economic development is the foundation of building a thriving community, business attraction and development is being met with considerable resistance in cities all over the United States, particularly concerning Big Box companies. Big Boxes strike fear in the hearts of local business owners who understand that the development of a Big Box company could mean the demise of local businesses, especially retail enterprises. City leaders, on the other hand, encourage Big Box companies to plant in their cities because of the massive tax revenue and affordable goods that they provide.

Wal-Mart is a perfect example of a Big Box companies that can be detrimental to local businesses. The chain's ability to sell goods more cheaply forms a profound threat to the viability of nearby retail establishments. Some small establishments will be forced to shut down when a new Wal-Mart opens its doors for business, unable to compete with the economies of scale that the retail giant enjoys, and others will be forced to downsize as their customer base declines.

Research sheds light on the astonishing fact that when a Wal-Mart store opens, it kills three local jobs for every two created in-house by reducing retail employment by an average of 2.7 percent in every county they enter (Neumark, David, Zhang, & Ciccarella, 2007). Particularly hard-hit competing businesses tend to be stores selling apparel, shoes, hardware, building supplies, paint and glass, groceries, fabric, and jewelry. A startling study shows that when a single Wal-Mart opened in Chicago in September 2006, 27 percent (82 of 306) of the small businesses in the surrounding neighborhood had gone out of business by March 2008 (Ailawadi, Zhang, Krishna, & Kruger, 2010).

The threat for small businesses and effects on local retail that Wal-Mart has had can be seen throughout the nation. Research has shown that supermarkets and discount variety stores sales decline anywhere from 10 to 40 percent after Wal-Mart's arrival (Stone, Artz, & Myles, 2002). Cities, consequently, have begun to turn their back on Wal-Mart in an attempt to preserve their local economy.

Inglewood, CA, home to 109,673 (2010 United States Census Bureau) and located in the heart of Los Angeles, dealt a blow to the retail giant several years ago. Wal-Mart had plans to design and develop a super-store in their city, but Inglewood voters rejected a measure that would have allowed the massive project. More than 60 percent of Inglewood voters said no to the measure on the ballot, then causing the local city council to turn down the project. Wal-Mart supporters, who include Inglewood's mayor, say that the complex would have brought jobs to a city with a high unemployment rate and offered goods at discounted prices. However, a coalition of opponents, including labor unions, local businesses, and activist Jesse Jackson, say Wal-Mart pays low wages, offers few benefits, and would hurt the city's existing businesses. Wal-Mart critic Daniel Taber hopes that the vote sends a message to the retail giant. He was quoted as saying, "while we may want to shop a discounted prices, we may want to have employment opportunities for out friends and families and seniors and young people, we will not sacrifice our rights as citizens and give you the opportunity to build in Inglewood any way you chose."

The defeat that the retail giant suffered at the hands of the electorate did not end with Wal-Mart simply not being allowed to develop in Inglewood; the company's loss may even make it more difficult to develop further in Los Angeles in the future. Evidence that supports includes that a number of Los Angeles leaders have drafted proposals to ban large super-stores from parts of their cities.

Cities around the country are recognizing the negative effects that the development of Big Box companies, like Wal-Mart, imply for their economies. With the realization that the value Wal-Mart adds to the economy will likely be less than the value of the jobs and businesses it replaces, cities, like Inglewood, are beginning to reject their development, deterring any future expansion of Big Box companies in their local economies. Companies like Wal-Mart have their place, but city managers should research the impact that the introduction of a Big Box company will have on their city. Cities managers cannot shortsightedly believe that the launch of a Big Box company will not create opportunity costs, realized in the loss of local businesses, but whether or not those impacts will create a net societal gain is a matter for local cost-benefit analysis and debate.

Guest Case: Wal-Mart: Negative Effects on Local Communities

By: Brad Petty

City leaders thirst for economic development. Similarly business leaders seek locations for their companies that present the most profitable environment. This thirst for economic development can be seen in communities around the country as it influences important business decisions. Evidence for this can be seen by the income and property tax advantages, relocation assistance, and fast-track permitting (just to name a few) that local communities offer companies as incentives for relocating.

Communities gain numerous advantages from bringing new corporations to their cities. Some advantages include new jobs, increased tax income, and the subsequent development of local suburbs increasing populations. As local communities compete to entice new business, companies look at environmental, economic, social, and political factors to determine which communities will foster the most profitable environment. According to Fujita, Krugman, and Venables, authors of the 1999 book, *Spatial Economy*, firms locate at the height in their market potential created by a concentration of other firms or by creating a new cusp altogether. A great amount of research by companies goes into these important decisions, which can ultimately determine the success or failure of a company in certain regions.

An example of a company that has taken advantage of local economic incentives coupled with solid research by in potential profitability is retail giant, Wal-Mart. According to the Global Fortune 500, Wal-Mart has grown to be the largest company in the world and has stimulated economic development in many local communities. A heated debate has spawned from the retail market takeover that occurs when Wal-Mart enters a community and whether this is advantageous or harmful to local businesses and economic development. Popular rhetoric suggests the entrance of Wal-Mart into a market negatively affects local businesses as well.

Bias in research has failed to take into account important economic factors that provide an accurate model of the effect of Wal-Mart in local communities. For example, Ken Stone of Iowa State University conducted an early study of Wal-Mart's effect in Iowa. This study concluded that Wal-Mart contributed to the loss of "mom and pop" stores and a reduction in retail employment. However, Stone failed to account for the 3.4% decline in population from 1983 to 1989, a drop equaled by few states even during the Great Depression (Hicks, 2006).

Furthermore, an extensive study of Wal-Mart, completed in 2009, outlines the effect of Wal-Mart's entry into the Florida economy from 1980-2004 and how it affected the entry and exit strategies of other local businesses. The study concluded that although some businesses were deterred by the entry of Wal-Mart, many businesses altered their business models and began offering more specialized products or luxury goods. This benefited communities by offering a diverse local retailer base. New businesses with non-competing products also began replacing competing-product businesses that were exiting (Paruchuri, et. al, 2009).

Taking a look at a more specific example provides a framework to consider the true effect the entrance of Wal-Mart has on local economies. While many cities such as Inglewood, California have worked hard to reject the building of Wal-Mart retail stores, an article written by Tom Van Ripper of Forbes magazine outlines a study released by the Federal Reserve Bank of Minneapolis that studied the effect of Wal-Mart on 89 different counties in its region from 1985-2003. He concluded that personal income, overall employment, and retail employment grew faster in counties with a Wal-Mart than in counties without one. In addition, Ohio University professor Richard Vedder, who has written a book about Wal-Mart, suggests that it forced the entire retail industry to improve (Riper, 2008).

Wal-Mart opened a store in Oakland in 2005 that further exemplifies the effect the company has on local economies. Oakland is typically seen as a low-income area. When Wal-Mart opened a new store in Oakland, there were 11,000 applicants for 400 jobs. After 5 years of operation, the net benefit of jobs created by Wal-Mart was still positive (Basker, 2010). This is a strong representation of the positive effect of Wal-Mart on local economies. In conclusion, the effect of Wal-Mart on local communities holds a positive outlook, which varies on economic and regional conditions.

Hedge Fund Agglomeration: An Intuitive Approach

By: Alan Feng

Technology has transformed high-wealth financial services. The speed at which trading strategies evolve is on par with speed at which information is exchanged. Nevertheless, technological growth does not change the most fundamental economic principle: firms seek to maximize profits. Even with supercomputers for big data analysis, and program trading for rapid arbitrage, hedge funds still exhibit a particular business behavior that can be found as early as the medieval times–agglomeration.

If hedge funds are information oriented, and information can be accessed anywhere via the Internet, why do hedge fund cluster in the same area? Why are there hedge fund localization economies in areas such as New York and London? Locating in such areas must benefit hedge funds in one way or another with respect to profitability. The answer to these questions emerges when we examine the factors of production that hedge funds use to generate their products, which may include portfolio management, risk arbitrage strategies, or derivatives investments. Labor pooling, social capital clustering, and knowledge spillover effects–benefits of localization economies–all contribute to higher returns for agglomerated hedge funds.

Hedge funds are private investment vehicles for high wealth individuals. Although hedge funds are often described as a tier of mutual funds because they maintain certain characteristics of traditional financial services, their investment objective, strategy, and behavior set them apart. Hedge funds are usually classified into four types according to their chief investment strategy: long-short funds, relative value funds, event-driven funds, and macro funds.

When comparing hedge funds and traditional mutual funds, long-short funds share the most similarity. Like mutual funds, they take long and short positions to create an optimal portfolio for given a level of risk. Relative value funds exploit securities' pricings to profit from the spread. Event-driven funds seek profits from major corporate events like mergers, acquisitions, or restructurings. Macro funds, as the name suggests, analyze macroeconomic trends to exploit profits. All four hedge fund types differ from traditional mutual funds in that they only serve high wealth investors, take higher risks, and operate with less federal regulations.

Naturally, high-risk investing requires careful management. Human capital and social capital are key factors of production for hedge fund products. Consider the difference between an experienced and well-connected hedge fund manager, and one who is inexperienced and poorly connected. The former better predicts market movements, invents new trading strategies as the market evolves, and works with other fund managers of the same caliber for mutual benefit. In contrast, the latter fund manager makes poorer investment decisions, uses outdated investment techniques, and falls behind due to the lack of mutual innovation.

Localization economies share the same labor pool, leading to a higher potential for human capital, ultimately boosting productivity and growth (Glaeser, Kallal, Scheinkman, & Shleifer, 1992). Considering hedge funds require workers to have a specialized set of financial skills, it is in their best interest to close the skills gap–the amount of training required to bring a worker with an existing skill set to the required skill set for the new job–by hiring those with experience in the fund management sector. Manhattan for example, has a cluster of high-wealth financial services. These existing clusters provide hedge funds with potential workers with a near-zero skills mismatch, which eliminates worker relocation costs and reduces training costs (Papageorgiou, Parwada, & Tan, 2012). Furthermore, employees from these industry clusters have up-to-date knowledge, as well as a preexisting stock of social capital to contribute to the new firm.

Social capital is another key factor of production contributing to the final quality of the products and services produced by the hedge fund. Because hedge funds do not operate in vacuums–they are service-oriented, after all–they need to position themselves within a social network of clients, service providers, and other hedge funds. According to De Figueiredo, Meyer-Doyle, & Rawley (2013), new hedge funds are typically spawns of existing ones. To retain the new fund's social capital, the manager locates near the parent hedge fund, further reinforcing the agglomeration of hedge funds in vibrant financial centers. This effect, manifested in hedge fund spawns, leads to outperforming non-agglomerated hedge funds "by approximately one percent per year" (De Figueiredo, Meyer-Doyle, & Rawley, 2013, p. 30). Ultimately, the stock of social capital translates into higher returns and profits. While one percent sounds small, this marginal benefit reoccurs each year, giving the new hedge fund a competitive advantage over other hedge funds that are outside of the industry cluster.

When viewed as distinct elements, human capital and social capital may not fully justify the need to agglomerate. The true benefit reaped from a localization economy comes from the dynamic interactions, known as knowledge spillover, between the two types of capital, unified by physical agglomeration (De Figueiredo, Meyer-Doyle, & Rawley, 2013). By locating near each other, hedge fund managers who share common know-how and social networks interact with each other to mutually innovate (Klepper & Sleeper, 2002). A trading technique practiced by one hedge fund may be learned by another. As a result, agglomerated hedge funds create a closed loop of mutual benefit, while non-agglomerated funds cannot reap these benefits. The interaction between human capital and social capital should be viewed as a multiplier to their inherent values. That is, the value of the final products and services for agglomerated hedge funds will be further enhanced by the element of synergy, knowledge spillover.

Further reasons for hedge fund agglomerations include image concerns and proximity to clients. As high-level financial service providers for wealthy individuals, how hedge funds present themselves will have a direct effect on the quality and quantity of the clients they attract. A Manhattan hedge fund will naturally radiate more prestige than one in Kansas. Just as important as human capital or social capital, the image of a hedge fund could directly affect firm success. To further boost firm-to-client relationships, hedge funds deliberately locate themselves in financial centers, which contain not only clusters of potential clients, but also other agglomerated financial services. This geographic advantage directly translates to a competitive advantage because it allows the firm to strengthen the relationship with its clients through convenience of access. That is, a high wealth individual, who is more likely to live near a financial center, will have easier physical access to face-to-face meetings with his or her respective hedge fund firm. This benefit, in turn, expedites the rate of growth of social capital for the firm, which further feeds the dynamic interactions within the hedge fund localization economy.

Despite the fast pace of technological innovation, physical space is still relevant in the world of financial services. Human capital, social capital, and the dynamic interactions between the two are relevant to the success of a hedge fund. While having the former two elements might lead to average returns, the synergetic knowledge spillover effect from localization economies distinguishes the best form the rest.

CHAPTER 5

MARKETING

Chapter Introduction

City leaders across the US have learned that marketing and promotion are low-cost techniques to attract firms to their city which could perhaps have strong impacts in the local economy. A common assumption in economic models is that people have perfect information and therefore make the best possible decisions. In reality, of course, we operate in the context of imperfect information and must follow the wisdom of Simon (1957) and use "bounded rationality," meaning we make the best decisions possible given the information we do have.

The profit motive drives private firms to make location decisions typically either 1) to be close to customers, or 2) to be close to important inputs. In the U.S. alone, there are over one thousand cities with populations over 25,000. The ideal city may not be known by a private firm, who therefore must operate in a suboptimal location. This is where marketing and promotion come in.

Industrial Motion, for example, is a company that supplies mechanical components for use by light manufacturing and laboratories. Around 2004 the company decided to move its operations away from its expensive location in Orange County to a lower cost location such as Reno or Phoenix (Covel, 2008).

Eventually the owners learned about Mooresville, North Carolina. Tax breaks and other incentives were not necessary to attract the company to the new location; it was the low cost land and labor that were enough. The marketing and promotion efforts of the city leaders successfully informed the company that Mooresville would be an ideal location for the firm.

Table 4.1 lists typical marketing and promotion techniques and the percentage of US cities using these techniques. The last five were dropped from the latter ICMA surveys so only the 1999 data are reported. Figure 4.1 shows the trends across three different time periods. Short descriptions of each technique follow. With the possible exception of trade missions abroad, all of these are relatively low-cost ways to promote your city.

Table 4.1 Percent of US Cities Using Marketing Policies for Business Attraction

	1999	2004	2009
Websites	70	64	64
Calling on companies	52	42	53
Media advertising	44	46	51
Trade show participation	50	39	50
Trade missions abroad	14	21	21
Ambassador programs	12	14	14
Promotional material	82		
Conference attendance	61		
Community resource databases	54		
Direct mail	40		
Hosting special events	30		

Figure 4.1 Percent of US Cities Using Marketing Techniques for Business Attraction

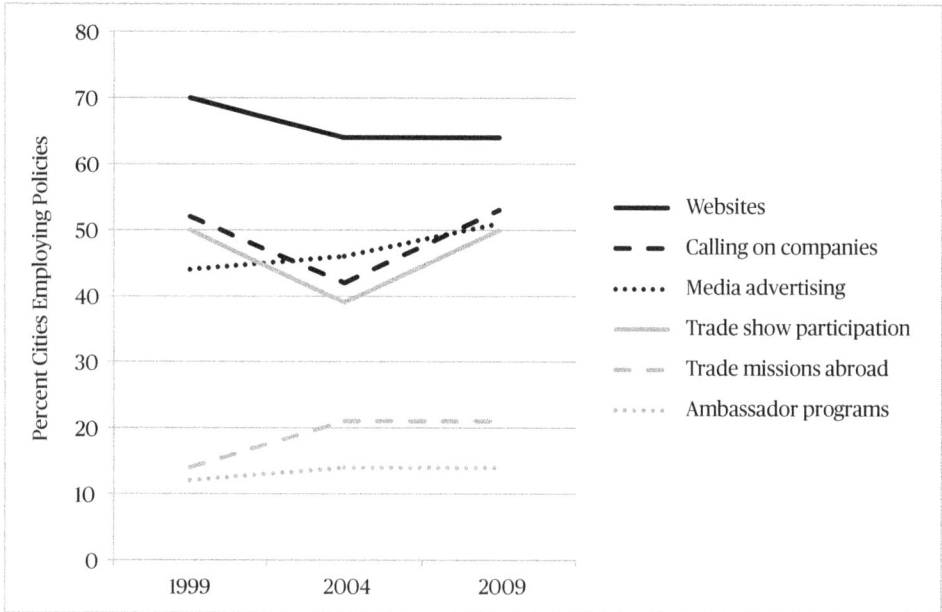

Websites are built by cities for a number of reasons, such reporting on governance issues, displaying municipal codes, permit applications, job applications, business assistance, and economic development. A typical website may describe properties available for development, and the standard economic development incentives offered by the city. Savvy business people contact city officials directly to negotiate additional incentives. Most cities in the US have a web presence but according to the ICMA data, only 64% are using websites specifically for economic development functions.

A city's website is perhaps the most important facet of an overall branding strategy. Morfessis and Malachuk suggest a city should "focus on building your brand globally, including in emerging markets" (2011, p. 26). They explain that BRIC-based companies are now considering their own global expansions and the U.S. is top of the list. But where to locate in the U.S? Foreign and domestic firms alike, when expanding seek locations typically to be close to suppliers, or to be close to customers. City leaders would do well to craft a brand that communicates the city's features that might appeal to outside firms.

The city of Corona, California created an aggressive marketing campaign which was successful in 2010 in luring a number of companies from nearby Orange County to Corons's inland location. In the aftermath of the Great Recession, Corona economic development officials attracted headquarters operations for clothing retailers Zumiez and Anchor Blue; Waggin Train, a pet food manufacturer; and Kobelco, a producer of compressors. During this time of expansion, Corona added more than 1,300 jobs.

Calling on companies is a proactive method of business attraction. It is difficult for city leaders to actively identify small businesses as targets, but national chains, especially retailers, are commonly targeted. The Trader Joe's boutique grocery chain is called on so much, they have corporate policies in place to ignore such calls. In 2009 53% of cities were calling on companies.

Media advertising is used by nearly half (51%) of US cities for business attraction. Typical outlets include industrial trade journals and business-focused newspapers such as Businessweek, The Economist and The Wall Street Journal. Businesses pay attention, not because the ads are particularly compelling, but because the city leaders who placed the ads are signalling their high level of willingness to assist companies with relocation.

A far more common method of advertising undertaken by cities (and counties and states) is to target individuals who might visit the locale with a wallet full of tourist dollars. San Juan County in Washington state has an aggressive marketing plan run by the local non-profit economic development agency. The group identified niche vacation ideas including heritage tourism, culinary tourism, volun-tourism, girlfriend getaways, "mancations" and others. In addition to producing brochures and a visitors guide, the group also utilizes magazine, newspaper, and online advertising especially in regional travel publications.

How effective is this advertising in recruiting businesses and individuals? Little research has been conducted on the former. On the latter, however, a number of studies have analyzed whether advertising can attract tourists to visit. Maumbe (2006) undertook a statistically robust analysis of the Travel Michigan campaign in 2003 which utilized television, radio and magazine advertising in the nearby cities of Indianapolis, Chicago and Cleveland. Effectiveness of marketing is often thought of in terms of return on investment. In one of Maumbe's examples, visitors indicated a desire to visit Michigan as a result of advertising. Conversion was 11.2% (those who actually visited) and the ROI was $10.47 (2006, abstract). Furthermore, she found that Michigan was "viewed by consumers most importantly as a family destination and also as a close enough destination for short get away trips" (p. 83) which gives the advertisers relevant feedback on which consumer market to target. The most important factor driving tourists to Michigan was not the advertisements; it was past experience as a tourist in Mighigan, then web searches, and then advertising.

Advertising obviously should extol the virtues of a place, such as Savannah, Georgia advertising its great beaches, but even negative characteristics can be capitalized on. The city of Winnipeg, Canada and the small town of Clute, Texas both play up their vibrant mosquito populations. Winnipeg has erected a large monument to the pesky insect and Clute hosts the Great Texas Mosquito Festival every July complete with live music, bingo, a barbecue, and a mosquito calling contest.

Trade show participation (50%) and **conference attendance** (61%) are practiced by city leaders actively seeking new businesses. To attract new retailers, savvy city representatives attend the Global Retail Real Estate Convention, sponsored by the International Council of Shopping Centers. This event, typically held in Las Vegas each May, is the largest gathering of retailers looking for new trends and new locations, and city leaders looking to attract new retailers to their city.

Cities looking to attract manufacturing or service firms do not have a one-stop-shop option. They will have to target a conference specific to a particular industry. The "WIndiana" conference in Muncie, Indiana is attended by numerous local government officials looking to bring wind power companies to their city.

Trade missions abroad provide an excellent benefit to city employees who enjoy a free trip overseas, but the benefits to the actual city (and its taxpayers) are uncertain. After the tsunami in Japan in 2012, South Carolina's governor attended the Japan-US Southeast Association meeting in Tokyo to pitch the state as a safer location for business; tsunamis and earthquakes are quite uncommon in South Carolina.

Ambassador programs engage citizens, usually local business leaders, to be the face of an economic development program. For example, the Staten Island Economic Development Corporation utilizes a manager from Faztec Industries, a concrete supplier, as the ambassador for its Green and Clean Zone, an area established to attract companies producing environmentally friendly products and services.

Promotional materials and **direct mail** are low cost way to quickly disseminate information about the city. The materials typically describe the city's demographics, economy, industrial base, and list economic development incentives and properties that might be available for new businesses. Direct mail is sent to firms that have expressed interest in the city in the past, industrial location consultants, and targeted companies. Some cities purchase mailing lists of prospective businesses.

Crab mallets (the tools used when eating crabs) were mailed to 2,000 CEOs of companies in New York, Connecticut, Pennsylvania and the District of Columbia. The mallets were part of a direct mail campaign inviting companies to relocate to the Mid-Atlantic region that includes parts of Virginia, New Jersey, Maryland and Delaware. The mailers were sent out by Conectiv, the regional electricity and gas provider. Two mailers were sent out. The first was a postcard explaining why the region is attractive for business: "a great location, a thriving economy, and a superior quality of life. (Not to mention some of the finest seafood in the world)" (PR Newswire, 1998). The second mailer included the crab mallets and pertinent information about low tax rates, labor force, seafood recipes and the crab mallet.

Community resource databases are little more than lists, typically on the website of the city or the local chamber of commerce, describing the various amenities in the city that might be of interest to prospective businesses. Listings might include shipping companies, materials suppliers, law firms, employment agencies, health-care facilities, waste management, schools and colleges.

Some **special events** specifically target businesses inviting business leaders to an event such as an after-hours mixer at a newly developed business park or indus-trial park. Many of these events, however, generally pitch the city as location for business, such as the Margarita Run in Haines City, Florida. People complete a short 5k run through the downtown, drink margaritas, and learn about the city's downtown revitalization efforts.

Chapter Summary

There are over six million private firms in the US, most of whom are not thinking of relocating to your city. Adding in the millions of non-profit organizations and government entities, a pool of nearly ten million employers could possibly move to your city and contribute to economic growth. If city leaders practice some of the simple, low-cost marketing and promotion techniques listed in this chapter it is possible to attract additional employers to the city.

Guest Case: Vacation Rentals:
Bane of the Neighborhood or Boon of the City?

By: Barbara L. Strother

Vacation rentals (VRs), those privately owned homes rented by the night or by the week to vacationing strangers, have become controversial in recent years. Across the nation cities big and small are instigating new laws that ban or substantially restrict vacation rental activity. Places as diverse as San Francisco, New York city, the Florida Keys, New Orleans, Portland, Austin, and many others have resorted to prohibitive VR regulations such as banning home rentals that are less than 30 days, capping the number of days a year a home can be rented to short-term tenants, requiring permits that are exorbitant or nearly impossible to meet the requirements or simply banning VRs outright. Examples include the $1000 permit fees for Islamorada, Florida (even though the average rental listing on AirBnB, for example, barely make $7000 per year), or the quirky New Orleans stipulations that the owner be physically on site during the rental period and that there cannot be a kitchen included. So what's all the fuss about? What is causing these cities to take such stringent measures against the vacation rental industry? Why shouldn't vacation rentals be allowed in a community?

Those U.S. communities that have picked a fight against the vacation rental industry are predominantly concerned about nuisances and economic impacts. Residents fear noise ordinance violations, party houses, increasing problems with traffic and parking, the loss of neighborly full-time home occupants to unknown strangers, and a decline in the environment of neighborhoods due to increasing numbers of rental properties. Local governments have increasingly taken an anti-VR bias over the loss of administrative control and tax revenue that comes with unlicensed or unpermitted vacation homes. And to add to the anti-VR din, local hotels and B&Bs bemoan the loss of business to the growing numbers of new little competitors, and threaten the loss of jobs if the competitive environment becomes too damaging to their business.

Despite the fears and complaints, the flip side of the vacation rental coin illustrates why communities might not want to be so eager to ban or even restrict the industry. Vacation rentals have direct fiscal impact for cities through the revenues they bring in, the transient occupancy taxes they pay, and the local jobs they support and provide such as housekeeping, janitorial, pool and spa service, catering, and home improvement. AirBnB claims their listed properties contribute $56 million annually in economic activity in San Francisco; $61 million in Portland, and $632 million in New York City, and support several hundreds of jobs in each place ("AirBnB Economic Impact," 2014). Similarly, research commissioned by the Realtors Association of Maui concluded that transient vacation rentals provided the following estimated economic benefits: $318.8M total sales output and 3,478 jobs throughout the state of Hawaii, $19.7M in Hawaii state tax, $191,000 in transient occupancy tax for Maui County, and $54M-$75M in direct Maui lodging expenditures by VR guests (Loudat & Kasturi, 2008). These are not insignificant numbers; on the contrary, these figures represent economic activity that could be devastating if lost.

Indirectly vacation rentals have an even greater benefit to local communities and account for significant tourism dollars generated by the consumption patterns of the typical VR guest. As high-value travelers, vacation home renters stay almost twice as many nights and spend about 1.5 times more than the typical tourist ("AirBnB Economic Impact," 2014), adding purchases such as groceries to the typical souvenir shopping and frequenting local restaurants on multiple days during their lengthier stay. For example, the total expenditures for VR guests in Maui was estimated to be as high as $160M per year (Loudat & Kasturi, 2008). Vacation renters also tend to bring more visitors with them and return more frequently as they make personal attachments to the local community. Staying in a local home makes you feel like a local, and often vacation rental guests will return to the same exact property partially out of a sense that it's *their* home away from home. In essence they are the best tourism customers a community could hope for.

Additionally, vacation rentals are an essential factor in drawing the levels of tourism that are often so critical for the economic viability of many locations. It could, of course, be argued that those tourists would visit anyways, staying in a hotel if no vacation rental were available. But recent industry trends highlight a growing preference for vacation rentals as the lodging of choice for many travelers, to the point that a growing percentage of travel bookings actually start with the hunt for VR lodging as the priority over the location destination, rejecting destinations that do not offer sufficient VR options. Increasingly travelers care more about staying in a cool house than a cool town; their immediate environment matters as much or more than the external geographic one due to the ways such lodging choices have direct and significant impact on the travel experience. Families doing a "staycation" in a vacation rental will more likely play games together, watch movies together, and cook together; all of which are much more difficult to do in a hotel environment. This uptrend in vacation rental preference dovetails into other national tourism trends, such as baby boomers taking their grandkids on trips and larger families and groups of friends traveling together, all of which often find the benefits of staying in a multiple bedroom home far exceeding the disjointed experience of individual hotel rooms. Today's traveling public demands vacation rental options in their vacation destinations, and to limit or ban these options is to reduce a city's competitiveness against comparable destinations that can provide what travelers want.

Small communities with limited lodging choices have considerably more to gain from vacation rentals. The tiny town of Wrightwood, California, is a perfect example. Sandwiched between mountain peaks, Wrightwood has limited geography for expansion, especially for commercial property. With just four motels or lodges representing no more than a couple dozen hotel rooms, there is little room for the hundreds of thousands of travelers that descend upon the town with the coming of snow. Since Wrightwood is just 90 miles from the heart of Los Angeles and is easily accessible to all of Southern California, there are close to 20 million people within a couple hours drive, and those millions live in locales that never see snow. When the snow hits the Wrightwood area mountain peaks, snow players, sledders, skiers, and snowboarders hit the road for the easy drive. Mountain High Ski Resort sees more than 500,000 visitors in a good year and as many as 10,000 visitors on a single good day. Many of those snow lovers would prefer to spend the night rather than face the cold dark drive home at the end of a tiring day of snow play. And they prefer to spend it cuddled up in front of a fireplace with hot cocoa in hand in a cozy local vacation cabin rental.

In contrast to the limited number of hotel rooms in Wrightwood, there are around 60 vacation rentals that can each sleep anywhere from four to twenty guests. These vacation rentals keep the tourism thriving in this little town, encouraging the snow players to stick around an extra day to empty their pockets at local restaurants and shops or return once more to the ski hills and tubing park. In fact, the #1 most booked property on the global HomeAway.com network in 2013 was, surprisingly, not located in Miami or Paris or Cancun, but in little old Wrightwood: The Hideaway, a tiny little 400-square-foot cabin best fit for just 2 people.

So what are communities to do? Welcome vacation rentals, or fear them? The evidence seems squarely placed on the side of the VR industry with significant benefits to local communities. But there must be wisdom in how the industry is managed, such as enforcing transient occupancy tax payment, requiring vacation rental permitting or licensing, and encouraging Chamber membership for property owners in the spirit of keeping standards high. Permits that limit the number of guests in relation to house size, prohibit amplified music, and limit parking based on driveway size prohibit the party house dynamic and other neighborhood nuisances, and provide a way for vacation rental owners to enforce such policies when they can use government regulations as the excuse for shutting down the party or evicting rule-breaking guess.

If communities can find effective ways to implement such measures, VRs can and will be a boon to the community, and should be encouraged increasingly by local policy support. For example, the Wrightwood Chamber of Commerce hosts the Wrightwood Lodging Association, an organization that requires all members to join the Chamber, pay the bed tax, maintain county permitting, and keep a minimum standard of excellence in their business operations. In exchange, VRs in the association are privy to exclusive discounts for their guests at several local businesses, including Mountain High Ski Resort, Big Pines Zip Lines, Admo Motorcycle Tours, and other local retail and attractions. As the Chamber hosts events, they specifically promote the Lodging Association member properties as lodging choices for event attenders. And the Lodging Association pulls its resources for cooperative marketing and advertising of all member properties. Such symbiotic relationships between vacation rental business owners, Chambers of Commerce, and local governments provide the accountability to avoid the potential negative impacts of poorly run vacation rentals while maximizing the economic potential for all involved - the city, the small business vacation rental owners, and the local community at large through the important direct and indirect economic benefits of the vacation rental industry.

Guest Case: The Little Beaver and the Big Swoosh: the Case of Nike in Small Town Oregon

By: Gina Christensen

As an Oregonian, it is always comforting knowing "Uncle Phil" is living up the road. Whether it's having the best dressed college football teams in the nation, or having your local hospitals receive $500 million dollar donations, Oregon residents cannot deny the benefits of having Phil Knight, founder of Nike Inc. and Oregon's only billionaire, as a fellow resident. But even better for the residents of Oregon, and more specifically, those of the Portland Metro Area, is the presence of this billionaire's world-leading athletic apparel and footwear company's headquartered in Beaverton, Oregon, a suburb of Portland.

Forbes reported $25.3 billion dollars of revenue for Nike in 2013, and the company employees over 44,000 personnel across the globe. The Nike World Headquarters in Beaverton employs more than 8,000 Oregonians, with the average annual income of $100,000; this is double the state's average. There are countless benefits to having a Fortune 500 company move into your city; from extensive job creation, to the possible tax revenue available.

Nike pays annual property taxes of $7.5 million alone. Most cities are not fortunate enough to have a company like Nike as neighbors, so it is imperative that cities do what they can to keep companies satisfied, encouraging them to stay and grow right where they are. Cities can implement specific policies to help develop the local economy by enticing large companies to stay within their city limits. Nike, and its relationship with the city of Beaverton and the Portland Metro Area as a whole, is an excellent example of these local economic development policies at play.

In 2005, the city of Beaverton attempted to annex Nike within its city limits. Up until that time, Nike had been unincorporated Washington County, surrounded entirely by incorporated Beaverton. This annexation would cause Nike an additional $700,000 dollars a year in taxes, clearly revealing the city of Beaverton's motivation.

After a legal battle ensued, Nike was granted assurance that they would remain an unincorporated island for at least the next 30 years. After the events that unfolded in 2005, Beaverton sought to become chummy neighbors with Nike, which has worked greatly in their benefit. The years after the annexation crisis, employment at the Nike campus rose 60%, employing a huge number of Oregonians during an otherwise rough economic patch. Not only does the presence of a Fortune 500 company create new jobs and provide tax revenue for a city, it can encourage other companies to follow suit. Adidas decided to move their North American headquarters from New Jersey to the Portland area in 1993, causing Portland to become an epicenter for the sports apparel industry.

Today, things are still better than ever between Nike and the City of Beaverton, as the two just announced a $93 million dollar deal. This is a welcomed sight for Oregonians after tensions rose between Nike and Oregon Legislature again in December of 2012. After proposed hikes in corporate tax rates, Nike threatened to expand its business elsewhere, upon which states including Texas and Washington attempted to make a play at obtaining this expansion plan. Out of fear of losing the Nike expansion and making waves with the existing campus, Oregon Legislature worked to secure a 40-year tax deal, in return for a promise from Nike to continue the planned business expansion within the state. The tax breaks on Nike were issued with the promise that Nike would undergo a $150 million dollar expansion, as well as add a minimum of 500 new positions by 2016. As of April 2013, the $93 million dollar plan was revealed, which includes a land purchase of over $61 million dollars to help Nike better accommodate recent and upcoming growth. It is thought that this expansion could create up to 6,000 new jobs in the Portland area in the coming years.

Although Oregon and the City of Beaverton may be losing some future tax revenues due to the recent deal they struck with Nike, they undoubtedly made the right choice. The future tax revenue and job creation that the Nike expansion will bring to the state and county will be exponentially more beneficial and economical in the long run than if they were taxing Nike higher but lost the expansion deal to another state.

CHAPTER 6

FISCAL INCENTIVES

This chapter describes some of the most commonly used fiscal tools in economic development practice. Firms use the three economic resources (land, labor and capital) to produce goods and services. Due to resource scarcity, many firms do not have sufficient financial capital to start, operate or sustain their business. City leaders, eager to develop their local economy have learned to mobilize public financial capital to encourage entrepreneurial activity in the city.

Critics are quick to call these fiscal practices unfair, inefficient and morally questionable. Why would a city government give money to a business instead of investing in socially worthwhile causes such as education, libraries, nutrition or poverty alleviation? City leaders who share public resources with private firms do so because they believe in the economic multiplier effect. Money invested in a private firm may result in job creation. When local residents are employed, they will spend their paychecks at local businesses within the city. Hopefully the net effect is much greater (i.e. "multiplied") than the initial investment.

In many cases local governments use borrowed funds to finance their fiscal incentive economic development efforts. These city leaders hope their economy will grow such that their increased tax revenues will more than offset their debt service obligations. Sbragia's 1996 book, *Debt Wish*, offers a critique of the practice of funding economic development programs through debt. As the book title implies, Sbragia suggests their chances of success are "wishful thinking," and that in the end, this practice can be a "death wish" for the city in fiscal terms. Nonetheless, fiscal incentives are widely offered across U.S. cities. The most common fiscal incentive policies are illustrated in Figure 6.1 and described below.

Table 6.1 Fiscal Incentive Use in U.S. Cities

	1999	2004	2009
Tax increment financing	50	32	49
Tax abatements	54	31	43
Grants	45	21	32
Low-cost loans	40	18	24
Revolving loan funds	59	23	24
Community dev. loan funds	55	63	22
Matching impr. grants	32	13	21
Revolving loan programs	36	22	20
Subsidized buildings	11	5	8

Figure 6.1 Fiscal Incentive Use in U.S. Cities

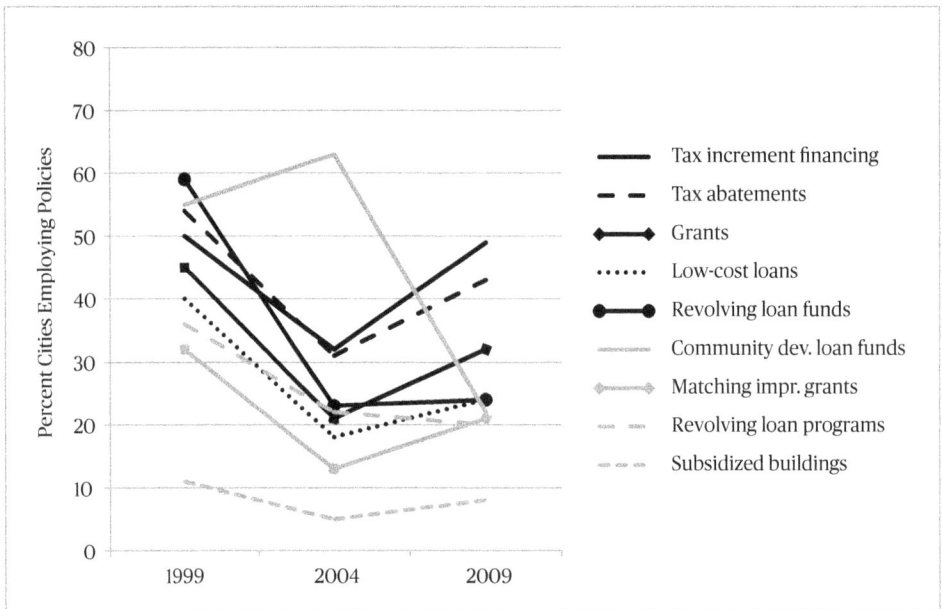

Tax Increment Financing (TIF) is a creative way for cities to finance development projects. Suppose a semiconductor company wants to open a small assembly plant in Bloomington, Illinois. The company selects a site that was previously a bicycle factory, but in its present state is considered a "brownfield," meaning it has some resident industrial pollution. As a brownfield, the property value is low, and therefore the property taxes derived from the site are low. Suppose the brownfield is only worth $10,000,000 which generates only $100,000 in property tax revenue for the city. After redevelopment, the site will be worth $50,000,000 which will generate $500,000 in tax revenue. This additional $400,000 is the "tax increment" that provides an incentive for city leaders to support the redevelopment project. In fact, they are so supportive, they will issue bonds today to finance the redevelopment project. Thus it is this future additional "tax increment" that is the impetus for "financing" the project today.

For the above example to work, the State of Illinois legislature would have had to have already passed laws making TIF's possible. The city government would have to designate the site a TIF site. The company and the city government would have to come to agreement on the terms of the redevelopment; for example, the city might clean up the industrial pollution, and the private company constructs the buildings.

The city would have to issue bonds to pay for the redevelopment of the site. The bond amount is usually limited to 50% of the tax increment. In the above example, the city will earn $8,000,000 in additional taxes over the next 20 years ($400,000 * 20 years). Therefore they can issue $4,000,000 in bonds. Over the next 20 years, as the city collects the $8 million in new tax revenues, the city can pay off the $4 million in bond obligations, but also have another $4 million in tax revenues to provide services to the site such as roads, police and fire protection.

In most cases the TIF designation covers a "district" such that any improvement in property values in the area results in greater tax revenue that flows into the TIF fund. For example, suppose after the city and the semiconductor company complete the redevelopment of the site that all adjacent properties increase their property values. The additional tax revenue would go into the TIF fund.

TIFs for economic development are complex and require cooperation from multiple levels of government and the private company. However, the data in Table 6.1 and Figure 6.1 show that TIFs are in use in nearly half of U.S. cities. In fact, tax increment financing, despite its complexity, is the most commonly used fiscal incentive for local economic development.

There are many criticisms of TIF districts. As the district improves, all property values rise which can drive up residential property values in the neighborhood which reduces the amount of available affordable housing. As other properties in the TIF district are improved without public assistance, the additional tax revenue flows to the TIF fund, rather than into providing services to the area. Politically connected developers often reap the benefits of TIF financing whereas other developers do not. And finally, TIF districts are designed to improve "blighted" areas, but sometimes public leaders assign TIF designations to greenfield developments, which has the effect of reducing future public service provision to the area in exchange for transferring funds to private companies at the time the site is developed. Because of these abuses, the state of California no longer allows TIF use.

Tax Abatements are contracts between local government and a private firm that reduce the firm's property tax payments. To encourage development, local government agrees that "some share of assessed value will not be taxed for an agreed time period" (Koven and Lyons, 2003, p. 192). The ICMA survey indicates that 43% of U.S. cities use tax abatement incentives as a tool of economic development.

"Abatement" is a euphemism for tax rates artificially lowered below the amount specified by law. Tax abatements typically apply to property taxes and gross receipts taxes. Property tax abatements typically cut the tax rate in half for a period of ten years. Real estate developers are savvy in negotiating these benefits prior to starting new development projects.

States derive much of their income from corporate income taxes. In recent years, however, private firms have exploited various tax loopholes enabling them to reduce their tax burden. Therefore many states have shifted to a "gross receipts" method of taxing companies. In this method, all company revenue generating transactions are taxed, similar to a retail sales tax. In many U.S. states and cities economic development officials offer abatements of the gross receipts tax to attract new businesses. Some of these efforts are industry-specific, especially high-tech. For example, 11.0% of the ICMA cities report that they reduce gross receipts taxes for new technology-related industries and businesses.

Proponents of tax abatements argue that the development would not occur unless the tax breaks are given. Critics of tax abatements argue that the development would occur, and that public officials are giving away public funds unnecessarily.

Table 6.1 and Figure 6.1 show that 43% of U.S. cities offer tax abatements as part of their economic development policy strategy.

A tax abatement becomes a **tax exemption** when 100% of the tax is not collected. South Carolina, for example, has many "cost of operation" automatic tax exemptions on items such as electricity and raw materials.

Tax credits typically allow a business to deduct a specific amount from their state income tax bill. Table 6.2 shows the tax credits that are available to Kentucky firms. Local government is often formally and informally involved in the receipt of these incentives. Similar tax credit programs exist in 24.5% of the ICMA cities.

Table 6.2 Tax Credit Programs Available to Firms in Kentucky

Program	Qualifications	Tax Credit
Bluegrass State Skills Corporation Skills Training Investment Credit	Sponsor occupational or skills upgrade training programs for the benefit of their employees.	Credit against Kentucky income tax of 50% of training costs, up to $500 per employee, and up to $100,000 per company.
Kentucky Jobs Development Act	For new and expanding service and technology related projects.	Projects may receive a 100% credit against the state income tax arising from a project and may collect a job assessment fee of up to 5% of the gross wages of each employee whose job is created by the project and who is subject to Kentucky income tax. Amounts can be up to 50% of project start-up cost and up to 50% of annual facility rental cost or rental value for up to 10 years.

Kentucky Rural Economic Development Act	For new and expanding manufacturing projects in qualified designated counties.	State income tax credits and job assessment fees for up to 100% of their capital investment for up to 15 years on land, buildings, site development, building fixtures and equipment used in a project.
Kentucky Economic Opportunity Zone Program	New or expanding manufacturing or service/technology companies in a certified Opportunity Zone.	An income tax credit of up to 100% of the Kentucky income tax liability on income generated by or arising out of the project; and A job development assessment fee of up to 5% of gross wages
Kentucky Industrial Development Act	For new and expanding manufacturing projects.	Approved projects may receive state income tax credits for up to 100% of its capital investment for up to 10 years on land, buildings, site development, building fixtures and equipment used in a project. Or, the company may collect a job assessment fee of 3% of the gross wages of each employee whose job is created by the approved project and who is subject to Kentucky income tax.

Source: Kentucky Cabinet for Economic Development

Tax stabilization agreements serve as guarantees from local government to the private sector that taxes will not be raised significantly in the near future. These are used "to assure potential investors of a stable tax environment" (Koven and Lyons, 2003, p. 193). The agreement need not be a burden on the municipality; it is only a promise to an individual firm that the tax rates will not be raised for a fixed amount of time, which is specified in the agreement. The city of Rutland, Vermont recently awarded 5-year tax stabilization agreements to The Vermont Farmer's Food Center and Keith's II Sports. Rutland typically offers 5-year exemptions, but can go up to 10 years according to its statutes.

Tax-exempt bonds are frequently used as a tool of economic development. Until the Tax Reform Act of 1986 cities often helped finance private sector projects. Rather than firms financing their own industrial construction through corporate bonds, cities would secure cheaper financing for firms by issuing municipal bonds. Government issues the bonds and transfers the proceeds to the private firm who then repays the money over a period of time. The net effect for the firm is that it gets access to cheap financial capital. This was an attractive incentive for private firms. Today this practice is mainly used for projects that are justifiably "public" in nature such as infrastructure.

MassDevelopment, the Massachusetts state economic development agency, recently issued $14.1 million in tax-exempt bonds to redevelop the Charles R. Wilbur School in the town of Sharon into 75 residential apartments. While the funds were used by a private developer, The Beacon Companies, the project is "public" in nature, because the building uses green design principles, and provides 15 units of affordable housing.

Low-cost loans are offered by 39.8% of the ICMA cities. Such loans "generally permit firms that have trouble obtaining loans through normal channels to secure financing at either market rates or below-market rates" (Koven and Lyons, 2003, p. 190). Such loans are often considered "gap" financing because they provide the firm with enough cash to use as collateral to secure significant venture capital.

The city of Minneapolis has a Great Streets development program that includes gap financing. The Chicago Avenue Fire Arts Center, a not-for-profit organization applied for and received a loan of $425,000 to redevelop a former theater and body shop into a building that suits their needs as an arts center.

Loan pooling occurs when a lender or multiple lenders contribute funds into a "pool" from which loans are made for economic development. In the case of Alabama's Regions Economic Development Loan Pool, officials with the state's

Commerce Department convinced the private Regions Bank to earmark $1 billion in funds to be loaned out to private firms who are either relocating to Alabama, or expanding their operations in the state.

Revolving loan funds can be a type of loan pooling. The distinction is that money loaned out is paid back into the same pool to be reinvested out later. The rationale for revolving the funds is to keep the benefits of the seed money within the community. However, the managers of the funds tend to have a bias towards local organizations, and they may not allow market mechanisms to determine the creditworthiness of the borrowers. For this reason, revolving loan fund use by city governments have dropped from 59% in 1999 to just 24% in 2009. It is possible the slack is being picked up by state governments.

New York state's Empire State Development agency has established a small business revolving loan fund of $50 million. Half of the funds were contributed by the state and the other half comes from private banks. The fund makes loans to small businesses up to 50% of a project's investment needs. The maximum loan amount is $125,000. **Microloans** are available as part of this program, which are often defined as loans less than $25,000.

Community development loan funds (CDLF) are another type of loan pool wherein a publicly chartered organization (the CDLF) is set up at the local level and funded with a mixture of public and private funds. The CDLF acts like a main street bank, in that it makes loans to local small businesses. If the CDLF meets certain criteria, they are eligible to receive funds directly from the U.S. Department of the Treasury through its Small Business Lending Fund.

Fargo, North Dakota has a CDLF that is managed by its regional economic development agency. City or county agencies within the region apply directly to the CDLF on behalf of private firms looking for funds to invest in real estate, equipment, inventory or working capital. Loans are typically $100,000 and the private firm must show the funds are tied to job creation. Table 6.1 and Figure 6.1 show that community development loan fund use has declined from 55% in 1999 to 22% in 2009.

Grants are offered by 32% of the cities surveyed by ICMA. While giving away money with no obligation of repayment seems irresponsible, with proper vetting, city leaders can stimulate economic development with grants while avoiding the administrative costs of managing loan programs. Grants are typically given by federal and state governments, but in many cases, such as with Community Development Block Grants, funds from the federal government are doled out by local government officials.

Grants may be issued for many purposes. The New York state economic development agency offers grants for acquisition of land, buildings, machinery or other equipment; environmental remediation; planning research studies; and many other purposes that are tied to economic development.

Matching Improvement Grants are given to firms who are making some physical improvement to their property. The city of Monticello, Illinois has issued forty "Façade Improvement Grants" to local businesses as part of their downtown renewal program. The matching grants are worth up to $3,000 (Monticello Main Street, Inc., 2004). Only 21% of the ICMA cities reported using these improvement grants.

Subsidized buildings are an economic development tool offered by just 8% of U.S. cities. The actual availability of subsidies may be larger, however, as subsidies are available through state and federal programs. Local officials face significant backlash from voters if they give money to builders who neediness does not compare to other worthwhile potential community investments such as schools.

Subsidized buildings can be good economic policy, however, in some cases. In Midland, Michigan, a business incubator was established which offers rent subsidies of up to $10,000 over an 18 month period to small business entrepreneurs. Dozens of companies have participated in the program.

Low taxes although typically not considered as an intentional local economic development policy actually may be the best idea offered in this chapter. Research by Stansel (2011) found strong relationships between low tax rates and higher economic growth from 1980 to 2007. Stansel analyzed data on taxes and economic growth for the 100 largest metro areas in the US which all had populations over 575,000. Cities with lower tax rates had higher rates of growth in population, employment, and real personal income. The ten lowest-tax rate metro areas had average state and local taxes of just 8.3% of personal income, and average real personal income growth of 157%. The ten highest tax metro areas taxed 12.4% of personal income and only saw person income grow 76%. Stansel's research verifies the wisdom of keeping resources in the hands of private firms and individuals, and is one of many empirical studies confirming the idea that Market Cities outperform cities with too much government intervention.

Chapter Summary
City leaders use a variety of fiscal policies to spur economic development in their regions. Many of these policies were harshly criticized by citizens and academics because public funds were given away to private firms whose neediness was

questionable. City leaders can make responsible decisions, however, such as pro-
curing funds from state and federal agencies and distributing those funds locally.

Guest Case: Decoding Intel's Move Out of Colorado Springs: A Case Study in Business Attraction & Retention

By: Brett Johnson

When semiconductor manufacturer Intel Corp. announced its $8 billion dollar plan for plant expansions in Hillsboro, Oregon and Chandler, Arizona in October 2010, the citizens of Colorado Springs, Colorado were left wondering why the high tech giant had left their city of 419,848 in such a hurry in 2007 (Heilman, 2010; City of Colorado Springs, 2012). Just a decade earlier, in 2000, Intel had announced its expansion into Colorado Springs with a $45.5 million purchase of a suburban 1.4 million square foot plant. The firm followed up the purchase of the plant with $590 million in upgrades and renovations until, in 2007, making the decision to shut down production and sell the facility (Heilman 2009; Heilman, 2010; Bainbridge, 2005). The 905 former employees of the Colorado Springs plant would find out just three years later about Intel's massive expansion plans, hundreds of miles away from the now motionless semiconductor plant in the Springs. So what pushed this manufacturer to abandon its 1.4 million square foot plant in Colorado Springs and spend over $8 billion at locations in Hillsboro and Chandler? What does this large scale move reveal about the mobility of capital? We begin our analysis of these questions in 2000, the year Intel announced its expansion into Colorado Springs.

In 2000, the high-tech manufacturing giant was the beneficiary of a combined city, county, and school district initiative to rebate a significant amount of personal property tax the company would need to pay on its manufacturing equipment (Heilman, 2010). To a physical capital-intensive, manufacturing firm like Intel, this resulted in a significant reduction in costs. As explained by Zodrow (2010), capital has mobility, and will seek out environments of low cost and low risk. Moreover, even with this rebate given to Intel, the local government of the Colorado Springs region would not suffer. Since its inception, the personal property tax rebates given to manufacturers, such as Intel, were reimbursed by funds from the state of Colorado (Heilman, 2010). Intel would benefit from a reduction in costs, and the city of Colorado Springs would gain roughly 1,000 new jobs within its expanding high-tech cluster. However, just three years later, the relationship between Intel and Colorado Springs would face a significant challenge that would test both the city and manufacturer.

In 2003, the Colorado state government faced a budget crisis, causing the state to decrease its tax reimbursement funding to the government of Colorado Springs. Colorado Springs School District 11, a primary beneficiary of the reimbursed tax revenue generated from the personal property tax on Intel's manufacturing equipment, was no longer receiving full reimbursement from the state. Faced with the decision to either significantly reduce the budget of the school district, or repeal the tax rebates given to Intel, local officials made the tough decision to stop rebating Intel's personal property taxes. The employer of nearly 1,000 Colorado Springs residents was now faced with a significant and unexpected increase in its production costs.

With the removal of the personal property tax rebate, the attractive, business-friendly environment of Colorado Springs had begun to morph into a more costly place of operation for Intel, as the manufacturer continued to pour new investment into its growing fabrication plant. The four years following the repeal of the personal property tax rebate proved to be simply too burdensome for Intel. Along with the removal of the personal property tax rebate, the semiconductor industry experienced a significant downturn, with global sales dropping up to 22% between 2007 and 2008 (Semiconductor Industry Association, 2012). Bill Mackenzie, an Intel company spokesman, identifies this latter statistic as the primary determinant in Intel's move out of the Springs. "I'm not saying that tax issues were irrelevant, but they weren't the determining factor," said Mackenzie in 2010 (Heilman, 2010). So while market factors may have pushed Intel out of Colorado Springs, it seemed that in 2010, certain incentives in Arizona and Oregon were too good for the manufacturer to pass up.

Intel attributed its $8 billion expansion to the favorable conditions found in the fabrication plants in Chandler, Arizona and Hillsboro, Oregon. Both the Oregon and Arizona plants were free of any corporate tax for production sold outside of their respective states, creating a massive opportunity for cost reduction to Intel. Colorado Springs could simply no longer provide an offer that could compete with Hillsboro and Chandler, so Intel responded accordingly.

Perhaps the greatest lesson from Intel's move out of Colorado Springs is the mobility of capital. Given the opportunity, capital-intensive firms will flee from risk (Heilman, 2010). Former Intel employee and Colorado resident Danny Tomlinson explained that, from Intel's perspective, the repeal of the personal property tax rebates signified a shift in the Colorado Springs economic climate, indicating a potential drop in local economic stability. "Capital flees from risk. Intel officials told me that 'as long as we know the rules and they don't change, we can do our due diligence and make decisions on whether to be here.' It comes down to predictability and stability," said Tomlinson (Heilman, 2010). If a capital-intensive firm has the means to, it will utilize its mobility and relocate to a more favorable place of operation (Younas and Nandwa, 2010).

Zodrow (2010) states that there is a "general agreement that capital is mobile and has become increasingly mobile over time" (p. 890). Firms, such as Intel, that rely heavily on costly physical capital for production will continue to make cost-benefit decisions and always be aware of favorable conditions that may exist in certain cities, and not in others. For now, the former Intel plant in Colorado Springs remains an empty, standing testament to disparity in business attraction conditions, and the mobility of today's capital.

CHAPTER 7

LOCATION INCENTIVES

Individuals and companies follow different criteria when making location decisions. Individuals choose to live in locations that provide the highest level of satisfaction, or "utility." Economic models of housing prices suggest an individual dwelling is assessed by its "hedonics," which are factors that make the house more enjoyable such as square footage, number of bedrooms and bathrooms, etc. Tiebout's (1956) public choice theory proposes that people choose to live in cities and neighborhoods that have the best basket of public amenities such as schools, parks and libraries. The same logic applies to private amenities such as shopping and entertainment. When all of these factors are considered equal, a transportation-based economic model suggests individuals want short commute times and therefore want to live near where they work. How about private firms? What about within a particular city? Private firms make location decisions based on a number of factors.

Bid-rent economic models explain company location decisions within a city. Office-based firms such as those in the FIRE industrial sector (finance, insurance, real estate) tend to locate in city centers because they trade primarily in tacit information. The closer they are to similar firms, the better. Manufacturing firms value proximity to freeways because they want to minimize the cost of shipping their inputs and outputs.

Understanding these location theories can assist city leaders in their economic development efforts. These theories are often called "bid-rent" models, meaning the land rent at more desirable locations will be bid up. A manufacturer will pay more to buy or rent a site adjacent to the freeway. Similarly, manufacturing rents decline further away from freeways. These bid-rent models hold up quite well empirically.

Figure 7.1 depicts Louisville, Kentucky which illustrates the bid-rent model. The office towers in the central business district house conventional FIRE firms and many buildings related to the health science cluster such as the Humana building. Freeways circle the city center, and manufacturing firms would locate along the freeways, including Rubbertown (home to chemical, tire and other plants) to the west, and GE and Ford to the south. Residential land use can be seen around the center of the city and spreading out into the suburbs.

Figure 7.1 Bid-rent in Louisville: the central business district, freeways, and residential land use

New Urbanism is an urban planning model which is a rebuttal to suburban sprawl land development popular in the post-World War II building boom. The planned communities of Levittown, New York and Levittown, Pennsylvania were created with much scientific rigor. Streets were layed out by a master planner, and cookie-cutter houses were hastily built. While these suburbs were marvels of city planning, architecture and construction, critics pointed out numerous social flaws of suburban development. The suburbs were primarily for middle class whites. The neighborhoods lacked character and important amenities were often missing such as shopping, pedestrian access, and public spaces. There was no public transportation, so everyone was dependent on the automobile for transport, leaving many stranded, especially the elderly, youths, and those unable to drive.

New Urbanism is a counter to the suburban model of development. It is primarily characterized by mixed-use development. New Urbanists shun traditional zoning systems, and suggest neighborhoods should have a mix of residential, retail, and offices. People can live, work, shop and play all within the same neighborhood. Less land is needed for transportation corridors such as the massive multilane freeways that dominate US cities today. High density is valued, such that people live near each other. This has social benefits and can also reduce crime. Jane Jacobs famously described more "eyes on the street" that can keep the neighborhood safe. In recent years New Urbanist ideas are influencing urban planning in the US, but real estate developers still prefer to leapfrog urban areas and convert open spaces and farmland into new developments because these methods are often less expensive and require less red tape.

Central place theory suggests cities emerged as places where society's needs for defense, worship and trade were met (Maki & Lichty, 2000). Central place theory assumes transportation is a major factor in economic decision making, therefore as the agrarian economy changed to an industrial economy people began to locate in cities for proximity to industrial work, and entertainment. This theory is a "purely market explanation for the emergence and location of cities" (Maki & Lichty, 2000, p. 85). People from the hinterlands gathered in a central place, and cities were born.

The **theory of the market area** simply explains that firms want to locate near their customers. Materials-oriented firms want to locate near their suppliers (fruit brokers near the citrus groves), but consumer-oriented firms locate near their customers (fruit smoothie shops at the shopping mall). The market area is the region in which a firm sells its product. Alonso observes, "Since the median of the distribution of customers will tend to be in large cities, this is one of the reasons why big cities tend to grow bigger" (1972, p. 18). Firms achieve profits through economies of scale, so firms seek to enlarge their market area or simply locate in the middle of the market area (Lösch, 1964). This creates an increased demand for land which in turn drives up the price of real estate in the city center. Paradoxically the customer base in an urban economy exerts a centripetal force pulling firms inward, while higher rents exert centrifugal force pushing firms outward.

Similar to the theory of the market area, a **theory of the resource area** explains that firms whose natural resources are expensive to transport will probably locate near those resources (Maki & Lichty, 2000). This explains why oil companies are headquartered in Texas, and limestone companies are headquartered in Indiana.

The **theory of agglomeration** suggests similar firms tend to locate near each other to benefit from shared technology, and to be nearer to suppliers and specialized labor (Marshall, 1920). For example, firms in the garment industry have tended to agglomerate in New York City to be near the pool of labor that specializes in garment-making. Houston, Texas is home to many chemical companies whose leaders understand the value of locating near their needed natural resources (oil), but also in proximity to other firms in their industry.

Unlike the concept of equilibrium that suggests growth flows to less costly areas, **growth pole theory** suggests geographic "poles" exist that attract growth (Perroux, 1983). Cities in Silicon Valley, for example, are growth poles that have attracted numerous high-tech firms.

Bid-rent models, suburban sprawl planning, New Urbanism, leapfrog development, Central place theory, the theory of market areas, and the theory of agglomeration are all relevant theories to explain the forces shaping the way cities are developing in the US. It is within this context that we make the case that city leaders can encourage economic development with a number of policies and programs which are described in this chapter. Many of the ideas require significant public resources to implement, whereas a choice few rely more on the power of the free market.

Location Incentives in Practice

Over the past four decades, US cities have aggressively used location-based economic development policies and programs to attract, retain and develop businesses within their city limits. Private firms have become quite savvy in negotiating land-based incentives from local governments. In many cases, local government officials literally "gave away the farm" to companies willing to relocate to the city. For example, the State of Kentucky purchased a number of family farms just south of Louisville in 2003 to assemble a site that would be given to the Hyundai company who had plans to open a car factory in the US. One stubborn farmer refused to sell his farm and Hyundai ended up moving to Alabama. Common location incentives are listed in Table 7.1 and illustrated in Figure 7.2.

Table 7.1 Location Incentives for Economic Development

	1999	2004	2009
Free land or land write-down	39	17	26
Federal/state enterprise zones	27	18	24
Special assessment districts	18	13	24
Local economic development zones	27	13	24
Zoning and permit assistance	72	37	12
Technology zones	89		
Enterprise zones	66		
Zoning flexibility	46		
TIF districts	35		
PPP for ED zones	14		

Figure 7.2 Location Incentives

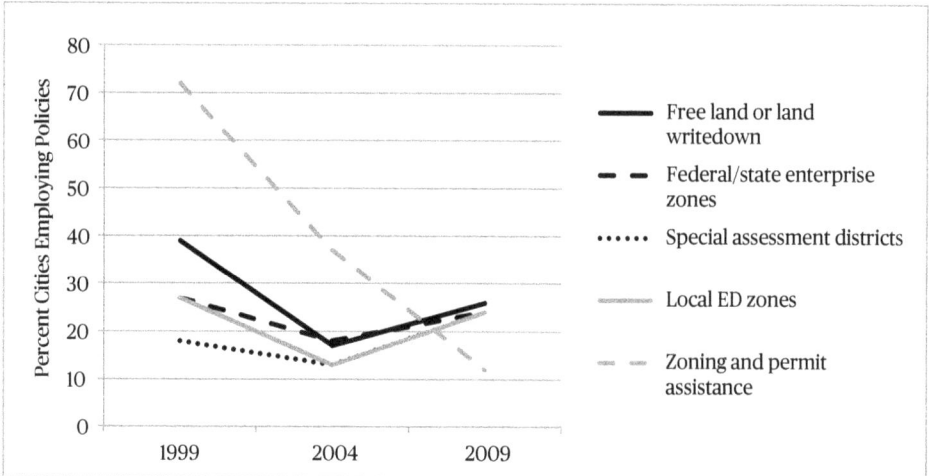

Local government economic development agencies often maintain databases of all industrial and commercial land and existing buildings in the community. Information on zoning, land availability, building costs, and utilities are in the database. Using this information and the location techniques described here cities can have more success in their economic development efforts.

Free Land is perhaps the most infamous economic development technique, but land grants have been a common economic development tool in recent years. While free market capitalists eschew giving away public assets such as land, land grants actually have a long history in the US. The federal government famously gave away land for railroad expansion, homesteading, and to establish public universities. These days land grants are more likely to be given out by state governments who hope to attract businesses that will make significant economic impact. According to the data in Table 7.1 land grants are given out in 26% of US cities in 2009. The data are unclear, but it is likely many of these cases consist of state and local government partnerships to give away the land.

In the case of Alabama attracting a new Mercedes factory in 1993, over $17 million of land was "sold" to Mercedes for only $100 (Koven and Lyons, 2003). To attract the Toyota Camry plant to Georgetown, Kentucky in 1984, the company secured free land from the Commonwealth of Kentucky. The region has been richly rewarded, as Toyota has built an industrial cluster that includes manufacturing facilities in Princeton, Indiana and Buffalo, West Virginia; and the company's North American headquarters in Erlanger, Kentucky. Respondents to the ICMA survey reported that 38.8% offer free land or land write-downs.

In 2006, city officials in the city of Azusa, California sold a large city block in the downtown area to a developer named Lowe's for $1. The site is at the corner of historic Route 66 and California Highway 39. For over 100 years the intersection was the most important commercial site in Azusa, which had historically been a major producer of citrus fruit. In the post-World War II economy, citrus groves began to be cut down and replaced with cheap tract housing developments. By the 1980s and 1990s, Azusa's downtown had lost all its vibrancy. The site, listed as "Block 36" on city maps consisted of mostly boarded up businesses except for Wimpey's Pawn Shop. Azusa's redevelopment officials purchased the parcels that comprised Block 36. Wimpey's was the last owner to sell the land to the city, and only after a sweetheart relocation package was offered and eminent domain was threatened.

The city assembled the various parcels into one property, upgraded the site's utilities and basically gave away the land to the developer. Lowe's had grand New Urbanist plans for the site including ground-level retail and offices, second-level condominiums, and underground parking. But in 2007 the Great Recession began and all construction in Southern California came to a halt. Seven years later the site remains unused. Azusa's redevelopment agency was closed, as were all such agencies in California by an order of the governor in 2011. Today some say the vacant site sits as a grim reminder of the follies of giving away land, but in years to come the development efforts will likely be revived and the intersection of 66 and 39 will likely regain some of its past economic vibrancy.

Land Write-Down is the practice of offering land to a business at a price lower than market value, so that a specified type of new development can be encouraged. In a typical scenario, the economic development agency acquires "blighted" land then invests in the improvement of the property. The land is then offered for sale to a business at a price lower than the fair market value. In exchange for the good price, the business agrees to follow stringent redevelopment requirements which are often the result of the local government's specifically defined use for the land. For example, the developers of the Broadway-Spring Center shopping center in Los Angeles received below market land in exchange for agreeing to build Biddy Mason Park adjacent to the shopping center.

Cities across the US have surplus land often called open space, public land, surplus property, abandoned property, etc. In an effort to build the local economy, these sites can be offered at below market prices. Land write-down is often practiced as an incentive for the new owner to build and industrial site that will create jobs, or for a housing developer to include so-called "affordable housing" as part of the site's development plan. Affordable housing for decades was defined as housing costing 25% or less than a household's income. In recent years this has been adjusted to 35%. It seems housing is less "affordable" than it used to be.

In 2013 the city council of Willmar, Minnesota adopted a land write-down policy. Willmar is a small farming town with a population of just under 20,000. City leaders hope to grow the non-agricultural part of the local economy by attracting industry. The new policy reduces the price of land located in the city's industrial parks. Companies qualify for the land write-down benefit if they provide jobs paying at least $12 per hour. City leaders expressed dismay at accepting lower than market value for the land, but they were willing to make the sacrifice if jobs could be created.

A **special assessment district** is geographic area designated by local government wherein the properties (usually commercial) receive some benefit, and are required to pay some tax. Many SAD's are set up for service provision such as a water or sewer district; the local government builds the water or sewer system and all properties within the SAD benefit from the project(s) but also must pay some tax. The district may also be "extraterritorial" meaning it extends beyond the city limits. In 2009, 26% of cities were using special assessment for economic development.

In terms of economic development, an SAD is typically formed to directly improve the business climate of an area. In Texas, the state government allows local governments to set up SAD's for purposes such as street and sidewalk improvements, mass transit improvements, parking, landscaping, business recruitment, marketing, and other purposes.

Officials in Kansas City, Missouri plan to use the special assessment district designation (in addition to local taxes, state support and federal support) to raise funds for the construction of a new streetcar system. Proponents cited economic development along the proposed route, while critics emphasized a funding shortfall and the failure to connect the streetcar line with the poorest neighborhoods in the city, such as a violent, low-income neighborhood in south Kansas City dubbed, "Murder Factory."

Business Improvement Districts are a type of special assessment district. The BID is a non-profit organizations that supplement local government services by providing additional services to improve an area. BIDs are usually established in retail areas with the objective of making the area more attractive to shoppers. They typically provide "added police services, local hourly clean ups, and joint merchant services" (Blakely and Bradshaw, 2002, p. 187) and sidewalk cleaning, graffiti removal, snow removal, and landscaping. BIDs are publicly sanctioned but run by the private members. The funding for BIDs generally comes in the form of a small tax on the businesses in the district.

For BIDs in Wisconsin this tax averages $2.52 per thousand dollars of assessed property value. BIDs have proven to be very effective ways to revitalize retail areas in New York and other cities (Blakely and Bradshaw, 2002).

In Seattle, a business improvement district was set up to support the Chinatown District. The BID is managed by a non-profit organization that exists to promote business, promote tourism, maintain public areas and put on cultural events. Businesses located in the district are charged a fee based on the size and value of their property. In some ways the Seattle is a market-based strategy in the sense that is managed privately and it is private companies who pay the costs and receive the benefits.

Zoning and permit assistance is offered by just 12% of US cities according to our data in Table 7.1. Zoning is a commonly used policy tool used by local government to manage the built environment. City leaders zone each parcel in the city limits according broad categories such as open space, industrial, commercial and residential. Each of these designations typically has numerous subcategories such as

R1 (single family residences), R2 (two single family residences) and R3 (multiple residences).

In economic terms, zoning is employed to reduce externalities such as pollution, congestion and crime. Zoning is favored by groups such as NIMBY (not-in-my-backyard) and BANANA (build-absolutely-nothing-near-anything).

In addition to zoning regulations, cities also limit growth by limiting the number of building permits, establishing growth boundaries (such as those in Oregon cities), through high taxes, and by limiting services such as roads, sewer and water. Real estate developers avoid these growth barriers by securing zoning and permit assistance, by providing their own services (such as private roads in HOA developments), or by practicing "leapfrog development."

In a market economy, growth limits create shortages of commercial and residential properties resulting in higher market prices. City leaders keen to practice market friendly policies will show flexibility in zoning and permiting when a project is deemed worthwhile in the local economy. Our data in Table 7.1 shows that 46% of US cities allowed **zoning flexibility** in 1999. This is a relatively low-cost market-based approach to economic development. When a business wants to rezone its land to expand, local bureaucrats should show some flexibility. Sadly that is often not the case.

The Columbine Baptist Church in Columbine, Colorado wanted to install an elevator in its aging building but city leaders took 11 months to approve the project saying the building had to first be rezoned. The church has less than 100 members with an average age of 68 years old. The seniors were pursuing a reasonable request that would assist their congregation, but the local city leaders chose to be the church's adversary rather than its advocate.

In St. Charles Parish in southern Louisiana, the Bayou Fleet company wanted to expand its business along the Mississippi River from just barge mooring, which was allowed under B-1 zoning, to ship repair and ship breaking, which is only allowed under B-2 zoning. The company had previously done B-1 and B-2 activities at the site, but the Parish government zoned the company B-1. In 1993 when the company decided to resume B-2 activities the Parish refused the rezoning request. The owner explained the business expansion was good for the local economy, jobs would be created the environment would not be harmed. Nonetheless, local officials refused the rezoning request, even after approving identical requests for two neighboring shipyards. Bayou Fleet sued the Parish to rezone the land, and for damages. After a 10-year battle, a Federal judge awarded the business $275,000 and the local officials were shamed for practicing cronyism.

Zoning simplification is used because private firms prefer to operate in areas with minimal government intervention and regulation. Overly restrictive zoning can be a deterrent to economic growth in a city. Rather than fight city hall, new firms might just choose to build in a municipality with less restrictive zoning. Economic development practitioners can use zoning policy to promote development by setting aside sufficient land for commercial and industrial use and by using flexible zoning rules. Incentive zoning, overlay zoning, and special districts are three types of flexible zoning practices. Respondents to the ICMA survey in 1999 reported that 72% use "zoning/permit assistance" and 46% of them use flexibility in special zoning. When land use is more flexible, a city is potentially more attractive to businesses.

Public private partnerships for economic development zones were practiced in 14% of US cities in 1999. PPP's take on many forms as explained in a later chapter of this book. The basic design, however, is that the public side of the partnership (usually a city or county government) provides land for the site and administrative support including permiting, zoning, tax incentives, etc. The private side of the partnership is often a key private company or a university.

In the case of the Gainseville (Florida) Technology Enterprise Center, a public-private partnership was formed between the city, Alachua County, the US Department of Commerce's Economic Development Administration and Cenetec a private company. The city contributed the land. A 30,000 square foot building was constructed with a city-run business incubator on the first floor with room for about ten start-ups, and Cenetec runs an accelerated business incubator on the second floor. Cenetec's mission is to commercialize new technology that was developed at nearby University of Florida, a top research university. Companies locating in Cenetec's incubator receive space, strategic guidance, legal guidance, marketing assistance and financing at no charge. Instead, the start-up contributes a portion of its equity ownership to the Cenetec company. This GTEC case illustrates how city leaders can encourage private enterprise to develop following market principles rather than government fiat.

Economic development zones, also called **Enterprise Zones**, are defined areas "where planning controls are kept to a minimum and attractive financial incentives are offered to prospective developers and occupants" (Blakely and Bradshaw, 2002, p. 234). The basic concept of the zone follows classical economic theory that economic growth is more likely to occur when government intervention is minimal.

The zones are usually established in "depressed areas, with the goal of encouraging investment and job creation" (Koven and Lyons, 2003, p. 188). Geographically-based programs, such as enterprise zones, "likely would assist low-income families who live in, or migrate to, the growing area" (Bish, 1971, p. 146). Enterprise zones were first introduced in the United Kingdom in the 1970s modeled after Hong Kong where regulations are minimal and economic growth is booming. As of 2002, thirty-seven U.S. states had enterprise zones, and in some cases, virtually entire cities are declared enterprise zones such as Toledo and Cleveland (Blakely and Bradshaw, 2002).

Louisiana has 750 enterprise zones. Distressed areas are defined as places with "high unemployment, low income, or a high percentage of residents receiving some form of public assistance" (Louisiana Department of Economic Development, 2003). A typical business is eligible for the benefits of the program if it increases its statewide workforce by 10%, or creates at least five new jobs. Of these new jobs, 35% must be filled by a member of "the Program's targeted groups" including enterprise zone residents, those receiving public assistance, people without basic skills, or physically challenged people. The benefits of the program for the business include a $2,500 tax credit per employee to be applied to the firm's state income or franchise taxes, and state sales tax rebates for purchases made during the construction period. The $2,500 tax credit is doubled if the new jobs are in the automotive or aerospace industries.

One criticism of enterprise zones is that they encourage existing businesses to relocate into the zone solely for the incentives, while no new jobs are added to the area. So government ends up subsidizing business development expenses that would have happened without any government intervention. These criticisms are difficult to measure, yet enterprise zones remain a common technique for economic development. In the ICMA, 66.3% of local governments reported that they use economic development zones.

Technology Zones are economic development zones that are designed to attract and develop technology companies. In the ICMA, 88.9% of local governments reported that they use technology zones. Technology companies locating in the zones are eligible for numerous incentives. The ICMA-surveyed cities reported that they offer these incentives in their technology zones: reduction in permit fees (24.0%), reduction in user fees (11.0%), flexibility in special zoning (46.0%), ordinance exemptions (10.0%), reduction in gross receipts tax (11.0%) and other (54.0%). Malecki (1984) notes that high tech companies prefer locales with universities, plenty of professional services, and diverse cultural and educational opportunities. Public investment in these areas should accompany the use of technology zones.

Tax Increment Finance districts (TIF) have been established in many cities as a way to stimulate redevelopment in areas that have a high number of vacant or dilapidated properties. A TIF is "an economic development financing tool used to attract private investment to blighted areas" (Fitzgerald and Leigh, 2002, p.117). Blighted areas typically have low property values, and therefore low property taxes. The property value of a new manufacturing facility in Chicago's Stockyards Commons TIF, for example, will be much higher than the property value of the vacant land prior to development. Properties that are redeveloped within a TIF district are taxed at their market value. However, any new tax revenue that is derived from a greater market value of the property over and above the pre-development baseline is reinvested into the TIF district through "improvements such as land acquisition and preparation, road and sewer construction, and streetscaping" (Fitzgerald and Leigh, 2002, p. 117). TIFs are established for a set period of time (no more than 23 years in Chicago) after which, all of the tax revenue goes into the general revenue fund of the city. Of the local governments in the ICMA survey, 49.6% reported that they use tax increment financing and 34.7% reported that they use TIF districts to fund economic development programs.

Planned Manufacturing Districts (PMD) are "designed to prevent competing land uses, specifically residential and commercial, from encroaching on manufacturing areas" (Fitzgerald and Leigh, 2002, p. 109). Normal zoning codes, which are normally contestable on a case-by-case basis, are suspended and the current industrial zone status is frozen. A common practice of real estate developers is to purchase low cost manufacturing land, have the zoning converted to residential, and build houses. Residential property values are higher per square foot than industrial property values. Additional residential developments can increase property values in an area resulting in major tax increases for preexisting industries, which can drive businesses away. Because Planned Manufacturing Districts work to prevent tax increases for industries, PMDs are effective tools of industrial retention.

In the late 1980s, leaders in Chicago established the Clybourn PMD which is a 41 acre area where manufacturing is the only allowable use. The area has good freeway and river access, and already housed dozens of manufacturing firms employing hundreds of local workers in high-paying manufacting jobs. At that time, many industrial areas were being converted to hipster mixed use sites with trendy boutiques at ground level and loft apartments up above. Rising property values and property taxes threatened to price out the manufacturers. The establishment of the PMD provided a stable environment for the businesses, such that twenty years later, the PMD has been deemed to have been a positive generator of economic activity for Chicago.

Industrial Parks are parcels of land "purchased by a local government for the purpose of subdividing it into lots for use by manufacturing businesses" (Koven and Lyons, 2003, p. 189). Local government typically provides the necessary infrastructure including roads and utilities, and in some cases erects speculative buildings. Industrial parks are built for the purpose of attracting new businesses to a city. Industrial parks have long been criticized because they contribute to urban sprawl and damage the environment (Jacobs, 1992). In response to this criticism, some developers have embraced "ecoparks," where "member businesses seek enhanced environmental, economic, and social performance through collaboration in managing environmental and resource issues" (Lowe, 2001, p. 2). The Choctaw Generation Plant is the core member of the Red Hills EcoPlex, in Chester, Mississippi. Other businesses in the EcoPlex industrial park manufacture products using waste products from the power plant ("Ecoparks Gaining Momentum" 2001). The industrial park managers are intentional in their efforts to conduct environmentally-friendly business.

Physical Infrastructure Development is one of the perennial tools of economic development officials for business attraction. This includes electricity, natural gas, telecommunications, water lines, sewage lines, public transportation, roads, railroads, waterfronts, and even airports. In the ICMA survey, 74.1% of the cities reported that they offer physical infrastructure incentives. Firms that are comparing potential sites for relocation prefer sites with existing functional infrastructure over undeveloped sites that require the firm itself to build and pay for its own infrastructure. To remain competitive, city economic development officials frequently offer infrastructure incentives to potential firms. "In almost all instances, the instrument is in the form of a direct grant" (Fisher and Peters, 1998, p. 42). Local government officials often secure the funding, on behalf of the private firm. State funds are often secured through Departments of Transportation, and federal funds are often secured through Community Development Block Grants.

Old Economy firms were more concerned with roads and utilities, while new economy firms consider telecommunications one of the most important infrastructure assets. In the ICMA survey, 74.8% of the cities reported that they consider their telecommunications infrastructure to be an economic development tool or asset.

The city of Cedar Falls, Iowa recently granted four acres of land worth $400,000 for the new Cedar Valley Data Center, which will serve as a Network Access Point

(NAP). NAPs serve as connection points for Internet service providers. Most NAPs are in California or the East Coast (Palmer, 2003). "Because it's cheaper to transport data with a nearby NAP, new economy companies have, for the most part, avoided Iowa, and opted for places like Silicon Valley, Seattle and Austin, Texas" (Palmer, 2003, p. 1). The new telecommunications infrastructure provided by the Cedar Valley Data Center is expected to help lure high tech industries to the area.

Speculative Buildings are built by cities in an effort to attract firms by reducing the firm's start-up time. Speculative buildings are typically built as "shells" with the interior mostly unfinished. Many of these buildings end up being used as business incubators. Blakely and Bradshaw (2002) recommend the use of speculative buildings by communities that have adequate labor forces, transportation and public services; yet lack a sufficient amount of industrial space.

Landbanking is the practice by public or nonprofit agencies of acquiring parcels of land to be used in a future economic development project. In many cases the economic development agency buys numerous small properties in an attempt to piece together a larger plot of land that will be used for some purpose such as an airport expansion, construction of an industrial park, expansion of a local firm, or simply to preserve open space. Landbanks often "receive vacant brownfield properties that are tax delinquent and environmentally contaminated" (Fitzgerald and Leigh, 2002, p. 93). The objective is to resolve the tax delinquency; decontaminate the site; and sell the property to an organization that will put the land back to productive use, such as a private firm.

In 1971 the Municipality of Anchorage created a land bank which came to be known as the Heritage Land Bank. Land in Anchorage is scarce, with 82% designated open space, 6% military, 3% tidal; leaving just 9% developable. The HLB obtained 12,000 acres from the state which it was able to offer in creative ways for economic development purposes. In some cases the land was sold at fair market value, other times it was sold for less, and in a few cases land trades were brokered. In one case a local business was able to trade its building at the airport in exchange for a building in the HLB. The business was able to double its operations including its employee count because the new building was twice as large. The local airport benefitted by receiving the traded building. They could use the building for expanded administration and they increased security by reducing traffic in and out of the airport.

Community Land Trusts are a type of landbank typically operated by charitable non-profit organizations. In an effort to create and preserve affordable housing, the trust will purchase land. The acquired properties are often in declining neighborhoods in central cities. These properties are improved and affordable housing is provided for lower income households.

Townscaping is the practice of improving the physical appearance of a central city following a theme developed by local merchants, city planners and citizen groups (Blakely and Bradshaw, 2002). The objective of townscaping is not only to attract tourists to the city, but also to encourage local residents to patronize their own downtown.

The Fourth Street Live project, part of a downtown revitalization plan in Louisville, Kentucky, can be considered a townscaping project. The project converts an underused shopping facility into a music- and sports-themed entertainment district spanning four city blocks. The project not only includes securing "anchor" tenants such as Hard Rock Café and the Premier Fitness Group, but also improving the cityscape including sidewalks, landscaping and a pedestrian walkway.

To wisely employ land-based policies, economic development practitioners should include land-use planners in analyzing a more comprehensive view. In New Jersey, for example, the state issued $137 million in tax credits to Panasonic and Bayer. The incentives were not to attract these companies from outside, but to help them move from one location to another within the state. While advocates of the incentives argued they prevented the departure of two major employers, many citizens criticized the state's use of funds. Kasabach (2011) warned that the moves will worsen pollution and congestion, as the employees of the two companies will likely have longer commutes. That is, the workers won't also move to new locations, but will continue living where they live and just drive further distances to work. In New Jersey, open space is disappearing fast. Kasabach recommends infill development as a higher priority for receiving incentives than greenfield development. Infill development already has infrastructure such as utilities and public transportation, whereas greenfield development also requires greater infrastructure development. Kasabach argues incentive should be "priced" based on proximity to urban areas.

Chapter Summary

While the major goals of economic development policy are attracting and retaining businesses, these goals are often only accomplished through policies related to physical space. Many local governments own land as one of their most significant assets. These assets can be put to use as part of an overall economic development strategy.

In the early years of "smokestack chasing" city leaders would give away land for free to businesses who were willing to move to the city or to expand existing operations in the city. These free land deals rarely met the most basic cost/benefit criteria in terms of the local community. In recent years, city leaders have become better stewards of our scarce public resources. They are employing a number of creative techniques that are less burdensome to the taxpayers. This chapter described a number of these market-based examples, contrasted with a few examples of irresponsible governance. Hopefully our local leaders will learn from the good examples and eschew the others.

Guest Case: Keystone Opportunity Zone

By: David Brumfield

Business retention policies, no matter how necessary, can leave communities with unexpected and unwanted results as companies take advantage of legislators. Without clear distinct procedures set up to track spending, program progress, or even safe guards to help protect communities, it can become easy to invest in an ineffective program that is doing more harm than good.

This became the case in the State of Pennsylvania when implementing the Keystone Opportunity Zone (KOZ) program. Although the program describes an ideal situation, companies used it to collect tax breaks without changing their usual business practices. The program was meant to inspire growth in the state of Pennsylvania by giving tax breaks to companies located in specific areas as well as tax breaks to draw companies into the zones. Unfortunately, this is far from what happened.

Nine years after implementing KOZ, state senate passed a bill establishing a committee to analyze the efficiency of the program. The response was shocking. The Legislative Budget and Finance Committee (LBFC) found there was a shocking shortage of performance measures built into the original KOZ. The committee could not determine how well the program was doing. No means to calculate job creation, which was the biggest criterion for tax breaks (the monthly average of full time jobs created multiplied by a preset rate), were ever implemented.

The data previously reported by the individual firms was formatted in several different formats. Some firms reported numbers in jobs created in a single year, while others provided data in a cumulative total ranging several years. With no detail as to when the jobs were created, it is possible that companies started strong but became stagnant after a year or two. Using the second practice, companies exploited credits, costing the state and local governments vital tax revenue.

Statewide, the LBFC discovered an underwhelming amount of job creation while researching the program. Throughout the state, around three-quarters of the participants recorded no job creation at all, leaving the majority of participants reaping unearned tax benefits. These companies managed to find loopholes in the wording of the law, increasing the burden on the taxpayers and taking advantage of lawmakers.

In Pittston, PA, discount retail giant TJ Maxx managed to hire unauthorized employees while also avoiding high wages as township supervisors felt were promised. Instead of hiring township residents at a minimum wage of $8 an hour, as officials expected, TJ Maxx hired workers starting with a wage of $6.50 an hour. It was soon discovered, amidst anger from township leaders, that 544 off of the employees were in fact illegal immigrants (Janoski, 2005). After these workers were removed and new staff was brought in, still only two-five of the employees were township residents according to then township supervisor Tony Attardo. Attardo went on to state his expectation of the company leaving the area in 2013, when the tax benefits had expired (Janoski, 2005).

Without a set of precedents to be followed, the LBFC found that some data had been duplicated or was a mix of actual data and estimates. In fact, the LBFC stated that there was no way to track how much the program was costing the state. Some local municipalities had been keeping records of the tax breaks, but without a comprehensive program, a full evaluation was impossible. In the report, the LBFC member reported that the only cost estimate they could form was $650 million based on a similar program in New York. Overall, the LBFC found that the program needed several major improvements to continue to ensure its success in the future and maintain the accountability of the state and the company it helps.

After the review, the governor signed a bill that approved an extension of the program. The new bill allows for companies to join the program until 2015, extending the duration of the program through 2025. In the new extension, amendments have been added to keep track of job creation as well as any other incentives used by the state. It is yet to been seen how improvements to the financial reporting systems have affected the program, but the future goal is to promote growth in the State of Pennsylvania while holding companies liable for creating jobs and, ultimately, helping the community.

Guest Case: Economic Development in the City of Roses

By: Michael Chrzanowski

Many cities across America are finding it more and more difficult during these poor economic times to attract new businesses and retain existing ones in order to maintain a stable operating economic environment. The Historical Californian City of Pasadena is no different; the city has implemented several growth and sustainment strategies that have allowed for continued success and development that are prime for times such as these. In order to attract new business, Pasadena has turned to hosting new events that draw large amounts of consumers to the area. The city is already known for the historic Tournament of Roses Parade, which originated on New Year's Day in 1890; now, however, the city has implored all new events and contests such as the Rock n' Roll Half Marathon, Clean Energy Challenge, Cheeseburger Week, and a variety of ethnic/cultural events to achieve their goal of growth and development. Because of the aforementioned history of the city, and the fact that it has always been a major destination of choice for various types of consumers, Pasadena already holds an advantage over many other cities, which allows it to take more risks. Now, however, more than ever; balance has become one of the city's top priorities in maintaining stability and growth.

Certain types of businesses can be profitable anywhere because of a unique array of products they possess; then there are those businesses that don't even offer any products for sale, therefore having no reason for being located in an area that draws a large consumer base, which means, for these two types of businesses, and several others, simply generating consumers is not enough to keep them there; this is where the city's use of fiscal tools plays a major role. Today, Pasadena's most notable economic strengths come from its scientific institutions, a large international engineering base, a regional health care cluster, and a broad retail sector, all of which require different sustaining principles to maintain.

Perhaps Pasadena's most prevalent use of fiscal tools lies within the boundaries of the *Pasadena Enterprise Zone.* Simply put, the State of California offers tax credits in order to promote business development and employment growth to all businesses in the Enterprise Zone. The first 15-year designation of the Enterprise Zone existed between April of 1992 to April of 2007. The current Enterprise Zone expires in April of 2022 and has expanded to include commercial and industrial zoned land located within the City of Pasadena. Under the Pasadena Enterprise Zone program, five tax credit incentives are offered, which reduce the cost of hiring new employees as well as investing in equipment within the zone. The incentives consist of the following: Hiring Tax Credit, Sales and Use Tax Credit, Business Expense Deduction, 15-Year Net

Operating Loss Carryover, and a Net Interest Deduction for Lenders. A major benefit to this program is that all forms of businesses located within the Pasadena Enterprise Zone, automatically qualify for benefits regardless if they are proprietorships, partnerships, or corporations; and there are no special fees or applications required to qualify.

The Hiring Credit is a five-year state tax credit, potentially worth up to $37,000 per employee. The Sales and Use Tax Credit permit businesses to claim a state tax credit equivalent to the sales and use tax paid on the purchase of various manufacturing, office, and computer equipment. This credit allows businesses to update equipment at a normal rate and use their funds toward other areas of the business in order to grow or maintain. Similarly, the Business Expense Deduction allows Enterprise Zone businesses a deduction of up to 40 percent of the cost of certain property purchased for the sole Enterprise Zone use during the first year of its service. The Net Operating Loss incentive gives businesses the opportunity to carry forward 100 percent of their net operating loss for 15 years. This tax incentive creates two possibilities; (1) businesses may receive a tax credit for applying the net operating loss to its past tax payments or (2) businesses can decrease the need to make payments in future periods by applying the net operating loss to future income tax payments, either way, the business benefits in the midst of troubled times. Finally, the Net Interest Deduction for Lenders creates an opportunity for lenders who give loans to Enterprise Zone businesses to receive a deduction from the income on the sum of the net interest earned on the loans. This establishes an incentive for loans in an otherwise poor economy where loans are difficult to come by and also decreases the risk of default due to asymmetric information and somewhat limits the possibility of a moral hazard.

These are five major tools that are currently being exercised to promote economic development in the City of Pasadena; however, they are not the only tools. The city also provides businesses with an Incentive for historic preservation of land, which saves businesses money on various development and architectural services and fees. A development currently in the making for Pasadena to attract new businesses is to offer free parking. Parking has been a major issue for many years in Pasadena and has often scared interested businesses away, however, in the midst of the economic drawbacks; the city is developing an effective means to manage the problem to promote growth.

Tax exemptions, tax credits, reduced taxes, low-cost loans, and infrastructure subsidies are all fiscal tools that the City of Pasadena currently uses, and though each of these tools is greatly important to the success of the city, the tangible incentives that each of these benefits create are just that: *tangible*. What makes the City of Pasadena stand out and continue to prosper in the midst of all the chaos of what is the United States economy, are the intangible ideals such as the rich history of the city, the desire of business owners to want to operate there, the consumer making it a destination of choice, the weather and climate, the social environment, and most importantly the perception of the city, is what will carry Pasadena through the various trials and setbacks that are inevitable in the world of business in America.

CHAPTER 8

BUSINESS RETENTION

Chapter Introduction

Over the past decades, we have seen the forces of globalization make the world economy much more interconnected. Consumers can buy products made virtually anywhere in the world. Similarly, businesses have many more location choices. Thanks to significant reductions in the cost of telecommunications and transportation, private firms these days are much more mobile. Given this newfound mobility of capital, many cities struggle to retain their existing businesses. This chapter describes some of the most common economic development policies employed by city leaders with the specific goal of retaining businesses within their borders.

Basic location theories explain that businesses either want to locate near their inputs or near their customers. Materials heavy industries, such as wineries, locate near their inputs; while customer focused industries, such as breweries locate near their customers. It takes three pounds of grapes to make a bottle of wine that only weighs one and a half pounds, so wineries choose to locate near vineyards and ship the lighter finished product out to their customers. Breweries on the other hand locate near their customers. Their lightweight inputs (hops, malt, and yeast) are distributed to breweries then mixed with the heaviest input, water. The finished product is heavier than the inputs so it is more economical for breweries to be dispersed in cities around the country.

Economic theory suggests that private firms locate near their inputs for economies of scale, labor pools, labor matching, knowledge spillovers and agglomeration economies. Companies who produce clothing take advantage of *economies of scale* when they locate in a textile cluster; inputs such as fabric, thread and buttons are all cheaper when offered in bulk. While much of our textile production has been offshored, the garment district in Los Angeles remains a good example of economies of scale.

Silicon Valley is an industrial cluster in the technology sector. Firms locate in Silicon Valley to take advantage of the *labor pool* of highly skilled tech workers. When their hiring needs grow or shrink it is relatively easy to grow or shrink their own labor force. Similarly, workers want to locate in labor pools because they can find employment at many different companies. This concept is often called *labor matching*.

Knowledge spillover is a term describing the informal gathering of intellectual capital between firms. If you and I have lunch together as friends, we will inevitably talk about work; if we are both tech workers in the Valley, it is likely that valuable intellectual capital will be shared informally during our lunch time. All of these positive effects drive private firms to locate in industrial clusters which are often called *agglomeration economies.*

While firms within an agglomeration economy enjoy many benefits, these same factors can drive companies to switch locations. For a start-up company, locating in what's been called an *urbanization economy* makes the most sense; this is a large urban center with many industrial clusters. A start-up manufacturer, for example, would benefit from proximity to financial firms to secure start-up funds, and engineering firms who can help develop prototypes and establish a manufacturing process. Once a firm is established, however, they may prefer to move to a more specialized location to take advantage of the benefits noted above, namely labor pooling, labor matching, and knowledge spillover.

The reality is that individual firms have varied reasons for their location choices. Most of these reasons are economically rational and can be predicted using the theories described above. Numerous business owners, however, are not economically rational and may make location decisions based on non-economic factors such as proximity to family or recreation or climate. In any case, city leaders would do well to get to know the key employers in their city so they might remain responsive to the changing needs of the business. In this new era of mobile capital, cities are at ever-increasing risk of losing key parts of their economic base. This chapter describes common economic development policies for business retention.

Business Retention in Practice

Table 8.1 reports the percentage of cities in the U.S. who practice various business retention techniques. The same data is show in Figure 8.1. Of the twelve policies listed, the most prevalent are local business surveys (52% in 2009), partnering with other local governments (47%), and business roundtables (35%). This data is relatively good news in the sense that all of these practices (and most of the others on the list) are not resource-intensive. In other words, city leaders are spending time getting to know local firms, which costs much less than other retention efforts such as fiscal incentives. In this way, the city leaders are employing market solutions to solve the problem of capital mobility.

Table 8.1 Percent of U.S. Cities Using Various Business Retention Policies

	1999	**2004**	**2009**
Local business surveys	60	43	52
Partnering with local gov'ts	42	37	47
Business roundtables	41	34	35
Publicity for local firms	32	24	26
Ombudsman programs	22	16	23
Revolving loan programs	36	22	20
Export assistance	11	9	8
Import replacement	3	2	
NGO partnerships for retention	78	58	
Calling on local companies	74	56	
Achievement awards	24	19	
Calling nat'l firm headquarters	22	18	

Figure 8.1 Business Retention Policies

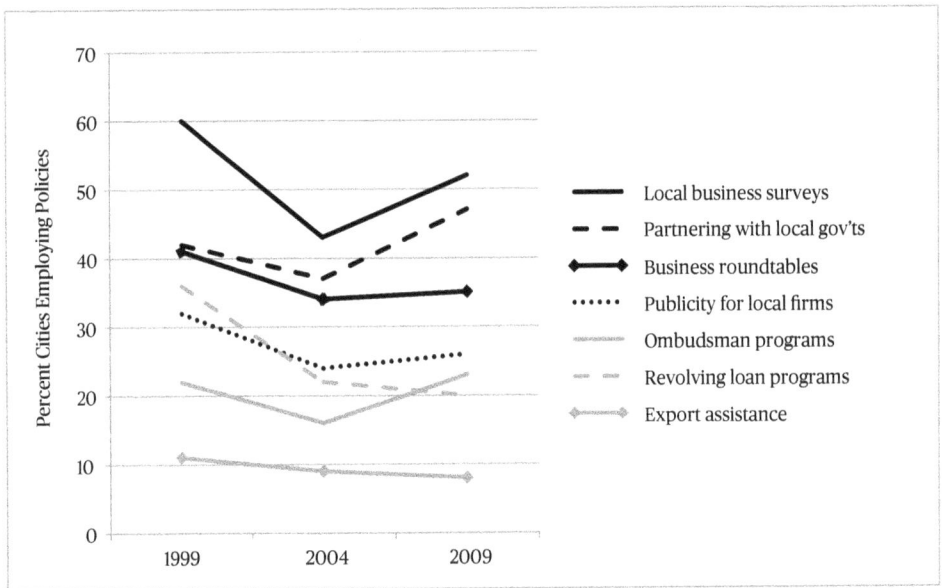

Local business surveys were practiced by 52% of U.S. cities in 2009, and have been prevalent over the past two decades. Business surveys are typically carried out by economic development officials or the local chamber of commerce. While the surveys rarely ask directly, "Are you thinking of moving your business?" the surveys generally ask broad questions which can alert the city leaders to a business that might be in distress. Common questions include, "Over the past five years have your business operations decreased, increased, or remained stable? Over the next five years, do you expect your business operations to decrease, increase or remain stable?"

These same type of questions are repeated with an emphasis on topics such as hiring, facilities, and so on. It is possible for city leaders to not only gauge the overall climate for business, but to also locate struggling firms who might be candidates to close operations in the city.

The City of Richland, Washington conducts its "Business Retention and Expansion" survey every 3-5 years with assistance from the local chamber of commerce and Washington State University. The stated goal of the survey is, "To capture business owners' thoughts, ideas, concerns, future plans, and valuable insight into City Services and Community Services" (2005, p. 5). The survey had a 25% response rate.

The results of the study allowed the authors to assess how well city services are meeting the needs of businesses, but also to predict over $37 million in future capital investments and over 500 new jobs to be created. Some reported barriers to growth included traffic, zoning, and the ominous presence of a massive nuclear facility in the neighboring city of Hanford. A few questions helped city leaders identify businesses that might be in danger of leaving Richland, such as, "Are there any employee skills that your business needs which are difficult to find in (the area)?" Overall the local business survey is an excellent way for city leaders to gain first-hand knowledge about the state of the local economy.

Partnering with local governments is practiced by 47% of U.S. cities according to the results presented in Table 8.1. These partnerships are typically entered into so the partnering governmental units can take advantage of economies of scale. It is common for county governments and numerous city governments to cooperatively create special districts, which are independent government agencies, usually formed for a specific purpose such as public education, utilities, or waste services. For economic development purposes, so-called "horizontal agreements" are formed typically by local governments within the same metropolitan area.

Savitch and Vogel (2000) point out that "regionalism" is a rising trend where fragmented local government units cooperate to boost their perceived diminished power in an increasingly globalizing economy. Regional agreements allow smaller governments to cooperate to battle urban sprawl and to provide a legal framework for development. Hawkins (2011) surveyed 206 city leaders in 12 metropolitan areas and found one of the main reasons cities had formed partnerships with other governments was because the higher level governments (county and state) had greater access to financial capital, especially funds distributed by the federal government. The federal government has designated certain Economic Development Districts, and some financial resources are tied to those districts.

In terms of business retention, these partnerships assist local governments in preventing local companies from leaving the city to go to another city within the same metropolitan area, because the economic development incentives would be the same in the new location. If the firm moved to an entirely different metropolitan area, the existing local partnership will be in a weaker position in terms of retaining the footloose firm.

Business roundtables were initially established in communities by local business leaders. Often they formed to pressure elected officials to make some decision such as removing some barrier to business. In recent years, business roundtables have become sophisticated organizations led by local business leaders, who now advocate not only for business interests, but other community interests as well, such as traffic and education. In the 2009 data, 35% of cities had business roundtables.

The Oakland County Business Roundtable was established in 1993 to encourage county government to make decisions that would help businesses thrive. These days the Roundtable is divided into four committees who advocate for economic development, quality of life, transportation and workforce development.

While business roundtables are led by businesses, savvy public officials would do well to cooperate with the roundtables. Sometimes business leaders just need to be heard, while at other times they are advocates for real change that will benefit the community. As part of a business retention strategy, city leaders should support the local business roundtable which will allow city leaders to learn what issues the business community is facing. Again, this is another low cost technique that may encourage free market economic development.

Publicity for local firms is practiced by 26% of the cities in the survey data. City leaders can assist in the marketing and public relations efforts of local businesses by regularly highlighting the firms' products and accomplishments in local media, websites, and publications such as chamber of commerce newsletters or tourist maps. Publicity can promote a local business, but also attempt to contradict unfavorable popular opinions, such as after a local business has a product recall. As an extreme example consider the case of Given Lubinda, the Zambian information minister who bungee jumped just to show the activity is safe for tourists.

An **ombudsman** is a local official who acts as an advocate for local citizens and businesses. The "classical" ombudsman is independent of local agency administrators and may report directly to the mayor or county commission. Staff in the office of the ombudsman typically try to resolve the complaints of local citizens or businesses, but may also refer the case to local judges. Citizens and businesses typically utilize ombudsman services when their issue is outside the scope of local agencies' duties, or if they feel the local agency has made an unfair decision.

Research by Hill (2002) describes the situation of an ombudsman in Hawaiian communities, one of five states cited to have "classical" ombudsmen. From 1969 to 1999 the most prevalent complaints the ombudsmen dealt with were public safety (32% of all complaints), social services and housing (15%), corrections (13%), and city and county government issues (6%). A number of complaints did, however, relate to local business including complaints about labor relations (4% of all complaints), commerce and consumer affairs (3%), taxation (2%), land use (2%), and business economic development and tourism (.2%). Of the 15,771 complaints the ombudsmen in Hawaii dealt with over this 30 year period, 90% had been satisfactorily rectified.

Revolving loan programs are a type of loan pooling wherein local companies obtain funding from the pool and then repay the loan back into the pool such that other local businesses might have the same opportunity in the future. These programs were described in greater detail in the previous fiscal incentives chapter.

In terms of revolving loans for business retention, the Poly-Tainer, Inc. case is illustrative. The company manufactures plastic products such as toy components and cosmetics cases out of recycled plastic. Poly-Tainer was founded in 1962 in Van Nuys, California which is part of the Los Angeles metropolitan area, but had moved a bit further out to the west in Simi Valley. Around 1998 the company was considering moving to Utah where real estate would be much cheaper and they could consolidate their three existing buildings into one larger and more efficient site. Two hundred and forty workers were at risk of losing their jobs. Local leaders assisted Poly-Tainer in securing a $1 million low-interest loan from a California loan program that targets environmentally friendly programs. Although not exactly a textbook example of a "revolving" loan program, nonetheless the Poly-Tainer case is a good example of local officials retaining an important local employer through the use of a loan program.

Export development assistance occurs when government helps businesses locate overseas markets for their products. Federal and state governments are more active in international trade, but 11.2% of the ICMA survey respondents affirmed that their local government provided export assistance to local firms. Besides the federal and state agencies located in the city, St. Louis firms can also gain export assistance from these local agencies: the St. Louis Regional Chamber and Growth Association (a private organization), the St. Louis Center for International Relations (a non-profit organization established by city and county government), and the World Affairs Council of St. Louis (another not-for-profit organization).

Import replacement is a simple concept–convince local businesses to buy from each other to create a multiplier effect in the local economy. For example, around 2002 when Mercedes announced it would be making its small-sized SUV in the US, many states competed to be the site of the new plant. Public officials had much to gain by winning the competition. The factory would employ hundreds of citizens and dozens of supporting firms who supply parts for the Mercedes assembly line were expected to open shop near the new factory. Additionally, the cachet of recruiting one of the world's most well-known luxury brands to the local economy proved to be an enticing achievement for local officials. In the end the state of Alabama won the competition. In addition to numerous incentives, the state of Alabama also agreed to purchase Mercedes vehicles for its state fleet. Some supporters thought this import replacement strategy was the "icing on the cake" that gave Alabama the win. Critics point out the irony that Alabama is one of the poorest states in the US, yet many of its bureaucrats now drive around in Mercedes vehicles.

In Eugene, Oregon, the "Buy Oregon" project helps local contractors because they alone are allowed to bid for regional manufacturing subcontracts.

Although import replacement can be an effective market-based economic development technique with little cost to taxpayers, only 2.7% of ICMA survey respondents confirmed that they use import replacement as a business retention tool.

In 1999, 78% of US cities were using **NGO partnerships for retention**. In 2004, the number dropped to 58%, and then in 2009, the ICMA dropped the question from its survey. Many of us think of international development aid when we hear "non-government organization" rather than the context of economic development in US cities, whereas the phrase "non-profit organization" seems more fitting in the context of the US. Nonetheless, NGO's are active in economic development in the US. NGO's tend to focus on family support, education, and workforce training. It is this last category where we see NGO's partnering with local governments for economic development.

In Baltimore in 1997, an NGO called America Works, was founded with one of its main missions the goal of preparing welfare recipients for the world of work. In 1996, Congress led by Newt Gingrich, had passed sweeping changes to the welfare system. Pressure was on to get people off the dole and into jobs. Unlike traditional job training programs that offer skills-based training, America Works focused on moving welfare recipients directly into jobs with the hope that the employers' on-the-job training would be sufficient. America Works counselors instead focused on soft skills such as work ethic, attitude, punctuality and so on. The program was deemed a success as 600 people out of 1,000 who were offered jobs were still employed one year later (Goldsmith, 1999, 70-71).

The support of NGO's/NFP's such as America Works can be instrumental in helping in business retention efforts. Many business faces a labor mismatch, which can be alleviated by job training and job placement services such as those provided by America Works. For a business to stay put, it must have an adequate workforce.

Calling on local companies is a key component in a city's efforts at business retention. Many businesses who are considering leaving a city will not make their intentions known, and when they do leave, a wave of unemployed workers creates bad faith between the company and the city. If city leaders will regularly call on key employers they might be able to retain those firms who were considering leaving. These efforts can be direct visits by city leaders to the company, but ideally city leaders develop deeper relationships with local business leaders through public events such as mixers and other events routinely put on by groups such as the local chamber of commerce.

Birch recommends city leaders move away from a "survey-focused, question-and-answer interrogation" and instead meet face-to-face with business owners, ask open-ended questions, and help them understand what economic development resources might be available to support the business (2009, p. 6). Established local businesses create more jobs than new businesses, yet more economic development emphasis is placed on attracting new businesses, while local businesses are ignored.

Calling national firm headquarters is similar to calling on local companies. The key difference is that large corporations have locations throughout the US, and their location decisions are not made by the local leadership but at the corporate headquarters. Unlike locally based businesses which have non-economic incentives to remain in the city, such as proximity to family, corporations are more likely to make location decisions solely on economic factors. In the 1999 ICMA survey 22% of cities were calling on national firm headquarters and the number declined to 18% in 2004.

Ambassador Programs establish an executive type person whose role is to communicate to the private sector regarding all of the various public sector programs that are available. Of the ICMA surveyed cities, 12.4% reported they use an ambassador program. Officials in Philadelphia designed their Business Ambassador Initiative such that individuals who work in private businesses can be designated as a Greater Philadelphia Ambassador. Their role is to help other local companies connect with Philadelphia's economic development officials for assistance with business expansion, regulatory assistance, grants, loans, and other assistance that could be offered by the local government.

The program uses the power of the free market in that the Ambassadors are folks who are already active in the local economy. They have an incentive to participate because they too want the local economy to prosper. Yet, the program uses few public resources. The city benefits from the assistance and expertise of local business people who offer to serve in the program. The Ambassadors also benefit, as their stature and reputation undoubtedly increases in the minds of others engaged in business in Philadelphia.

Achievement Awards are a low cost market-based retention technique practiced by 24.0% of the surveyed economic development agencies in 1999. City leaders, such as the directors of the local chamber of commerce, select a number of businesses each year to be recognized as a key contributor to the local economy, usually in terms of employment. The businesses who earn the award can use the accolades in their marketing and public relations efforts. In some places, awards are given to individuals rather than companies, such as in Pensacola, Florida, where the chamber of commerce annually recognizes a number of business leaders in categories including emerging leader, professional leader, community leader, business leader, Pioneer Award, and the Spirit of Pensacola award.

Chapter Conclusion

By many measures the city of Bridgeport, Connecticut was in decline around 1990. The population was shrinking, and the local economy was suffering from the effects of deindustrialization. A number of manufacturers had closed their doors as they moved out looking for more attractive locations. Around 1993, city leaders received word that two additional manufacturers were planning on shuttering their plants and laying off their workers.

Conco Medical Company announced its intentions to lay off its 140 workers. The company had been producing flexible bandages in Bridgeport for 20 years, but wanted to be closer to its suppliers in the "textile belt" of South Carolina.

Meanwhile the Casco company, which had been in Bridgeport for 75 years was considering generous incentive offers from Virginia and Arkansas. The Casco facility manufactured a number of automotive components. Each day Casco's 280 workers produced 85,000 automotive cigarette lighters. Around this time, American automotive manufacturing was beginning to shift from Detroit, to lower-cost, and more centrally-located places in the South. A new "auto belt" was forming which stretched from Ohio (Honda), through Indiana and Kentucky (Toyota) down to Alabama. Casco's move was imminent.

City leaders, including Bridgeport's mayor, joined with state officials to attempt to retain both Conco and Casco. They put into practice many of the business retention techniques described in this chapter. The efforts failed to retain Conco, but in the curious case of Casco, the company's leadership team decided to close its existing location in the west side of Bridgeport and move into a location in the east side of town. The location was the former site of Conco. In addition to finding Casco this new site, public officials had also put together a grant package from the state of Connecticut worth $1.5 million. Surely these funds were the linchpin in Casco's decision to remain in the city. In the end Casco's 280 jobs were retained, and 100 more were added. Ironically, Casco's new site was the former location of the Conco company.

Guest Case: Zooming Out of Los Angeles

By: Kyle Calvillo

On March 5th 2010, the Los Angeles City Council met and was faced with a crucial decision. As a result of a change in the tax code made by Los Angeles' Office of Finance, the city was forced to decide between millions of dollars in tax revenue, or the risk of capital flight of many highly valued Internet businesses. According to the Los Angeles Chamber of Commerce, this dilemma came as the result of the Office of Finance's reclassification of many Internet-based businesses from multi media to professional service providers. The new classification increased the taxes imposed on the businesses' gross receipts by more than 500%. Needless to say the decision stirred up a storm of outraged companies.

When taken in the context of Charles Tiebout's theory that people "vote with their feet," it is easy to guess what happened next. Through a combination of the tax increase and Internet companies being very mobile, it became clear the reclassification was going to result in Los Angeles losing many of its Internet-based companies and their relatively high paying jobs. The L.A. Chamber noted that while many companies and thousand of jobs had already left the city, Los Angeles had much more to lose if the tax code was not modified. A noteworthy example took place within the Hollywood offices of LegalZoom. Since Hollywood is located in Los Angeles County, LegalZoom was one of the many companies hit with the 500% tax increase. As a result, the company had no problem making it known that they were preparing to leave Los Angeles and planning to move to Austin, Texas.

As the pressure mounted, the City Council had no choice but to recognize the need to review the reclassification. On March 6th 2010, the Los Angeles Times reported that when faced with a likely $3.4 million loss in tax revenue compared to the potential flight of many of the 1,400 businesses affected by the tax increase, the council unanimously approved a new classification for Internet companies. This new category put the majority of the companies back in the same tax bracket they were in prior to the previous reclassification. Although substantial damage was done by the decision of the Office of Finance, the move made by the Council saved the city from further losses and the potential obliteration of an Internet presence in Los Angeles.

Some of the companies who were retained by the modification include Shopzilla and MyLife.com. Unfortunately, LegalZoom was not included in the reclassification. As a result, the company decided to move their offices and 600 jobs to Glendale, California and Austin, Texas where they are currently located.

Guest Case: Long Live the Kings!

By: Matthew Pereira

Talented athletes have thrilled and excited zealous fanatics into squandering exuberant amounts of money to observe their beloved professionals' extraordinary abilities. Economists have struggled to calculate the benefits provided by superstar athletes and professional sports teams. While financial analysts can compute how a sports team impacts a city monetarily, the psychological advantages of hosting a team are far more difficult to quantify. On paper, many professional franchises actually cost cities more than they are worth fiscally. In Sacramento, the city faces the difficulty of deciding whether building their team, the Kings, a new arena is a wise investment.

As long as professional sports teams contribute sufficient emotional benefits to offset net monetary losses, their survival will remain economically rational. According to Stanford Economist Roger Noll, in reality, sports arenas fail to yield net economic gains to cities. Moreover, in their 1997 essay, *Sports, Jobs, and Taxes*, Noll and Zimbalist proceed to estimate sports arenas tend to cost the host city $10 million a year. Nevertheless, not only do sports stadiums continue to exist, but society constantly provides the funding to construct new and improved stadiums across the United States. Thus, professional teams must be providing advantages that reach beyond simply the economy. Besides the more quantifiable monetary revenues, Malcolm Gladwell asserts professional sports franchises also yield "psychic benefits" to owners, local communities, and other fans all over the nation. Furthermore, despite Noll's emphasis on the net economic loss sports teams generate, he acknowledges they "create a 'public good' or 'externality'–a benefit enjoyed by consumers who follow sports regardless of whether they help pay for it" (Noll, 1997).

In Sacramento, city officials are facing the obstacle of retaining their professional sports team, an excellent illustration of the necessity of including "psychic benefits" in deciding whether a sports team is beneficial to a community. The lackluster Kings, who have failed to make the playoffs since 2006, are in desperate need of a new arena because their primitive facility currently lacks sufficient seating capacity and reasonable proximity to hotels. According to the *Sacramento Bee*, an estimated $391 million dollars is required for the construction of a new arena. A recent proposal from city officials designates the city of Sacramento to supply 65 percent of the total cost. The private sector, consisting of the Kings' organization and Anschutz Entertainment Group, would shell out the remaining 35 percent. Since Sacramento voters firmly rejected a general tax increase to finance the new arena, a majority of the money will be raised through parking revenues collected from Sacramento's downtown parking garages.

A careful analysis of the risks involved in both building and not building the new arena is crucial in determining whether the new sports complex should be constructed. If the city decides to fund the new stadium, Sacramento will also have to resolve the issue of backfilling lost parking revenues. Additionally, since parking revenues are heavily reliant upon estimations, the city may need to provide other methods of funding the new stadium if parking revenues insufficiently cover the cost. Aside from the financial risk of providing the Kings with a new arena, much uncertainty still remains if the city elects not to construct the new sports complex. Due to the presently inadequate facility, the Sacramento Kings are expected to relocate to either Seattle or Anaheim if a new arena is not built in Sacramento. With the city of Sacramento already facing a serious economic depression, the loss of a pivotal attraction like the Kings could have devastating effects for the future of the city.

Despite the potential pitfalls involved in the decision, the benefits accompanying the construction of a new arena may compensate for the risks. First, the city would receive a percentage of net profits earned by the arena operator. Additional possible returns on investment include job creation, cultural development, economic growth, and civic pride. A professional sports team creates compounding economic growth because the team attracts new businesses and tourist spending to the host city. As additional new spending occurs within the host city, a "multiplier effect" ensues. Increased income on the local level results in additional spending and job creation within Sacramento. Nevertheless, the most substantial reward of a new arena may be the "psychic benefits" created by retention of a professional sports team that has been in Sacramento since 1985. If the city of Sacramento fails to keep possession of their beloved Kings, the team will surely be missed as the community loses a treasured public possession.

CHAPTER 9

BUSINESS DEVELOPMENT

Chapter Introduction

Besides attracting and retaining businesses, the development of new businesses is an important ambition for city leaders. According to those subscribing to neo-classical economic theory, it is the private sector that is primarily responsible for economic growth. However, city leaders can implement non-burdensome market-based policies that can encourage growth. Many cities across the US have robust business development policies and programs in place to assist entrepreneurs in their pursuit of profits which also widely benefit others in the locale.

When entrepreneurs succeed, the economic multiplier phenomenon informs us that many others in the city will benefit. Entrepreneurs hire workers, who in turn spend their wages in the local economy. Additionally, the entrepreneurs also inject cash into the locality by purchasing supplies from other local firms. The economic multiplier varies by industry, but research shows every $1.00 paid to employees is multiplied and creates value in the local economy from $1.50 up to $3.00.

Business Development in Practice

This chapter describes techniques that cities are using for business development. They are listed in Table 9.1 and illustrated in Figure 9.1. The figure shows business development techniques were much more prevalent in 1999, declined in 2004, and then stayed down in 2009. Perhaps this is the result of macroeconomic trends. In the 1990s, the US economy experienced GDP growth of 5.5% on average per year. Perhaps city leaders decided they no longer needed to assist the development of businesses because the economy was already quite robust. On the other hand, perhaps city leaders decided these business development techniques were not bearing much fruit, and therefore decided to scale back their efforts. In either case, the data reveal that business development efforts have been in decline. The remainder of this chapter describes these business development techniques in detail.

Table 9.1 Percent of U.S. Cities Using Various Business Development Policies

	1999	2004	2009
Small business dev. centers	49	26	25
Revolving loan funds	59	23	24
Training support	36	16	23
Matching impr. grants	32	13	21
Marketing assistance	29	16	22
Business incubators	25	14	16
Mgmt. training	17	10	10
Executive/mentor on loan	14	5	7
Vendor/supplier matching	9	4	6

Figure 9.1 Business Development Policies

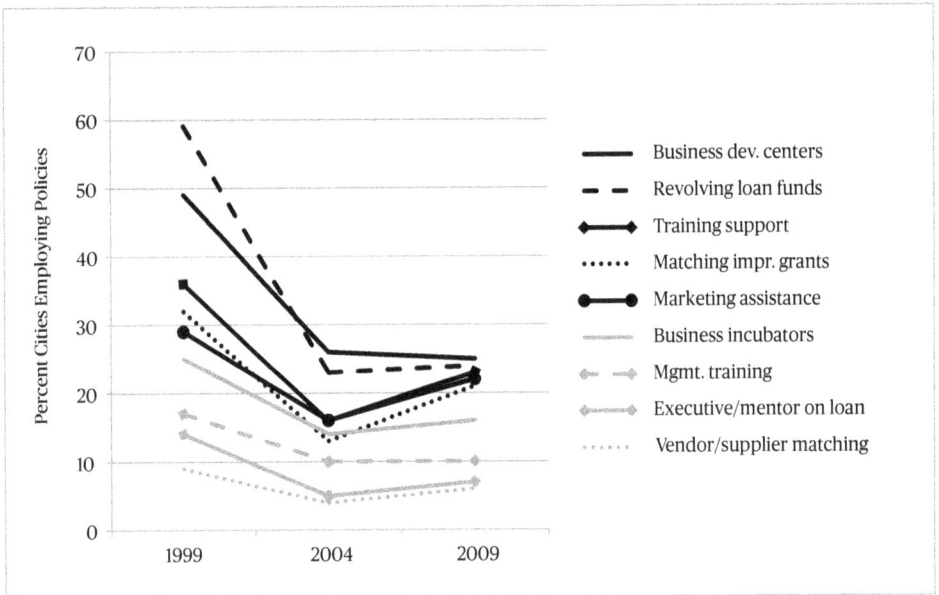

Small Business Development Centers serve as one-stop centers to help local entrepreneurs start a company. Centers typically contain information of interest to small businesses, such as local regulations, local development plans, local economic indicators, local labor market statistics, land availability, building permits, taxation, grant funding, loans, and miscellaneous regulatory assistance. Businesses benefit from these centers because they can interact with government in a single place cutting through the red tape of dealing with multiple agencies, and government benefits by having a greater involvement and understanding of small businesses in the community.

SBDC's are a function of the federal Small Business Administration which began in the Eisenhower Administration in 1953. The main function of the SBA is to guarantee loans from private banks to small businesses, but the managerial assistance offered at the SBDC's can be equally valuable to a new business start-up. Today there are approximately 900 SBDC's across the US, many of which are located in community colleges or state universities. Table 9.1 reveals that SBDC prevalence is actually on the wane, as only 25% of cities in 2009 reported having an SBDC, whereas it was 49% in 1999. Anecdotally, this is likely a result of city leaders not seeing enough immediate results from the centers. It takes a while for a start-up company to develop into a thriving company, and many start-ups never make it.

Business Incubators often share facilities with small business development centers. Business incubators are speculative buildings used to house start-up businesses. The start-up firms rent space in the incubator and receive "shared business services, management training and assistance, financial assistance, and an opportunity to network with each other" (Koven and Lyons, 2003, p. 186). The ICMA survey indicates that 24.6% of U.S. cities use business incubators as a small business development tool.

Early models of business incubator focused on space and operational services, whereas current models focus on providing managerial advice, mentoring and networking (Mattare, Ashley-Cotleur and Masciocchi, 2012). Earlier models also focused on mixed use; meaning the center would allow multiple types of business to start-up at the incubator; these days incubators tend to be "single segment" especially high-tech. Another trend is that incubators previously were started, funded and managed by government, whereas nowadays incubators are housed at universities. Many inventors are professors or students, and the university community offer important support services including engineering labs who can help develop product prototypes, and business schools who can commercialize an invention.

A rich body of research exists which evaluates the effectiveness of business incubators to produce sustainable businesses. Key success factors include business expertise, mentoring, access to financing, education, networking (Mattare, Ashley-Cotleur and Masciocchi, 2012). When these supports are available, business start-ups thrive, create jobs, and ultimately "graduate" from the incubator and move on to operate in their own facility.

Microenterprise Programs are characterized by small loans or grants made to "micro" enterprise entrepreneurs such as self-employed persons and those starting home-based businesses. The loan is usually no more than $1,000, and the entrepreneur is required to complete a business training course. The *MicroEnterprise Journal* defines microenterprises as "small businesses employing fewer than five people and needing less than $35,000 in initial capitalization costs." Many of these firms are home-based businesses and the business owner only works at it part-time. With proper support, especially mentoring and funding, a microenterprise can grow to be a "small" business, moving out of the house and beginning to employ workers.

Of the ICMA survey respondents, 26.6% indicated that they use microenterprise programs to promote economic development. When a city reports that a microenterprise program exists, they are typically affirming that a microenterprise business can get start-up funding. The funding is in the form of a Community Development Loan Fund offered by a Community Development Financial Institution. CDFI's are typically small community banks, credit unions, loan funds, and even venture capital firms. When a CDFI is certified, it is eligible to receive funds from the US Treasury to make loans to local businesses.

For example, the Fresno, California CDFI offers nano-loans (up to $10,000), microenterprise loans (up to $50,000), and enterprise and community development loans (up to $250,000). The Fresno CDFI also specializes in helping new immigrants and offers services in English, Spanish, Hmong, Lao, Thai, Indonesian, Tagalog, Hindi and Punjabi. A recent loan to SL Alteration and Designs allowed the company to remodel its store.

Executive on Loan programs allow small businesspeople to be mentored by corporate executives or retirees. Perhaps the greatest benefit offered by SBDC's is the opportunity to work with SCORE, which is usually housed in an SBDC. Formerly known as the Service Corps of Retired Executives, this non-profit organization exists to connect experienced (usually retired) business people with entrepreneurs to help them through the start-up process. SCORE assists with business plan writing, securing loans, marketing and management. Of the 2009 ICMA survey respondents, only 7% related that they use executive on loan programs directly. Perhaps survey respondents thought of SCORE as an external program, because SCORE's 11,000 volunteers work across the US in 321 SCORE chapters.

Revolving loan funds have been described in the previous chapter on fiscal incentives; here we will offer an illustration of revolving loans for business development. In 1993 the US Congress decided to close six military bases in Alameda County, California. A few years later, a revolving loan fund organization called the East Bay Conversion and Reinvestment Commission was created with contributions of $650,000 by Bank of America, and $900,000 by the US Department of Commerce. Within the first five years, $1 million had been loaned out to eight businesses who helped repurpose the military bases and created over 75 jobs. The businesses were targeted as those owned by women, minorities, veterans, or companies previously doing business with the military bases.

Training support is offered by 23% of cities in our data set. The goal of training support is to bridge the skills mismatch problem which is the situation of workers have a skill set that is different from the skills demanded by local employers. An existing company, especially a large company, can afford to train new hires using on-the-job-training. Start-up companies, however, cannot afford the OJT model because their resources are too scarce.

Consider the example of the Colorado First training program. In the 1980s as Colorado's economy began shedding jobs in mining and drilling, workers found themselves ill-trained for other jobs. The Colorado First program, funded by the state, was created to train or retrain employees at various companies. The companies typically covered 40% of the training costs. Many of the classes were held on community college campuses. A model called "cluster" training mixed workers from different companies in the same classes, which facilitated knowledge spillovers. Much of the training was in the fields of software, computers, manufacturing and electronics. The Colorado First program offers training grants to existing businesses who are adding jobs or to new companies who want their new staff trained.

In 1996 the Bal Seal Engineering company opened for business in Colorado Springs. The company manufactures seals, coil springs and connectors for use in aircraft and underwater craft. The manufacturing process is not simple, and new employees must undergo specialized training to be competent in the workplace. Bal Seal participated in the Colorado First program to train its new employees. By 2014 the company had expanded its Colorado operation by building a new facility and employing 81 people.

Management training is offered by just 10% of surveyed cities. Management training is already well-covered by community colleges and universities offering business degrees including the graduate MBA degree. These same schools also offer non-credit management training. For example Savannah Technical College in Savannah, Georgia offers management training for hotel and restaurant staff. Elizabethtown Community and Technical College in Kentucky offers an array of non-credit management courses, such as a course in human resource management.

Private organizations such as the American Management Association also offer management training, although it is not for college credit. FranklinCovey, for example offers "7 Habits" management workshops in cities across the US. The key example of cities assisting businesses in management training are the SBDC and SCORE examples described above.

Vendor/supplier matching programs link local suppliers with local purchasers. The creators of these programs understand the value of the economic multiplier effect and seek to encourage local businesses to support each other by doing business with each other. These programs have very low-costs, and are environmentally friendly, in that less fuel is used and less pollution is created, because companies are buying local instead of ordering supplies from far away. Only 6% of ICMA cities reportedly have vendor/supplier matching programs, however, local city leaders and chamber of commerce leaders encourage buying local even if no formal program exists.

The Georgia Department of Economic Development operates a formal vendor/ supplier matching program that encourages business-to-business purchasing within the state of Georgia. Avoiding the cumbersome step of asking companies to register, the program instead has created a long list of Georgia-based companies. Data is gathered from Hoover's, a subsidiary of Dun and Bradstreet, that collects and provides information on US companies and industries.

The City of Marshfield, Wisconsin created a Buy Local project. The committee obtained a list of local business's top non-labor purchases and then matched those needs with local suppliers. Efforts were made to inform the companies of local suppliers. A website www.buylocalmarshfield.com was created listing the local companies. The website is not very robust, likely the result of the town being small and not having many firms. Therefore purchases from outside the city will likely continue. However, the program creates excellent publicity for the concept of buying local to develop the local economy.

Marketing assistance is offered to small businesses by economic development agencies in 22% of the ICMA cities. Marketing serves a vital economic function in that buyers can learn of a seller that has produced something the buyer can use.

The Miami County Economic Development Authority offers a grant program called Marketing Assistance Program. The program offers grants to assist local companies in marketing their products at relevant trade shows. The program is small, with only a $5,000 annual budget which can be spread out among ten businesses each receiving up to $500. The funds are to cover the partial cost of registration at a trade show.

In Maine, the Department of Economic and Community Development created a program to market and promote products made in the state. The program dubbed "Maine Made America's Best" now has over 2,000 member companies. The products are offered on the program's webpage www.mainemade.com and each producer is allowed to include the program logo in its marketing and packaging materials. Most of the participating companies are small businesses producing tangible goods such as art, high-end bicycles, sailboats, furniture, and foods, including a fresh lobster mail order company. The companies are not charged a fee to participate in the program.

Matching improvement grants are offered in 21% of surveyed cities. "Improvement" typically refers to the physical built environment, such as roads, green spaces, and building facades. Improvement grants usually reimburse the business owner for a third or up to a half of the cost of the improvement. The grants are typically offered by local governments to small, locally-owned businesses. Larger companies typically receive government grants from state or federal sources.

The City of Hollywood, Florida around 2007 began offering matching improvement grants for hotels with less than 50 rooms. The goal for the city was to establish itself as a Certified Superior Small Lodging Destination which is thought to increase the number of tourists visiting the city.

In South Bend, Indiana, a small camera shop improved the building and built a parking lot using a matching improvement grant of $20,000. The owner contributed $42,000 of his own money for the project.

Shopsteading encourages the development of new retail businesses in urban areas undergoing revitalization. In a typical shopsteading situation, entrepreneurs rent or purchase dilapidated retail property. Like homesteading, shopsteaders take possession of the property and make improvements at their own expense. The shop keepers benefit by having low rent, and the city benefits from a new firm added to the local economy. In order for shopsteading to work, a retail market must exist and the shopsteaders must follow an agreed upon property rehabilitation schedule.

Chapter Summary

In addition to attracting and retaining businesses in the local economy, city leaders do well to develop their local economy by creating a business climate that encourages entrepreneurship. Some cities are better at this than others.

CNN Money recently released a list of the most business-friendly cities in the US. The results are based on a survey of over 8,000 US businesses. The criteria included ease of starting a business, government support of entrepreneurs and other factors. The top five cities are Austin, Virginia Beach, Houston, Colorado Springs, and San Antonio.

Fortune Magazine regularly releases a list of "10 Hot Cities for Entrepreneurs." They consider factors such as talent pools, distribution networks, business community, venture capital support, and you guessed it, local economic development incentives. The top five US locations are Silicon Valley, Atlanta, Seattle, Boston, and Los Angeles. Boulder, Colorado was not far down the list.

Entrepreneur Magazine also conducted a study of world cities to find entrepreneurial "hot spots." Three of their top criteria included differentiation (many business start-ups in varied industrial sectors), government support, and art scenes. They argue a strong correlation exists between large art and music scenes and a successful entrepreneurial ecosystem. They also consider the percentage of female entrepreneurs which was highest in Santiago, Chile (20%) and comparably low in Silicon Valley (10%). Education levels were also a factor, and Paris, France was top with 97% of entrepreneurs possessing master's or Ph.D. degrees compared to just 42% in Silicon Valley. Top US locations in the study were Silicon Valley (1st place), Los Angeles (3rd), Seattle (4th), New York (5th), and Boston (6th).

Business start-ups choose their location based on a number of factors. Materials-oriented firms, such as wineries, will only locate near their inputs, the vineyards. If there are no vineyards nearby, it is pointless to attempt to attract wineries to a city. Consumer-oriented firms, such as breweries want to locate near their customers. Across the country, numerous cities have attracted new microbreweries who tend to locate in downtown restaurant neighborhoods. Some firms make economically irrational location decisions, such as the desire to operate in a hometown, near family, or near some amenity such as the beach. The point here, is that businesses have their own location criteria, and city leaders are unlikely to directly sway a business owner's location decisions. These decisions are typically market-driven decisions. However, the policies and practices described in this chapter can assist a city in its business development efforts.

The business development policies and practices described in this chapter can serve as tie-breakers between different locales. The Bal Seal company noted above was considering expanding its business by opening a new location in either Southern California or Colorado Springs. The Colorado First training program was just enough of an incentive to sway the business owner to choose Colorado Springs. Today, over a decade later, the company employs nearly 100 workers and makes large expenditures in the local economy. These wages and purchases are multiplied over and over to make a huge economic impact in the city.

Guest Case: Garden Walk Hotel Project

By: Shelby Farmer

The City of Anaheim gave a $158 million dollar tax break to a hotel builder planning to build two four-star hotels inside Anaheim's Garden Walk. In 2009 a similar, yet much smaller proposal by the city was given to the same builders. This plan consisted of a $76.3 million dollar subsidy to build two four-star hotels inside Anaheim's Garden Walk. The $81.7 million dollar jump came as a result of the builders' claim that their projected budget had increased, and more money was needed to finish the project. The developer ensured the project would be finished as long as they received their Transient Occupancy Taxes (TOTs) back for the 15-year period. This subsidy consists of the builders recovering 80% of the bed tax on the hotels for a 15-year period. The hotels would, however, still be required to pay all property and sales tax. In a typical city, property tax revenue make up 73% of all taxes, and sales and gross receipts came in at 17%. Knowing this, the Garden Walk Hotels will bring in much revenue to the city of Anaheim.

The vote by the City Council was 3 for this tax break and 2 against it. This divide between the council was rare and resulted in controversy among the citizens. Many came to protest at the next two city council meetings and spoke their opinions during public comment. The first meeting had 19 citizens and business owners who were against the Garden Walk Hotel Project and 25 for it. In the next meeting there were 11 against the project and only one for it. Additionally, at this meeting there were numerous protestors whom were not allowed inside due to fire regulations.

The citizens and business owners in favor of the project defended their position, citing the creation of 3,200 construction jobs, 1,300 permanent jobs through hotel positions and shops as a large benefit. Additionally, they noted that the lot the hotels would be on was currently empty, thus generating no revenue for the city. After the 15 year period the hotels would make the city about $20 million dollars in new revenue. Many of the people who attended the City Council meeting were union and construction workers who believed this project would create jobs for them. However, the city did not specify in their contract whether or not the construction workers hired during the process of building the hotel would be their workers, or if they would contract with outside help.

The citizens and business owners who opposed the project brought up many issues: other hotels and other businesses had opened with little to no help from the city and they felt it was unfair to give so much aid to these developers, and libraries were shutting down and putting their librarians out of work because the city has no money. They felt the money would be better used employing more police officers and firemen to protect the city and its neighborhoods. The general feeling of those opposing this project was that the city should be giving any extra money back to the community, rather than wealthy developers.

This tax break divided the community, but also caused a political divide among the council. Council member Kris Murray, who voted in favor of the project, initiated the removal of Lorri Galloway's position of Mayor Pro Tem for her vote opposing the project and her obvious disapproval of its result. Lorri Galloway was removed as Mayor Pro Tem, and Harry Sidhu, a council member in favor of the hotel tax break, was voted into her place.

With the community divided, as well as the council, the citizens of Anaheim are taking drastic measures to ensure this will not happen again. A group of citizens put together an initiative petition hoping to put a measure on the ballot that would prevent any hotel development without the vote of the people. If the initiative proponents acquire signatures of at least 10% of the registered voters then the City Council must please the measure on the ballot for voter approval. Although extreme, this is one way the citizens can show the council that the people are still in charge. Not only will this petition drive hotel developers away from the city, it will decrease development all together. Hotels will have to campaign for their developments to win the vote of the people. If the citizens feel this strongly about hotel tax breaks, who is to say they will not feel this way about any developer tax breaks? The citizens of Anaheim are making their city a little more exclusive than its officials had in mind.

In a poll of 288 hotel developers taken by Meeting News, 37.3% said incentives have no effect on their decisions to develop, while 19.4% said that it did in fact play into their decision to develop. This makes one think the developers of The Garden Walk Hotel project may not have needed that $158 million dollar tax break in order to build. In actuality, is possible that without the offer of incentives given by the city, the developers would have gone ahead with the project anyway.

Despite the poll's results and the opposition of the citizens, The Garden Walk Hotel Project was a good move for the city of Anaheim. These two four-star hotels will bring in more people, generating revenue in the restaurants and retailers in Garden Walk, as well as creating jobs in the city. Also, with developers still paying property and sales tax, the city is only receiving money for an otherwise empty lot. It is also proven that when a city obtains new, higher-end hotels, they bring up the value and room rates of surrounding hotels, which, in turn, gives the city more money in TOT's. After the 15 year period is up, the hotels in Garden Walk will pay their full TOT's in addition to their property and sales tax, which is expected to bring in over $20 million dollars. At this point, the citizens of Anaheim will be grateful after the hotels are built and making money for their prestigious city.

Guest Case: The Blight of the Sierra Madre Bathrooms

By: Chris Siraganian

Early in February 2012, The California Supreme Court upheld the ruling of ABXI 26, resulting in the elimination of the California Redevelopment Agencies (CRA's). The stated purpose of these agencies was to remove blight from local communities by investing tax monies in redevelopment. Many proponents of the agencies claim that they are crucial in spurring economic development in cities. Giving money to agencies whose sole purpose is to help the less fortunate and make our cities better places by creating affordable housing, schools, and jobs is an ideal concept.

Though the intentions for the agencies were positive, there were abuses of the system that are hard to ignore. There was a city park in Lancaster that was paved over including taking down 100 trees to build a new Costco using the Redevelopment Agency funds. In Los Angeles $52 million of Redevelopment Agencies money was approved to fund the building of a parking structure for the billionaire Eli Broad's museum. These examples are just a few of the many seen throughout the state of California. Sierra Madre is an example of a small town that used these funds in a questionable manner. The city is known for being the "Village of the Foothills", less than three square miles, and brags about not having a single stop light in the city. The acronym BANANA, Build Absolutely Nothing Anywhere Near Anything, is an economics term that sounds ridiculous but is a perfect way to describe Sierra Madre. This then begs the question as to what redevelopment money would be spent on in a town that brags about not having a single stoplight and no intentions of building anything?

Some of the local citizens have brought up the concerns of the use of the Sierra Madre Redevelopment Agencies money, seeing it as irresponsible. The Sierra Madre Tattler rants about the most current expenditures for a $25,000 parking study and $30,000 market study, which are very costly for a city with a population of under 11,000. When looking at the report of Sierra Madre Redevelopment Agencies expenditures over a one year span, you can see that $30,000 was spent on pressure washing the sidewalks of downtown. Other large ticket items include replacing a fully functional playground with a new one for $138,000. There is $271,460 allocated towards Internal Services and $345,576 more for Staffing Costs, expenses that are not clearly defined and have been used to fund employee salaries. Money was also spent to waive permit fees for a wine tasting room in one of the local liquor stores, as well as the $100,000 Kodiak restroom at Memorial Park (Sierra Madre). The restroom is a top of line, luxury restroom that, according to the builders website, can withstand a category E earthquake, 150 mph wind load, and up to 250-pound per square foot of snow. It is this kind of excess that seems to be characteristic of the spending done by Sierra Madre using Redevelopment Agencies funds.

The median household income in Sierra Madre from 2006-2009 was $82,675, which is considerably above the average for neighboring cities Arcadia, $77,024, Pasadena, $65,422, and far above the state average of $60,883 (US Census Bureau). Sierra Madre is clearly an affluent city, which brings into question the need to obtain funds from a state that is already in a deep financial predicament. These funds were meant for blighted communities and redevelopment, but it appears as if Sierra Madre felt that their restrooms were worth spending $100,000 of "free money" to help with their "blight."

The case of Sierra Madre shows an example of how a city abused what was seen as "free money". Chris McKenzie, Executive Director, League of California cities stated, "Redevelopment is indispensable to cities to spur economic development, create jobs and improve communities"(PR Newswire, December 29, 2011, p. 2). Looking at the case of Sierra Madre, it is hard to see how the hundreds of thousands of dollars that were spent promoted any of the activities that Mr. McKenzie speaks of. Now that these agencies have been eliminated, the State of California should find better ways to use tax-payers money than allowing it to be wasted by Redevelopment Agencies.

CHAPTER 10

HUMAN CAPITAL AND EQUITY PLANNING

Chapter Introduction

Throughout this book, we have extolled market-based policies as strategies for local economic development. Such policies, rooted in neoclassical economic views, typically suggest improving the local economy by supporting its businesses. When businesses succeed, employees directly share in the success of the business through wages earned. Other citizens benefit indirectly as the wages and business expenses are multiplied throughout the local economy. In this chapter we diverge from such neoclassical economic thinking and put on a Keynesian economic hat, which looks a bit like the liberal political hat. In other words, this chapter introduces local economic development strategies and policies which focus more on the individual than the private firm.

Recall earlier in this book a discussion of the "waves" of economic development policy. So-called first- and second-wave economic development efforts were led by the states, but third-wave strategies shift the focus on localities. First-wave strategies were "place-based" in the sense of attracting firms to places, whereas second-wave strategies are "firm-based" because they rely on retention and expansion of existing businesses. The third wave does not replace earlier techniques but emphasizes a local economic development strategy characterized by: public and private sector local leadership (not just a state agency); a strategic local plan (rather than just a state plan); an emphasis on developing specific industrial clusters (rather than general smokestack chasing); involvement of multiple agencies and creating public-private partnerships; and equitable job opportunities for the poor (Fitzgerald and Leigh, 2002). This chapter describes two "third wave" strategies, which are human capital strategies and equity planning.

Human Capital Economic Development

Land, labor and capital are considered the three economic resources necessary to produce a finished product. After World War Two it was observed that countries such as Germany and Japan recovered more quickly than nations such as Poland or China because of greater human capital endowments. While these nations may have had somewhat equal access to primary economic resources (land, labor, and capital) many economists in the 1950s attributed the rapid economic recoveries of Germany and Japan to the human capital endowments of their citizens. In other words, German and Japanese citizens were relatively better educated in terms of knowledge and skills, such that these nations were able to rebuild relatively quickly. Gary Becker's 1964 book *Human Capital* amply describes how a worker's education, skills, and training are just as valuable as physical capital in terms of economic development.

Human Capital Economic Development in Practice

This book is about local economics, and just as on a national level, human capital is correlated with economic growth, we might assume the same on the local level. City leaders understand the importance of human capital. Higher education is consistently linked to success in economic development (Reich, 1983, 1991, 1998; Asefa and Huang, 1994; Koven and Lyons, 2003).

As low skill jobs consistently move off-shore, U.S. cities must invest in their own human capital. Cities with more educated workforces are more capable of retaining and attracting new economy jobs. A full 46.6% of ICMA survey participants cite a lack of skilled labor as a barrier to economic development. A city's public schools and colleges are economic assets that can contribute to a better educated workforce.

Investment in education is a large share of the typical local government's annual budget. In addition to K-12 education, many cities also support adult learners through job training programs, community colleges and other programs. A number of human capital economic development techniques are listed in Table 10.1 and then illustrated in Figure 10.1.

Table 10.1 Percent of U.S. Cities Using Various Human Capital Policies

	1999	2004	2009
Customized job training	19	63	34
Training support	36	16	23
Employee screening	16	8	10
Management training	17	10	10
Executive/mentor on loan	14	5	7
PPP to provide job training	19		

Figure 10.1 Human Capital Policies

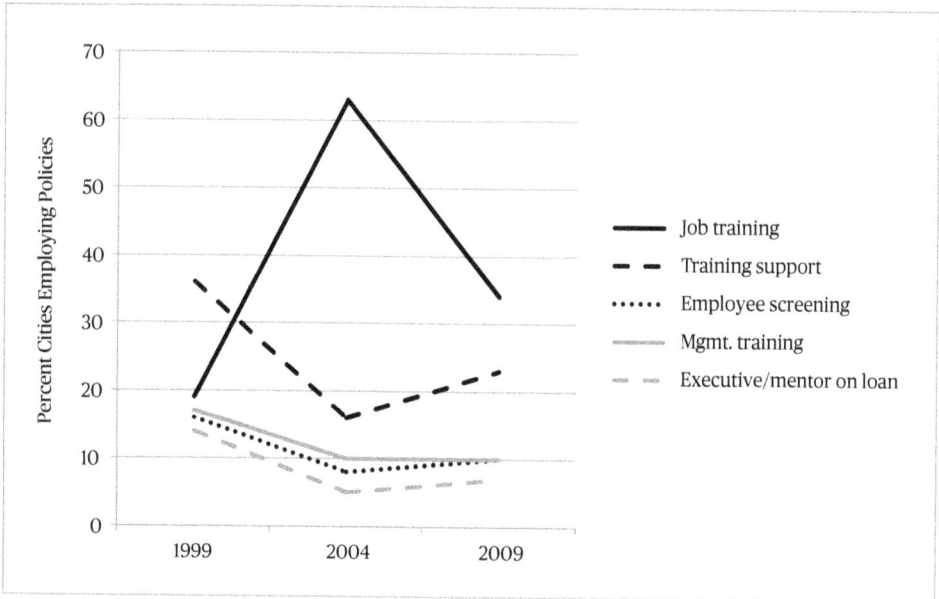

Customized job training is a frequently used economic development tool. Koven and Lyons note that "customized training is the most common industrial incentive financed directly from state resources" (2003, p. 49). Training programs are often accompanied by job screening programs to ensure that a new employer has a sufficient workforce. These programs typically include pre-employment training, technical training, on-the-job training, and management training. Training is often delivered by community colleges or technical education centers.

The West Virginia Development Office explicitly voices their willingness to pay for training and explains that their "overall funding levels will be based on the wages and benefits, location, and the number of net new jobs created."

In New York City, the Department of Small Business Services offers a number of training services as part of its overall "NYC Business Solutions" program including general courses on business operations, legal matters and selling to government. Additionally they can fund and develop specialized training for the employees of local firms. For example, the "Made in NY" Media Employee Training program offer grants to small and medium-sized media businesses to help pay for functions such as filming, post-production, or other technical work in New York City. Etsy. com, the leading online marketplace of handmade and vintage items, founded and located in Brooklyn, participates in the "Made in NY" economic development program. Kickstarter, a website for creative project fundraising, is another successful media/tech start-up supported by the "Made in NY" program.

In the ICMA survey, 34% of local governments reported supporting job training programs, which is down from 2004 (63%), but still higher than in 1999 (19%). The 2004 survey asked whether the job training was intentionally linked to the city's economic policies and 36% of respondents reported this was the case.

Training support is offered by 23% of ICMA cities in 2009. Training support takes on many forms such as offering city facilities as classrooms, arranging trainers, or sending trainers to local firms. But these efforts are not limited to the public sector only. In Pittsburgh in 1994, a number of local corporations pooled resources to create a supplier training center. The efforts were led by Miles, Inc., a producer of chemicals, pharmaceuticals and film, and Duquesne University. The center was established to train local suppliers on the latest manufacturing techniques and total quality management, a popular manufacturing management system at the time. This is an example of a market-based solution to a market problem, which is made more interesting by the fact that many of the cooperating firms normally see each other as competitors in the marketplace for their products.

Employee screening is often used by local governments to attract new business into its locale. New foreign firms especially need this service as they are often unfamiliar with the local labor force and local hiring practices. In the 2009 ICMA survey, 10% of local governments reported offering employee screening as an economic development incentive.

Many private firms offer employee screening services, such as the venerable Pinkerton company, famous in detective novels for its indefatigable private eyes.

While these firms normally investigate an individual's background, such as a person's education and career history, a city government can also investigate more deeply whether a person will be a good "fit" for the company.

In recent years, foreign manufacturing firms, have opened new facilities in small cities across the US, but especially in the South. In the 1980s foreign auto firms, such as Toyota and Honda, began building cars in the US to avoid paying high import tariffs while still having access to US markets. These days the cost of global labor is on the rise and many foreign firms can now afford to produce in the US for the US market while hiring US workers. But these same firms seek out locations with low cost labor which tends to be in small cities, especially in the South.

One of these cities, Washington, Georgia, located in Wilkes County near Savannah offers job screening as a part of its standard economic development incentives. Like many southern cities, Washington's economy has not grown at the same rate as the rest of the US. Despite early innovation (Eli Whitney invented the cotton gin in 1795 in Washington) most of the city's jobs are in the manufacture of lumber and healthcare for the aged. While these jobs pay living wages, city leaders are eager to attract new companies to the city. If a new firm is considering locating in Washington, city officials are ready with a number of economic incentives to assist in the new firm, including employee screening.

Management training was offered by 10% of cities in the ICMA 2009 survey. Community colleges and universities offer management training to the business community, but a few city governments also offer this incentive to local firms. The training frequently consists of a mentor, such as a member of SCORE, who teaches the local entrepreneur basic management skills. In the 2009 survey, only 7% of cities had such an *executive/mentor on loan* program.

Public private partnerships to provide job training were practiced by 19% of cities in 1999. Presumably these practices continue today, although the question was dropped from the ICMA survey. The next chapter describes a range of PPP schemes; here we offer a single illustration of a successful PPP. In Philadelphia, a public-private partnership was formed between the Lincoln Technical Institute, Philadelphia Workforce Development, and a private company, Cottman Transmissions. The program trains workers to be automobile transmission installers, a job paying 3-4 times the minimum wage. All program costs were borne by a federal grant which trickled down to the local level. Tuition is free for the students, but they must be willing to relocate, even out of state, after completing the 16-week course.

Equity Economic Development

Equity economic development strategies are designed to bring the poor into full economic participation, especially by helping them get jobs. Goetz (1994) hypothesized that the equity development paradigm is becoming more prevalent in economic development policy that has traditionally been dominated by pro-growth economic development policy. Goetz used regression analysis to examine the economic development practices in 173 U.S. cities to determine what factors correlate with equity economic development policies. Equity development was measured by considering seven economic development techniques (such as requiring developers to provide low-income housing, and transportation mitigation fees), and certain housing policies (such as rent control, and requiring developers to replace demolished low-income housing). The study's findings suggest that alternate development policy is becoming more prevalent and "the grip on local policy enjoyed by business interests is not as strong as once believed" (p. 102).

This section analyzes the prevalence of certain equity economic development practices and short descriptions of the equity policies found in the ICMA data. Table 10.2 reveals that equity policies peaked in 2004, but then declined in 2009. Economists might call this a counter-cyclical phenomenon, meaning that when the business cycle is in the expansion phase, such as was the case in 2004, city governments can afford to look out for the poor and put equity policies into place. When the economy shifted from expansion to contraction in the Great Recession of 2007, city leaders retrenched their equity efforts, choosing instead to focus their energies (and their discretionary resources) toward private firms. The data below, although scant, support this counter-cyclical view. A cynic would suggest city leaders care for the poor only when it is affordable to do so.

Table 10.2 Percent of US Cities Using Various "Equity" Economic Development Policies

	1999	2004	2009
Job training	19	63	34
Community Development Corp.	53	68	33
Local ED zones	27	13	24
Community dev. loan funds	55	63	22
Microenterprise	27	57	8
Welfare-to-Work	49		

Figure 10.2 "Equity" Economic Development

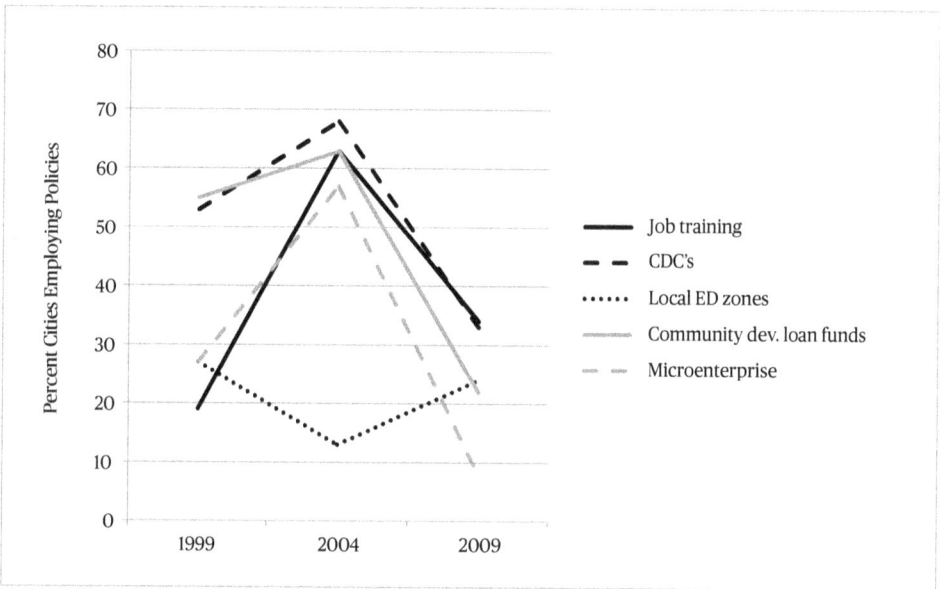

Typical "equity" techniques are described in this section. Many of these techniques involve federal programs. They are included here because local governments can use these programs in their economic development efforts.

Job training was briefly described above in the human capital section, but let's consider why only 34% of cities have an active job training program. Fitzgerald and Leigh (2002, p. 195) explain that job training and economic development are linked because a skilled workforce is an important component of a robust business climate. Nonetheless, in many US cities the economic development department focuses on land use, economic analysis and interacting with private firms, while job training programs are managed by social workers. Economic development officials may look down on social workers, and in some cases may even sabotage jobs programs (Fitzgerald and Leigh, 2002, p. 196).

Jobs programs and economic development agencies measure success differently. The former count the number of people trained, whereas the latter focus on new jobs created. Because of "frictional unemployment," the lag time between completing training and starting a new job, a newly trained worker might not be tracked by the economic development officials. Training programs led by social workers have been known to be out of date. After completing training a "skills mismatch" may still exist between what the individual learned and what companies are looking for.

Jobs training programs must be market-based. That is, employers must be the drivers of the program while the economic and workforce development agencies fulfill a supporting role. The Seattle Jobs Initiative put about 50,000 people into training programs such as skilled trade apprenticeships from 1995 to 2005. The program was initiated by local leaders but made possible with $5 million in funding from the Annie E. Casey Foundation, a private organization. The SJI program is an example of successful integration of the private sector and multiple public agencies. For a jobs program to work this meaningful integration must take place.

Community Development Corporations are reportedly present in 33% of US cities. The phrase "community development" usually refers to improving low income and inner city neighborhoods by providing administrative and funding support. CDC's tend to invest in worthwhile projects such as job creation, affordable housing, access to education, eliminating blight, creating new community assets such as parks, and entrepreneurship.

Funding local projects is the key function of CDC's. Initially, CDC's received direct funding from the federal government, which was later replaced with the more broadly distributed and more locally controlled Community Development Block Grants. CDBG's are federal funds distributed by locals according to local needs. Nonetheless, funding for CDC's was generous, leading to many cities starting their own Community Development Banks.

Community development venture capital organizations complement the function of the CDC's. Low-income and inner city residents have low access to investment capital, despite the fact that inner cities are full of viable businesses and robust consumer spending. Unlike the CDC's, which had easy access to government funds,

CDVC's operate as free enterprises. The initial funding of CDVC's is typically from companies, foundations, or government sources. Once funded, however, CDVC's face pressure to be profitable, therefore their project selection criteria is much stronger than the criteria the CDC's face.

The East Los Angeles Credit Union is one of the 30 initial CDC's started in the 1960s. TELACU operates as a single parent CDC that owns 13 for-profit subsidiaries including a bank, financial services companies, construction companies, a restaurant, and property development companies. The for-profit companies intentionally engage in community development ventures and pay part of their profits "upstream" to the non-profit parent CDC. TELACU uses these funds to support 5 non-profits that provide services to seniors, housing assistance, educational assistance, community capital, and a faith-based non-profit organization. TELACU generates $130 in annual revenues and has created over 10,000 permanent jobs.

Of the 30 initial CDC's started in the 1960s, only two are viable today, one of which is TELACU. Why are they successful today nearly fifty years later, while all but one other CDC have failed? TELACU, although many of its units are not-for-profit, operates as a free enterprise. Once again, we see that when organizations follow market principles, they achieve success much greater than organizations created, funded and managed by government bureaucrats.

Local economic development zones are considered "equity" development policy because the ED zones are designated in economically distressed areas, especially in inner cities or in former brownfields. Of the cities surveyed, 24% report having local economic development zones. See Chapter 7, Location Incentives, for more information on local economic development zones.

Community development loan funds are designed to provide financing and investment that will create or save jobs for lower income persons. The federal department of Housing and Urban Development (HUD) provides funds to states through Community Development Block Grants (CDBG) and these funds are supplemented with principal and interest payments from previous borrowers. Local agencies administer these programs. To earn a loan, businesses submit applications and they must prove that 51% of the jobs that are being created or saved are for lower or middle income persons. In the ICMA survey, 22% of local governments reported that they have a community development loan fund. CDLF's are frequently managed by the previously described CDC's or CDVC's.

Microenterprise programs (MEP), also called microcredit programs, provide very small loans to entrepreneurs. While microcredit has existed informally for

generations, the recent success of the Grameen Bank has encouraged community development organizations to start their own microenterprise programs. In
the U.S., MEP tend to be operated by nonprofit organizations who function as a
lender of last resort, meaning they give loans to borrowers who couldn't secure
funding from any other sources. To receive a microloan, the borrower is usually
required to complete business training on topics such as marketing and bookkeep-
ing. Microloans range from $100 to $25,000.

In addition to only giving small loans, MEP's are distinct in that the borrower joins
a group of entrepreneurs. Initially, MEP's in the US followed the Grameen model
where entrepreneurs were accountable to each other. These days peer accountability is on the wane, but entrepreneurs are still linked through the revolving
loan pool.

Koven and Lyons (2003) report that many microentrepreneurs started their businesses out of necessity because they suddenly became unemployed and had few
options to replace their income. Most are members of minority groups (66%),
women (76%). Most are high-school educated, and over 1/3 have college degrees.
Surprisingly, half own their own homes. These facts give some evidence that traditional financing is unavailable not only to the poor, but to other members of
society also.

Welfare-to-Work is a federal program designed to move people off of welfare
and into economic self-sufficiency. Businesses that hire a welfare recipient and
employ them for 180 days can claim a tax credit up to 35% of the employee's first
year wages, and up to 50% of the employee's second year wages. A "local agency"
must certify that the employee was on welfare. In the ICMA survey, 48.7% of local
governments reported that they support Welfare-to-Work as an economic development initiative.

Wage subsidies is another equity policy (although not included in the ICMA data).
The subsidies provide a tax credit to employers for hiring low-skilled workers.
Wage subsidies can be offered at the local or state level, but often local govern-
ments aid local businesses in obtaining federal work subsidies. Through the Work
Opportunity Tax Credit, a 1996 federal program, businesses earn tax credits up to
$2,400 for each employee they hire. To qualify for the program, employees must
be in a "targeted group," such as disabled, or those on welfare.

Chapter Conclusion

The great debate in economics is whether the free market system is better than
an economy directed by experts. This debate is captured in the labels of classical

economic theory and Keynesian economic theory. Both theories have ample representation in the theoretical economic literature. The lion's share of the empirical literature, however, confirms that capitalism routinely delivers better results than an economic system managed by bureaucrats.

Classical and Keynesian economists actually agree on much. Both groups value economic prosperity and full employment. The Classical economists also value production and profits, while the Keynesians value spending and consumption. We can see the end goals are very similar. It is the means to achieve these goals where the two camps differ. Classical economists focus on the supply-side, meaning businesses should succeed for the economic goals to be achieved, whereas Keynesians focus on the demand-side, meaning it is the individual's welfare that we must be concerned about. Much of this book fits in the Classical camp with an emphasis on supply-side economics, but this chapter is a diversion where we've emphasized human capital training for the individual and equity policies which aim to help the poor.

Senator Ted Kennedy was influential in the 1960s in writing the legislation that birthed the CDC's as a part of LBJ's overall War on Poverty. While his conservative opponents may have disagreed with Kennedy's policies, they certainly couldn't disagree with his motivations. Senator Kennedy said,

"My own center of belief moved toward the great Gospel of Matthew, Chapter 25 especially, in which he calls us to care for the least of these among us, and feed the hungry, clothe the naked, give drink to the thirsty, welcome the stranger, visit the imprisoned. It's enormously significant to me that the only description in the Bible about salvation is tied to one's willingness to act on behalf of one's fellow human beings."

Guest Case: The City of Bell Scandal and the Responsibility of City Officials

By: Brian Sprague

 The City of Bell scandal was a critical blow to the opinion and trust citizens once had in city officials. In, city officials managed to find and exploit loopholes in the law, such as the misappropriation of taxes and embezzlement, and began drastically increasing their salaries well beyond the national averages of their counterparts, which ranges from $42,973 to $172,241.The City of Bell and its relative size and demographics played a key role in uncovering the fraudulent practices transpiring in Bell. The City of Bell is comprised of 35,477 (2010) people who are of Hispanic or Latino descent, 93.1%. These numbers show that there are not enough citizens living in Bell to justify a city manager being paid $787,637 especially when the median household income is just $29,946.

 This raises two questions regarding whether or not city officials are being held accountable for their actions as well as creating a wall of distrust between citizen and city official. What is the role of a city official and what is their role in ensuring that the city functions as a cohesive unit? At the head of the city is the City Manager. The city manager is appointed by the City Council and is responsible for running the day-to-day operations of a city with a clear understanding of how the different components of a city best function together. One crucial responsibility of the city manager is forming a budget and then applying that budget to the city. The reason this responsibility is important is because former Bell city manager Robert Rizzo managed to weasel his way to a salary totaling $787,637 and if the LA Times article hadn't exposed the anomaly then who knows how much higher it would have gotten. Robert Rizzo was using money that belonged to the City of Bell, more specifically the citizens of Bell, to fill his own pockets. This isn't even about greed; this goes much deeper than a corrupt city manager. This is direct a violation of duty. The citizens of Bell put their trust in the city manager to fulfill his responsibilities as an elected official While Rizzo was busy embezzling money from the citizens what was happening in terms of city growth or business attraction? In fact, the city was doing the exact opposite by randomly making certain businesses make payments in order for them to continue operating in the city.

How much blame should be placed on the City Council? It is the responsibility of the city council to elect a city manager that they feel will best represent their city and ensure it operates at as close to maximum potential as it can. The city council is also responsible for passing bills as well as creating laws that will benefit the city and its citizens. The citizens of Bell trusted that he city council would perform their duties in a manner that would uphold their expectations; however, corruption nullified rational thought and the council members allowed themselves to be bribed by the city manager in order to maintain absolute secrecy and participation. An uproar as caused when the, already struggling, citizens of Bell learned that public funds and tax money had been misappropriated totaling 6.7 million dollars.

In general, the role of public administration is to perform their tasks and responsibilities consistent with the policies adopted by the City Council as well as federal and state laws, and regulations as directed by the City Manager and their department director. The citizens of any given city put their trust in their city officials to make decisions on behalf of the city that will prove to be beneficial. The city officials of Bell failed to uphold the duties of their appointed position and because of that much trust was lost between citizen and city official not only in Bell, but in cities throughout California, such as Irvine, Temple City, La Puente, and many other cities. This scandal should be a call for citizens and city officials to closely scrutinize themselves and to hold each other accountable in order to prevent greed from ever threatening to destroy confidence in businesses and trust of people. Citizens can keep officials accountable by becoming familiar with the roles the city officials are hired to perform and then establishing a presence in the city that leaves the city officials without a doubt in their mind that they are being closely watched. If nobody in the city raises his or her voice against injustice then how can they expect anything to change. Now is the time for the citizens to look upward and onward. This is a time when the businesses in Bell should unify themselves instead of attempting to do things individually. Recently, the state has agreed to pay back 3 million dollars of tax money to the residents of Bell. This may not fully cover the intrinsic damage done to the residents of Bell but it is a step closer to a new Bell, a reformed Bell, and an economically unified Bell.

CHAPTER 11

PUBLIC-PRIVATE PARTNERSHIPS
BY STEVEN G. KOVEN AND STUART C. STROTHER

Chapter Introduction

A public-private partnership is a formal complementary relationship between two or more public and private entities to achieve a common objective in which all parties derive some benefit. The formal partnership arrangement delineates each partner's roles and responsibilities; states the level of investment and risk of each partner; and describes how financial and non-financial benefits will be distributed between the partners. Although partnerships represent government "power-sharing," they also entail "risk-shifting" from government to the private sector (Linder, 1999). The basic purpose of partnering is "to take advantage of the potential for all parties to gain greater benefit than they could on their own" (Mullin, 2002, p. v.).

When public-private partnerships are tendered for the purpose of economic development, the overall objective of the partnership is usually to increase the number of jobs or the number of employers in a region, or to revitalize the physical assets of an urban area. This chapter relates why public-private partnerships are on the rise in economic development practice; offers examples of typical partnerships, describes different models of partnership arrangements for service delivery and infrastructure development; and concludes by projecting future trends and directions for economic development public-private partnerships.

The Rise of Public-Private Partnerships

The use of public-private partnerships is on the rise because they allow governments to provide services that otherwise would have had to wait until funds were available (Williams, 2003). City leaders primarily enter into public-private partnerships because "they are seeking additional capital for economic expansion" (Walzer and Jacob, 1998, p. 16). Local governments often lack the funds to build needed infrastructure so they partner with private organizations to leverage private capital. In certain cases (which are explained further below) private contractors finance, build and operate a public good such as a new toll road. After a period of time, during which the contractor earned a profit, ownership of the public good is transferred to the government. In this instance a worthy good was made available to the public, the private firm earned a profit, and the government took ownership of the public good with virtually no expenditure.

Another reason why the use of partnerships is on the rise is that government decision-making has been decentralized from the national government to local government. Local governments often lack the fiscal resources necessary for public projects. Therefore creative entrepreneurial approaches, such as partnering with the private sector, are useful to provide needed public goods and services. Now local public administrators have a greater stake in their own economic development. A local economy experiences growth when it increases the number of jobs and firms. Partnering directly with those firms for economic development projects represents the new entrepreneurial approach to public administration.

A third reason why public-private partnerships are becoming more prevalent is that they provide a better more efficient alternative to the traditional bidding process for government contracts (Williams, 2003). In the traditional competitive bidding process, private firms competed with each other and contracts were typically awarded to the lowest bidder. This often resulted in an adversarial relationship between the government and the contractor, because the low bid often meant the project would not receive sufficient resources and funding. In a typical partnership the public agency looks for expertise rather than economy, and the private sector actor is chosen based on their technical qualifications. This results in more realistic management of resources and a collaborative working relationship rather than a competitive relationship. But this does not mean partnerships are more expensive than the traditional model, because in many partnerships, the private actor invests much, if not all, of the capital resources.

A final reason for the rise in partnerships between government and industry relates to structural changes in the macroeconomy. The new marketplace is a globalized economy with firms competing across national boundaries. National governments now have more of a stake in the success of its firms. In the so-called "New Economy," economic growth occurs through technological advances and corporate strategy (Carayinnis and Alexander, 2000), so we see a rise in technology partnerships between public and private actors (Stiglitz and Wallsten, 1999). One such example is SEMATECH, a partnership formed in 1987 between U.S. computer chip makers and the federal government, who provided funding and research. At the time the U.S. lagged behind Japan in semiconductor market share (Caryinnis and Alexander, 2000). After almost a decade, the U.S. became the world leader in the semiconductor market and SEMATECH withdrew from federal funding. SEMATECH now allows foreign firms to join the partnership.

Public-Private Partnerships for Economic Development

State and local public actors enter into partnerships with private organizations to accomplish a number of economic development objectives that often fall under the broad context of the revitalization of urban areas. Some of the most common objectives of an economic development public-private partnership are: to improve the business climate of the region, to develop real estate, to retain an existing employer, to develop small businesses, and to provide assistance to workers. Some public-private partnerships are designed to develop the business climate of a region and to market the region to outside firms that might be attracted to locate to the region.

The 1999 survey of economic development officials by the International City/County Management Association (ICMA) revealed that 40% of U.S. cities have partnerships with private organizations, and 21% of them have a private economic development foundation. These private foundations typically engage in activities such as developing promotional materials and websites, providing media advertising, hosting special events, and sponsoring trade missions abroad. Table 11.1 reports the prevalence of public private partnerships in US cities as found in the 1999 ICMA survey. These questions were removed in subsequent surveys, so unlike previous chapters in this book, we cannot report partnership trends over time.

Table 11.1 Percentage of US Cities with Public Private Partnerships in 1999

PPP with NGOs	70
PPP to develop ED policy	42
PPP with other governments	41
PPP to provide job training	19
PPP for ED zones	14
PPP to support CDC's	12
PPP to support Welfare-to-Work	11
PPP for microenterprise	7

Public-Private Partnerships with NGOs

Retaining firms in the local economy is a third objective of some partnerships. Local government partners with non-governmental private organizations such as chambers of commerce and private firms to prevent a local firm from exiting the area. The ICMA survey reveals that 70% of participating cities had such partnerships. At the end of this chapter, we describe a case in Louisville, Kentucky where the state's largest employer threatened to close its facility because the firm did not have enough part-time labor for its third shift. City, state, and business leaders created an innovative partnership that addressed the employer's needs. Private and public resources were invested and the employer was retained.

Forty two percent of US cities use **public-private partnerships to develop economic development policy**. In the most common cases, a city government partners with a local business organization, such as the local chamber of commerce, who has input into the policy making process or even administers some of the programs. But in some cases, a new public private partnership totally replaces the former government economic development agency, which was the case in Wisconsin.

In 2011 the newly-created Wisconsin Economic Development Corporation replaced was touted by some as, "The successful transformation of a bureaucratic maze into a nimble job-creating enterprise that leverages private sector expertise" (Maynard, 2012). The WEDC immediately went to work spending federal funds it received from Community Development Block Grants to help businesses expand their operations in Wisconsin. The creation of the WEDC by Republican Governor Scott Walker faced strong criticism, especially by government employees whose functions were being privatized. In fact, Walker entirely closed the state's Department of Commerce. HUD got involved and began monitoring WEDC. The results, however, speak for themselves. The Business Retention and Expansion Investment Program invested $9.9 million in 20 companies resulting in 1,160 new jobs created and 1,942 jobs retained. This is an average investment of $3,223 per job.

Although the WEDC is still relatively new, evaluations of the WEDC reveal that the benefits of privatization of the economic development function far exceed the costs. The leadership in Wisconsin understands the free market is more effective in economic development and job creation than traditional bureaucratic government efforts.

Table 11.1 also reveals 41% of US cities enter into **public-private partnerships with other governments**. Similar to the Wisconsin case, in Ohio, Republican Governor John Kasich signed a bill in 2011 to create a new state-funded nonprofit corporation called JobsOhio. Many existing state programs are consolidating into the JobsOhio organization. The main business of JobsOhio is to use state and private resources to encourage companies to create or retain jobs in Ohio. Although paying a company to create a job seems counterproductive, analysis shows the return on investment breaks even after just one year. When JobsOhio provides a company an incentive of $4,000 to create one job, that state will earn back the $4,000 within one year in the form of taxes paid back to the state. Additionally the employee's wages will be spent locally which benefits the local economy. Once again, we see the market function as an economic development force more powerful than the efforts of public agencies.

Many public-private partnerships are created to provide **job training** for a city's residents. Of the cities in the ICMA survey, 16% report that public-private partnerships are used to provide job training, and 9% report that partnerships are used to manage the federal Welfare to Work program. This program allows participants to continue on welfare while going through an approved skills training program.

Public-private partnerships for Economic Development Zones

Another objective of public-partnerships is to develop, or redevelop, public infrastructure or real estate. An example of a public-private partnership for infrastructure development is described above. In a typical real estate development partnership, an economic development zone is created. Private firms develop the land and the physical structures. In some cases public land is given to the developer. Both the developer and the new firms locating in these zones are eligible for tax incentives. In the survey cited above, 14% of participants reported that they have used public-private partnerships to create such economic development zones.

Public-private partnerships to support CDC's exist in just 12% of US cities according to the ICMA data reported in Table 11.1. Recall from the previous chapter that Community Development Corporation is non-profit organization funded by Community Development Block Grants. The goals of the CDC are broadly to improve poor and inner city neighborhoods. CDC's invest in worthwhile projects in education, public space, housing and entrepreneurship. CDC's have many partnerships, so it is surprising that only 12% of US cities report this, despite 33% of US cities having a CDC present. CDC's typically partner with government social services agencies and sometimes with privately-operated Community Development Banks and Community Development Venture Capital.

Eleven percent of US cities report having **public-private partnerships to support Welfare-to-Work.** The phrase, Welfare-to-Work, broadly refers to policies that encourage welfare benefit recipients to enter the labor market. The concept was a key component of the Personal Responsibility and Work Opportunity Act of 1996 led by Newt Gingrich and signed by President Clinton. The bill represented a shift from giving cash payments to the poor, to requiring the poor to seek work. People criticized the cash payments as a disincentive to work, and so the law was hailed as a great reform of the welfare system.

Public-private partnerships for microenterprise are useful to develop small businesses. Of the surveyed cities 9% report that they use public-private partnerships to provide community development loan funds and 7% use partnerships for microenterprise programs. Through community development loan funds, public and private funds are loaned to entrepreneurs at below-market rates to help them start new businesses. Microenterprise programs, such as business incubators, provide capital, technical expertise, training, and networking assistance for entrepreneurs. In these ventures, the private actor is often a non-profit organization, such as a Community Development Corporation (CDC), whose invested funds are matched by a local government entity. CDCs are nonprofit 501c3 organizations that often specialize in housing and business development (Clarke, 1998).

Partnership Models for Service Delivery

The level of collaboration between public and private actors in a partnership varies from case to case. Many public services have traditionally been provided directly by the government with no collaboration with the private sector. Intergovernmental agreements (such as a county and city sharing jail facilities, road maintenance responsibilities, or an airport) represent an example of collaboration between multiple public organizations. But the public sector is increasingly looking to the private sector for partners who can produce public services. Savas (2000) lists models of public-private partnerships where a private entity acts as a producer of public goods and services: 1) contracts, 2) franchises, 3) grants, and 4) vouchers. Goods and services can also be provided in the free market, by voluntary service, and by self-service.

Contracting involves government payment to a private entity to provide a specific service. Virtually all governments procure some goods or services by contracting with private firms. Services related to economic development that are often provided by contractors include economic development attraction activity, road and building construction, convention center management, industrial development, and urban planning.

Franchises are awarded by governments to private firms who agree to provide a unique public service such as airport operation, utilities, and toll roads. Government gives the firm permission to operate in a specific geographic area and citizens pay the firm directly for services.

Grants are resources given by government to private firms who can then provide more affordable good or service to citizens. Grants are often subsidies, in the form of money, tax exemptions, tax abatements, or low-cost loans. For economic development, many state and local governments give away land at no cost to new firms.

Vouchers are subsidies given directly to consumers to purchase goods such as food (food stamps) or education (school vouchers). Unlike grants where the government decides which producers get the resources; consumers decide where to spend their vouchers. Job training vouchers and the G. I. Bill are voucher programs designed to increase human capital and are therefore relevant from an economic development perspective.

The examples above mention partnerships with private firms, but numerous partnerships exist where the private-sector partner is not a firm, but a non-profit organization.

Partnership Models for Infrastructure Development

The potential for economic growth in a region is enhanced when physical infrastructure (such as roads, airports, mass transit, and utilities) and social infrastructure (such as hospitals, housing, jails, and schools) are fully developed. When public funds are available, governments can produce and provide needed infrastructure. But governments often lack the funds (and the expertise) to build needed infrastructure, therefore they look for partners in the private sector that have both capital and technical expertise. A typical partnership is characterized by the public entity providing political and bureaucratic resources, and the private entity providing capital and technical expertise. Savas (2000) and Williams (2003) describe a range of public-private partnerships each with varied degrees of privatization. Numerous models exist, but four representative models are illustrated in Figure 4.7.

Figure 11.1 The Range of Privatization

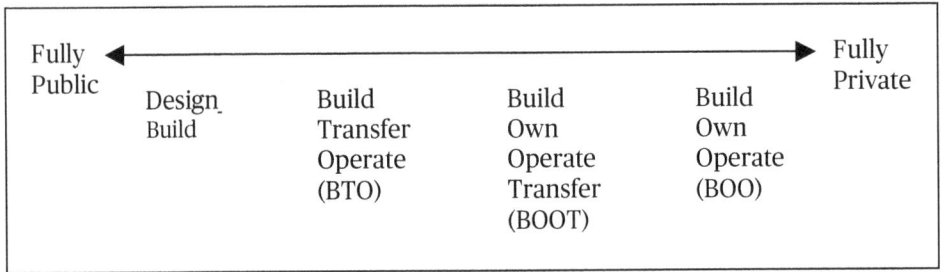

Based on: Savas, 2000.

The first model, design-build, represents traditional infrastructure development where the private contractor provides architectural and construction services. The public entity provides financing, retains ownership of the newly created asset, and earns any user fees from the project.

In the build-transfer-operate model, the private partner provides their own funding. After construction is complete, ownership of the asset is transferred to the government partner. The private firm then leases the facility back, operates the facility and earns reasonable income from user charges.

The build-own-operate-transfer (BOOT) model is an excellent way for governments to acquire infrastructure assets without fiscal hardship. The private firm builds, owns, and operates the facility for a period of time, then transfers the asset to the government. Chinese local government officials entered into a BOOT public-private partnership to avoid the high costs of constructing a bridge across the Hangzhou bay from Shanghai, China to Ningbo, "Non-governmental private enterprises" provided a large part of the initial investment. Through the formal partnership arrangement a government clause guarantees the private enterprises will recoup their investments through years of earning bridge tolls (Wu and Wu, 2003).

The build-own-operate "resembles outright privatization" (Williams, 2003). Private firms build and operate a public infrastructure asset, and there is usually no provision for ownership to be transferred to the government. The "chunnel" connecting England and France is an example of public infrastructure that followed the BOO model.

Chapter Conclusion
Public-private partnerships are on the rise for many reasons. Decentralization of political power from national governments to local governments, a new entrepreneurial public sector management style, and fiscal stress are driving local

government to secure private funding for economic development projects. The use of partnerships will especially increase for infrastructure construction projects (Klitgaard and Treverton, 2003). Because partnerships are found to be more efficient and less adversarial than traditional bidding contractual arrangements, the use of public-private partnerships might be on the rise. However, one hindrance to the rise in public-private partnerships is the appearance of cronyism and impropriety–private firms appear to be enriching themselves with public resources. And the "risk-shifting" aspects of partnerships can result in poor performance according to "the criteria of equity, access, and democracy" (Rosenau, 1999). In general, however, public-private partnerships have proven to be an effective tool for economic development projects and it is expected that they will continue to be utilized in the future.

Louisville United Parcel Service Case Study

In 1997 it was announced that United Parcel Service (UPS) was considering closing their headquarters operation in Louisville, Kentucky and relocating to another U.S. city. Due to their difficulty in staffing their late night package handling positions in Louisville, UPS began looking for another city that could meet their labor demands. Facing the immediate threat of losing the city's major employer, government and private sector leaders in the Louisville area developed a plan aimed at satisfying UPS's work force needs. Typical economic development initiatives were engaged to prevent the departure of UPS from the Louisville economy, but the creation of the innovative Metropolitan College program became the key component in retaining UPS. This brief case study provides a description of the Metropolitan College program.

The Problem

Since its founding in 1907, United Parcel Service has grown to be the largest package distribution company in the world. The company's 359,000 employees work at 1,748 operating facilities in over 200 countries and territories throughout the world (United Parcel Service 2001a). Louisville has served as the corporate headquarters and the main U.S. air hub. In addition to being the largest employer in the city and in the state, UPS was thought to be one of Kentucky's "industries of the future" that could take advantage of increased deliveries generated by Internet commerce. Many believed that growth in this sector could balance recent job losses in other parts of the metropolitan area, due to manufacturing decline. If UPS relocated to another city, the area would not only lose existing jobs, but also future jobs that were part of UPS's planned billion dollar expansion.

The Economic Development Response

To convince UPS to remain in Louisville, city leaders employed numerous traditional incentive programs. Certain fiscal incentives were offered including elimination of the jet fuel tax (attractive to UPS given their massive air fleet of 51 jet aircraft and 384 chartered aircraft), and property tax abatements for construction of the new "Mega-Hub." Whole neighborhoods were removed (using eminent domain), and brownfields were decontaminated in a massive airport expansion program. Local government and local firms agreed to exclusively use UPS for their shipping business. But the initiative that was most important in the retention of UPS was the creation of the Metropolitan College program. The program produced a large pool of labor that was willing to work as part-time package handlers.

The Metropolitan College program was developed in an emergency atmosphere since the threat of job loss mandated a quick response. This quick response led to collaboration among three local colleges, state officials, city business leaders, and UPS. The collaborative plan was innovative in its use of public universities as tools of economic development.

As part of their "Hub 2000" program, UPS invested over $1 billion to expand its Louisville operation. In 2001, the Louisville hub required a total of 4,800 part-time package handlers during the peak season, and according to John Kinney, Workforce Planning Manager at UPS, they were usually "a couple hundred short" going into the peak holiday season. Metropolitan College allowed UPS to hire 2,200 part-time package handlers in 2001. This figure surpassed their year 2005 objective of 2,100 part-time package handlers (J. Kinney, personal communication, October 2, 2001). Table 11.2 shows the overall composition of part-time package handlers at UPS.

Table 11.2, Composition of Part-time Package Handlers at the Louisville UPS Facility

School to Work	$400
Earn & Learn	$400
Metro College	
University of Louisville	$960
Jefferson Community College	$1,100
Jefferson Technical College	$70
Other Package Handlers	$1,870
Total	**$4,800**

Source: UPS, 2001.

The Program

Through the Metropolitan College program, student-workers who agree to work at the UPS Next Day Air operation have free tuition at Jefferson Technical College, Jefferson Community College, or the University of Louisville. The commonwealth of Kentucky assumes responsibility for half of the tuition, and the other half is paid by UPS, if not already covered elsewhere by federal grants or college scholarships.

Metropolitan College students who fulfilled their work requirements at UPS, attended classes regularly, and received at least 18 credits during a given year were eligible for housing stipends which were 103 dollars per month in 2001. A new dormitory, Bettie Johnson Hall, was opened on the University of Louisville campus July 2000 with Metropolitan College students in mind. The housing program was designed specifically to help recruit workers from outside the Louisville area. Using the housing stipend, UPS recruiters attracted about 400 people from the Appalachian mountain region of the state where residents faced many obstacles such as high unemployment (Jones, 2000; J. Kinney, personal communication, October 2, 2001). Many of the Appalachians have since returned home.

UPS also offered a loan program to their student-workers. Students can borrow up to $2,000 per year from UPS for living expenses. The loan is renewable for a total of four years. If the student-worker stays with UPS for a full year, UPS forgives 50 percent of the loan. After two years, UPS forgives 75 percent of the loan up to $3,000. After three years, the company forgives 100 percent of the loan up to $6,000, and after four years, 100 percent up to $8,000 (United Parcel Service 2001b).

The program also provides certain non-financial benefits. To accommodate the late night schedules of package handlers many classes were set up for late afternoons and early evenings, and some classes are offered at the UPS facility. Many classes end by Thanksgiving to enable students to work extra hours over the peak shipping season. Workers who enrolled in the Metropolitan College program also receive free bus passes for public transit, and special bus routes were established from the three college campuses to the company's sorting center (Holmes 1998).

In October 2001, Metropolitan College enrolled about 1,100 students at Jefferson Community College, 965 students at the University of Louisville, and about 65 students at Jefferson Tech (J. Kinney, personal communication, October 2, 2001).

The Impacts of the Program

The Metropolitan College program has been perceived as a "win-win" situation, providing positive impacts to UPS, local politicians, colleges and the student-workers.

Benefits to UPS. From the perspective of UPS, the main objectives of Metro College were to reduce turnover and to grow the labor pool. These objectives were met, largely due to implementation of the Metro College program. Significant advances were attained in terms of the turnover issue. Part-time package handler turnover was a steady 80 percent per year before Metro College, but by the year 2001 this figure dropped to 15 percent. Regarding overall retention rates of Metro College and non-Metro College workers, the Louisville location consistently ranks second or third place among all 47 UPS "Mega Hubs." Each retained employee represents significant cost savings for UPS. The average cost of recruiting, hiring, background checks, training and the "productivity curve" was estimated to be about $1,450 (J. Kinney, personal communication, October 2, 2001). Helped by the lower rates of turnover, UPS was able to meet its hiring objectives by adding an additional 1,500 positions.

Perhaps the most significant benefit of this program for UPS is the improved efficiency of the workforce. UPS Louisville witnessed an increase in the "piece per hour" rate of packages handled, an internal measure of worker productivity. In addition, the number of mis-sorted and damaged packages has decreased as well as the number of work-related injuries. The young, healthy, dedicated work force contributed to these increases in efficiency. Metro College also was credited with creating "residual benefits" which were "immeasurable, but clearly positive" (J. Kinney, personal communication, October 2, 2001).

Benefits to Government. Political leaders protected and expanded their tax base by keeping the largest employer in the state within the Louisville metropolitan area. The multiplier effect was significant in terms of keeping the present jobs as well as adding 1,500 jobs. Wages to UPS workers helped to fill government coffers through additions to property, income and sales tax revenues. Politicians were also able to reap a positive public relations coup as citizens began to see government leaders from the perspective of protecting jobs and ensuring future prosperity for the state.

Benefits to Universities. Local colleges and universities were able to augment their enrollment base and increase their revenues from added tuition. College presidents were able to claim that they were "team players" in economic development, in the hopes of receiving more funding from state leaders in the future. They avoided negative publicity that would have been received if they refused to participate in the program. Leaders of public colleges, recognizing that large proportions of their funding came from state allocations, did not want to jeopardize future allocations.

Benefits to Students. The program expanded opportunities for students who might not otherwise have been able to attend college. By 2001, over 3,000 students had participated in the Metro College program. Table 11.3 shows the annual financial benefits a student earns by participating in the program.

Table 4.3, Combined Metro College Annual Benefits

Tuition		
50% paid by United Parcel Service	$1,822	
50% paid by Commonwealth of Kentucky	$1,822	
Book Stipend		
$65 * 8 classes =	$520	
Housing Stipend		
$103 * 12 months =	$1,236	
Wages		
80 hours per month * $8.50/hour * 12 months =		$8,160
Forgivable Loan		$2,000
Total Metro College Benefit:	$5,400	
Total Annual Benefit:		**$15,560**

Sources: University of Louisville, Metropolitan College. (Based on a full-time undergraduate student taking 12 credit hours per semester at the University of Louisville).

Case Conclusion

The Metropolitan College case illustrates the use of public and private resources and innovative economic development policy to retain a major firm, and to enhance the human capital of a city. Metropolitan College is credited with changing the external work force environment in order to retain the largest employer in the state of Kentucky and to lock in a major expansion of future jobs. In contrast to the ideal of exclusively attracting high paying, highly skilled, professional employees, the Metropolitan College experience illustrates that employers have needs for both higher skill and lower skill employees. The Metropolitan College case study suggests that, while companies often decide to relocate, such decisions are not unmalleable. Companies that face difficult decisions can be influenced by coordinated public sector efforts. This is illustrated in Kentucky where fiscal incentives combined with innovative use of public universities convinced UPS to stay in Louisville.

CHAPTER 12

EMPIRICAL CONCLUSION

Chapter Introduction

This book has described the history of economic development policy in the US in Chapter 2. Chapters 3 and 4 offered economic and political theories that illuminate the rationale behind economic development policy and practice. The subsequent chapters 5 through 11 described nearly a hundred different policies, practices and programs that city leaders, both public and private, employ to improve their local economy.

While the book has mainly been descriptive and objective, throughout the book I have also presented an argument that "Market Cities" are the cities with robust economies. The term, "Market Cities" refers to a city whose leadership, public and private, embraces free market principles in its policy decisions. And rather than have bureaucrats steer the economy, resources are put in the hands of (or more accurately, "left in the hands of") private individuals and businesses. While government serves many necessary and irreplaceable functions (national defense, rule of law, law enforcement, and so on), the private sector more efficiently manages economic resources.

Anecdotes have been offered throughout the book of this "Market Cities" principle, and now in this final chapter, we introduce an empirical model that asks the question, to what extent does economic development policy actually impact the economy? In the end, we'll see that policy is only about ten percent correlated with economic growth. Does this mean city leaders should give up on local economic development policy? Actually, cities should continue their economic policies intended to attract, retain and develop businesses, largely to keep the playing field level. In other words, every other city in the US is offering incentives to businesses, therefore cities must follow suit to remain competitive. However, the mix of policies and incentives should be steered towards market-based programs.

The remainder of this chapter is an empirical research project that analyzes the correlation between economic development policy and actual economic development.

Introduction to the Empirical Study

This study uses cities with populations greater than 25,000 as the unit of analysis and analyzes economic growth from one period to another. Two primary data sources are used in this study. Data regarding economic conditions in U.S. cities are from the 1994 and 2000 *County and City Data Books* from the U.S. Census Bureau. Data regarding the economic development practices of U.S. municipalities come from the 1999 *Economic Development* mail survey conducted by the International City/County Management Association (ICMA). The 912 ICMA records were merged with the 1,070 Census records resulting in a final data set consisting of the 412 cities that were found in both the ICMA data and Census data. Difference of means tests confirmed that the 412 sample cities are largely representative of the population of 1,070 cities.

Figure 12.1. Map of 412 Cities Used in This Study

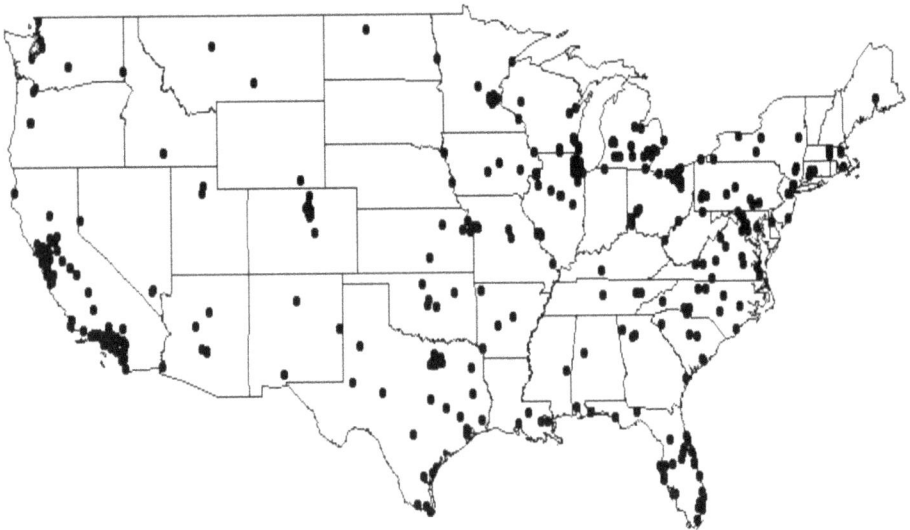

Dependent Variables

Because economic development policy is designed to have wide impacts on a local economy, this study considers changes in the number of firms, jobs, and income as evidence of economic growth. To measure economic growth across time, the difference in a particular economic indicator is calculated from an earlier time period (typically 1987) to a later time period (typically 1997). Financial data are expressed in constant 1997 dollars–that is, the 1987 figures have been adjusted for inflation. Table 12.1 lists the dependent variables and displays the descriptive statistics for these variables.

Table 12.1. Descriptive Statistics for Dependent Variables, Measures of Economic Growth

	n	Minimum	Maximum	Mean	St. Dev.
Dependent Variables Related to the Number of Firms					
Growth, mfg. firms	410	-343.0	182.0	-1.5	45.0
Growth, retail firms	412	-6,772.0	123.0	-477.3	647.7
Dependent Variables Related to the Labor Force					
Growth, jobs	412	-21,043.5	208,471.4	7,733.8	16639.5
Growth, mfg. employees	366	-48,764.0	20,823.0	-1,740.5	5,627.2
Growth, retail employees	412	-39,978.0	4,371.0	-2,244.0	4,145.7
Dependent Variables Related to Income*					
Mfg. value-added growth	352	-$4,869,558	$3,705,732	$33,102.0	$611,492
Retail sales growth	412	-$1,004,363	$3,103,016	$136,767	$391,928
Per capita income growth	412	-$33,809	$54,191	$4,964	$11,615
*Expressed in 1997 constant dollars.					

Sources: U.S. Census, County and City Data Books, 1994 and 2000.

Independent Variables

It is thought that economic development policies and programs are positively correlated with economic growth in cities, so variables from the ICMA data set that measure economic development policy and practice serve as independent variables in this study. These variables represent the four principal economic development objectives of attraction, retention, business development, and equity planning. Table 12.2 shows the descriptive statistics for these independent variables.

Table 12.2. Descriptive Statistics for Independent Variables, Measures of ED Policy

	n	Min	Max	Mean	St. Dev.
Independent Variables Related to Economic Development Policy					
Capita Per ED Staff	295	1,843	1,205,278	43,856	79,575
ED Budget Per Capita	363	$0.0	$421.6	$16.1	$45.7
Total E.D. Initiatives	412	0.0	55.0	24.7	12.6
Public-Private Partnerships	412	0.0	9.0	2.3	1.7
Independent Variables Related to Business Attraction and Retention					
% Time On Attraction	352	0.0	100.0	25.1	18.2
Attraction Techniques	412	0.0	13.0	5.4	3.6
Use Of Incentives	412	0.0	15.0	5.2	4.0
% Time On Retention	362	0.0	100.0	29.0	21.7
Retention Techniques	412	0.0	12.0	4.6	3.0
Independent Variables Related to Business Development					
% Time On Development	358	0.0	100.0	38.1	25.0
Use Of Sm. Bus. Dev.	412	0.0	9.0	2.0	2.1
Use Of Loans	412	0.0	4.0	1.5	1.5
Independent Variables Related to Equity Planning					
Use Of "Equity" Techniques	412	0.0	6.0	2.6	1.8

Source: ICMA Economic Development Survey, 1999.

Control Variables

Certain control variables that represent factors that affect city economies are also included in this study. Economies are quite complex, and it is unlikely that the total variation of an economy can be explained by any collection of variables. Perhaps the variation in urban economies will be more accounted for by the control variables rather than the economic development policy variables. A complete list of the control variables and their descriptive statistics is shown in Table 12.3. Three variables are dummy variables (0 = *no*, 1 = *yes*), which are manufacturing economic base, technology economic base, and mayoral form of government.

Table 12.3. Descriptive Statistics, Control Variables

	n	Min	Max	Mean	St. Dev.
1990 Population	412	25,063	1,111,030	87,951	119,913
Pop. Growth 1990-2000	412	-48,496	332,062	11,161	27,713
Manufacturing Economic Base	412	0	1	0.16	0.36
Technology Economic Base	412	0	1	0.04	0.20
Taxes Per Capita	397	$67	$2,173	$434	$256
Expenditures Per Capita	397	$301	$4,088	$987	$539
Mayoral Form Of Gov't	412	0	1	0.15	0.36
Crime Rate 1990	412	-	37,903	6,580	4,044
% Hs Grads, 1990	412	26	97	78	10
% College Grads, 1990	412	1.7	71	24	12
January Temp, Avg.	412	5.9	68	38	15

Sources: ICMA Economic Development Survey, 1999, U.S. Census, County and City Data Books, 1994 and 2000.

Methodology

The objective of this study is to determine whether the economic development policies employed at the local government level are statistically significant and positively correlated with measures of economic growth in U.S. cities. The multiple regression statistical technique is used to examine correlations between the incidence of economic development practice and actual economic growth. Three models are used: the firm growth model, the job growth model, and the income growth model.

In each of the three models, economic indicators serve as dependent variables. Using SPSS software, the independent variables are entered into each model in blocks. The first block contains all of the control variables, and then the second block adds the economic development policy variables. The coefficient of multiple determination (R^2) indicates the amount of the variance in the dependent variable that is explained, or accounted for, by these independent control variables (Lind, Marchal, and Wathen, 2003, p. 435). Because R^2 tends to be overestimated (Tabachnick and Fidell, 2001, p.147), this statistic is adjusted according to the guidelines proposed by Wherry (1931). The change in the adjusted coefficient of multiple determination (adjusted R^2 change) from the first block to the second block indicates the additional amount of the variance in the dependent variable that is accounted for by the economic development policy variables. Consistent with previous research, this analysis is expected to confirm that control variables explain much more of the variance in economic growth than do economic development policies.

In the regressions, missing values were replaced with mean scores, a common technique described by Tabachnick and Fidell (2001, p. 62). In a few instances, multicollinearity problems were discovered and the offending variables were eliminated from the analysis. In the case that a control or independent variable is multicollinear with the dependent variable, the offending control or independent variable is removed from the analysis and noted in the tables.

Firm Growth Models

The **firm growth models** test the hypothesis that cities that are more proactive in their efforts to attract, retain, and develop firms are those cities that experience growth in the absolute number of firms. Growth in the number of manufacturing firms and growth in the number of retail firms serve as the dependent variables.

Table 12.4 reports that about 32% of the variance in manufacturing firm growth is explained by the control variables (adjusted R^2 = .319). The standardized regression coefficients for control and independent variables are shown in the "Beta" column. Population growth is statistically significant and positively correlated with the dependent variable ($p < 0.001$, $\beta = .527$) which confirms the parallel migratory patterns of individuals and firms described by Koven and Shelley (1989). The technology economic base variable is also significant and positively correlated with the dependent variable ($p < 0.05$, $\beta = .099$). This confirms the role of high-tech as a driver of economic growth.

Evidently cities with higher populations ($p < 0.001$, $\beta = -.548$), higher taxes ($p < 0.001$, $\beta = -.191$), and higher crime rates ($p < 0.1$, $\beta = -.094$) are experiencing a decline or slower growth in the number of manufacturing firms. These results confirm the trends of manufacturing firms deserting larger, high-crime cities in favor of smaller growing cities that are most likely in suburban locations.

When the policy variables are entered in the second block, only an additional two percent of the variance in manufacturing firm growth is explained (adjusted R^2 change = .024). The percent time spent on attraction variable is significant and positively correlated with increased numbers of manufacturing firms ($p < 0.05$, $\beta = .126$). Although the standardized regression coefficient is small, we have some evidence that cities focusing more time on attraction are more likely to experience growth in the number of manufacturing firms. Conversely, the number of attraction techniques variable is significant and negatively correlated in this regression ($p < 0.1$, $\beta = -.103$). Perhaps this finding is evidence of the inefficacy of a "shotgun" policy approach. Rather than employing a vast array of attraction techniques, cities might consider focusing their attraction efforts according to their economic base, such as is suggested in the literature espousing cluster-strategies (see for example, Porter, 1998).

The number of retention techniques variable is also significant and positively correlated in this regression ($p < 0.05$, $\beta = .157$). Cities employing a wider array of retention policies are more likely to expand their numbers of manufacturers.

Overall, the regression coefficients for these policy variables are small, indicating weak correlation. The overall interpretation of these regression results is that economic development policy variables only have a modest impact on the number of manufacturing firms in a city over and above that of the controls.

The **retail firm growth model** uses the number of retail shops added as the dependent variable. Table 12.4 reports that the block of control variables explains about 41 percent of the variance in the dependent variable (adjusted R^2 = .409). Because the absolute number of retail firms is in decline (median = -307) this variable is more of a measure of slower decline rather than actual growth.

Population growth is significant and negatively correlated with retail firm growth ($p < 0.001$, $\beta = -.559$), which is perhaps explained by the trends of suburbanization and consolidation. By 1987 (the first time period of this study) much of the migration of retail firms from the urban core to suburban locations (i.e. shopping malls, strip malls) was complete. By 1997 (the second time period of this study) the absolute number of these retailers was shrinking, perhaps due to consolidation, as big box retail stores, such as Wal-Mart, Target and Best Buy, have replaced smaller retail shops. Places with higher population growth (i.e. suburban cities) may have lost more retail firms simply because they had more small shops to lose.

The significant negative correlation of the local tax variable ($p < 0.001$, $\beta = -.146$) again illustrates private firms' preference for low tax areas. Crime rates are also negatively correlated with retail firm growth ($p < 0.001$, $\beta = -.250$), which is expected as retailers tend to avoid areas with many negative externalities, especially crime.

The average January temperature is a significant positive predictor of retail firm growth ($p < 0.05$, $\beta = .095$). This is expected because retail firm locations are based on the presence of a retail market. As Americans migrate from colder states to warmer states it is understandable that retail firm migration would follow the pattern of customer migration. The national migration trend reported by the U.S. Census Bureau shows that the South and West (warmer areas) are experiencing positive net migration, while the Northeast and Midwest (colder areas) are experiencing negative net migration (Franklin, 2003). In other words, as Americans move south with their retail shopping dollars, the retailers follow them with their wares.

Entering the policy variables in the second block explains only an additional two percent of the variance in retail firm growth (adjusted R^2 change = .021). The number of attraction techniques is the only policy variable positively correlated with retail firm growth ($p < 0.05$, $\beta = .116$). This can be interpreted that the cities employing a greater number of attraction techniques are more likely to experience growth in the number of retail firms.

The number of incentive techniques variable is significant and negatively correlated with retail firm growth ($p < 0.05$, $\beta = -.165$). It is unlikely that the offering of more types of incentives exerts a causal effect on the number of retail firms. More than likely, the significance of this variable reflects the reality that cities experiencing retail decline are probably experiencing many other economic hardships also. Such declining cities are known to offer more fiscal incentives to businesses than offered by prosperous cities. In desperate times, city leaders have been known to make riskier speculative decisions with public funds.

The fact that policy variables only exert minimal influence over retail firm location decisions is not surprising. It is unlikely that economic development incentives can change the minds of retailers who choose their locations primarily based on market surveys and potential profits. The overall interpretation of these regression results is that economic development policy variables only have a modest impact on the number of retail firms in a city.

Table 12.4, Firm Growth Model Regression Results

	Mfg. Firm Growth				Retail Firm Growth			
	Block 1		Block 2		Block 1		Block 2	
	Beta		Beta		Beta		Beta	
Control Variables								
population	-.548	***	-.552	***	†		†	
population growth	.527	***	.494	***	-.559	***	-.572	***
mfg. economic base	.005		-.015		-.014		-.007	
tech. economic base	.099	**	.102	**	-.050		-.043	
local taxes (capita)	-.191	***	-.210	***	-.146	***	-.159	***
mayor form of gov't	.001		-.011		.022		.024	
crime rate	-.094	*	-.087	*	-.250	***	-.251	***
% high school grads	.041		.045		.061		.008	
January temp. avg.	.058		.048		.095	**	.066	
Policy Variables								
ED staff size (capita)			-.046				-.034	
ED budget (capita)			-.044				-.047	
% time on attraction			.126	**			.029	
attraction techniques			-.103	*			.116	**
% time on retention			-.005				-.047	
retention techniques			.157	**			-.028	
% time on development			.000				-.042	
develop. techniques			.091				-.011	
loans			.041				-.033	
incentives			-.042				-.165	**
PPP			-.034				.001	
n	412		412		412		412	
F	22.41	***	11.71	***	36.57	***	17.30	***
Adjusted R^2	.319		.343		.409		.430	
Adjusted R^2 change			.024	**			.021	**
* $p < 0.1$ ** $p < 0.05$ *** $p < 0.01$								
† excluded due to multicollinearity								

Job Growth Models

The job growth models test the hypothesis that cities that are more proactive in their economic development efforts experience growth in the number of jobs. The dependent variables in these models are growth in the overall number of jobs, growth in the number of manufacturing jobs, and growth in the number of retail jobs. Growth is measured as the absolute difference in the number of jobs from 1987 to 1997 as reported in the 1994 and 2000 *County and City Data Books*.

The **overall job growth model** results are shown in Table 12.5, which reports that only about six percent of the variance in overall job growth is explained by the control variables (adjusted R^2 = .060). Similar to a previous regression, the technology economic base is significant and positively correlated with overall job growth ($p < 0.05$, β = .108). This reflects structural changes as the macroeconomy takes on more characteristics of the so-called New Economy, or Information Economy. Cities with technology economic bases (only four percent of the study cities) are experiencing greater job growth than cities with other economic bases. The high school graduate percentage variable is also significant and positively correlated with job growth. This underscores the important role of human capital development as an essential part of economic growth.

Crime rates are also significant and positively correlated with overall job growth ($p < 0.001$, β = .219). This unexpected finding is perhaps explained by the dynamism that has created jobs may also have attracted non-law abiding citizens. The local tax variable is again significant and negatively correlated with economic growth ($p < 0.1$, β = -.094) again illustrating the inclination of businesses to avoid high tax areas.

When the policy variables are entered in the second block an additional two percent of the variance in overall job growth is explained (adjusted R^2 change = .024). The development techniques variable accounts for much of this change. It is statistically significant and contributes to prediction of overall job growth more than all of the other variables in this regression ($p < 0.001$, β = .220). This indicates that the cities experiencing more job growth are more entrepreneurial cities that use more business development techniques such as revolving loan funds, small business development centers, matching improvement grants, marketing assistance, business incubators and vendor/supplier matching. These results emphasize the important role entrepreneurial development policies play in economic growth.

Economic development staff size is also significant and positively correlated with overall job growth ($p < 0.1$, β = .081). City governments employing larger (per capita) numbers of economic development practitioners are experiencing more job growth than cities with smaller staffs.

Noting that this regression only explains about eight percent of the variance in job growth (adjusted R^2 = .084) illustrates that job growth is perhaps more dependent upon market factors not included in the model rather than economic development policy and the control variables included in this regression. However, the regression coefficient for the business development techniques variable is larger than any of the others which suggests that these techniques are more likely to foster job growth than the other techniques.

Using **manufacturing job growth** as the dependent variable, Table 12.5 reports that the control variables in the first block explain about thirty five percent of the variance in manufacturing job growth (adjusted R^2 = .351). Most of this manufacturing job growth is accounted for by the population variable which is significant and negatively correlated with manufacturing job growth ($p < 0.001$, β = -.687). This finding is consistent with a massive body of literature that documents the decline of manufacturing jobs in larger cities. Three trends explain the losses of manufacturing jobs from large U.S. cities: mechanization (labor replaced by machines), globalization (labor replaced by cheap overseas labor), and suburbanization (production moved from cities to suburban sites). Manufacturing jobs have been shifting away from highly populated central cities to lesser populated suburban cities. Suburban cities are smaller than central cities and have higher population growth rates which explains why the population growth variable is statistically significant and positively correlated with manufacturing job growth ($p < 0.001$, β = .382).

Local government taxes are again statistically significant and negatively correlated with job growth ($p < 0.001$, β = -.155), which can be interpreted various ways. Perhaps the firms that are creating new jobs are tax-averse and avoid locating in high-tax areas. Or perhaps the loss of jobs (or lack of growth of jobs) in a city forces that city to place higher per capita tax burdens on the workers that remain employed. Cities experiencing economic decline, such as many Rust Belt cities, are often saddled with crumbling infrastructure which requires greater public investment for maintenance.

Adding the economic development policy variables to the regression in the second block results in no change in the explained variance in manufacturing job growth (adjusted R^2 change = .000). The economic development budget per capita variable is the only statistically significant policy variable ($p < 0.1$, β = -.079). The correlation is negative, indicating that cities investing more money in economic development still experience less manufacturing job growth. The small regression weight indicates that this variable is a weak predictor of the dependent variable.

The final column in Table 12.5 reports results of the **retail job growth model**. The control variables explain almost twenty four percent of the variance in retail job growth (adjusted R^2 = .239). The significant positive correlation of the January temperature variable ($p < 0.05$, β = .132) reveals that retail job growth largely follows the general migration patterns of Americans from the North and East, to the West, and especially the South.

The local tax rate variable is statistically significant and negatively correlated with the dependent variable ($p < 0.001$, β = -.222) again underscoring the relationship between higher tax rates and slower economic growth. Population growth is also significant and negatively correlated with retail job growth ($p < 0.001$, β = -.331) which is perhaps further evidence of the trend of retail consolidation, where smaller retail shops are replaced by big box retailers. It is no surprise that retail job growth is lower in growing cities than non-growing cities. Also, cities with severely declining populations may have already lost much of the retail base and would not show any additional job loss. The crime rate variable is also significant and negatively correlated with retail job growth ($p < 0.001$, β = -.274) which perhaps reflects retailers' aversion to high-crime areas.

Adding the policy variables into the regression improves the prediction of retail job growth by about two percent (adjusted R^2 change = .018). The incentives variable is significant and once again negatively correlated with the dependent variable ($p < 0.05$, β = -.171). This demonstrates that cities offering more types of fiscal incentives to businesses are more likely cities that are losing retail jobs. Incentives are more likely to be used by cities experiencing slower economic growth. The fact that economic development policy has little positive correlation with retail jobs is expected because economic decisions are driven by profit potential, not the amount of government programs. This finding confirms the idea that offering financial incentives to retailers may not lead to the anticipated outcome of economic growth.

Table 12.5, Job Growth Model Regression Results

	Overall Job Growth				Mfg. Job Growth				Retail Job Growth			
	Block 1		Block 2		Block 1		Block 2		Block 1		Block 2	
	Beta		Beta		Beta		Beta		Beta		Beta	
Control Variables												
population	†		†		-.687	***	-.673	***	†		†	
population growth	†		†		.382	***	.359	***	-.331	***	-.344	***
mfg. economic base	.054		.043		-.003		-.021		.025		.041	
tech. economic base	.108	**	.099	**	-.010		-.014		-.028		-.020	
local taxes (capita)	-.094	*	-.108	**	-.155	***	-.160	***	-.222	***	-.237	***
mayor form of gov't	-.050		-.033		-.016		-.007		.031		.035	
crime rate	.219	***	.218	***	-.043		-.056		-.274	***	-.288	***
% high school grads	.158	**	.197	***	.039		.036		.053		.001	
January temp. avg.	.076		.054		.037		.032		.132	**	.108	**
Policy Variables												
ED staff size (capita)			.081	*			-.040				-.048	
ED budget (capita)			.005				-.079	**			-.043	
% time on attraction			.003				.051				.066	
attraction techniques			.045				-.007				.059	
% time on retention			-.076				.010				-.050	
retention techniques			.047				.059				-.069	
% time on develop.			.024				-.025				-.061	
develop. techniques			.220	***			.006				-.042	
loans			-.079				-.001				-.039	
incentives			-.019				-.001				-.171	**
PPP			-.051				-.017				-.026	
"equity" techniques			.023				.036				.081	
n	412		412		412		412		412		412	
F	4.74	***	2.97	***	25.71	***	11.49	***	17.11	***	8.13	***
Adjusted R^2	.060		.084		.351		.349		.239		.257	
Adjusted R^2 change			.024	**			.000				.018	**

$* \ p < 0.1 \ ** \ p < 0.05 \ *** \ p < 0.01$ † excluded due to multicollinearity

Income Growth Models

The income growth models test the hypothesis that economic development policy has positive impacts on personal and corporate income. The dependent variables are growth in per capita income, growth in manufacturing value added, and growth in retail sales. Growth is measured as the inflation-adjusted difference in income from 1987 to 1997 as reported in the 1994 and 2000 *County and City Data Books*.

The **per capita income growth model** shown in Table 12.6 uses inflation-adjusted per capita income growth from 1987 to 1997 as the dependent variable. Using the global test and the F distribution it was found that this regression model is invalid. The null hypothesis that all the regression coefficients are zero could not be rejected in the first block ($F = 1.53$, $p = .135$), nor in the second block ($F = 1.27$, $p = .193$). From a practical standpoint, this means that the independent variables do not have the ability to predict the dependent variable. In other words, neither the control variables nor the policy variables have a statistically significant effect on per capita income growth. The variation in per capita income growth must therefore be explained by other factors that are not included in this analysis.

The **manufacturing value added growth model** uses value-added as a proxy measure of the aggregate profitability of all manufacturing firms in the study cities from 1987 to 1997. The control variables in this regression explain thirteen percent of the variance in manufacturing value added growth (adjusted $R^2 = .130$). This entire variance is accounted for by two variables. The population variable is significant and negatively correlated with manufacturing value added ($p < 0.001$, $\beta = -.254$). The population growth variable is also significant but is positively correlated with the dependent variable ($p < 0.001$, $\beta = .490$). This indicates that the value added of manufacturing firms in larger cities is not growing as much as it is in smaller cities. Inspection of the data revealed manufacturing value added actually dropped by an average of $123,624 in the largest quartile (103 largest cities). The smallest quartile of study cities experienced an average manufacturing value added growth of $78,238. The fact that firms have greater value added accretions in smaller cities and growing cities is no doubt a reflection of two trends: the shift of manufacturing from larger Rust Belt cities to smaller Sun Belt cities, and the shift of manufacturing from urban core cities to the suburbs.

Adding the policy variables to the model did not improve the prediction of the dependent variable (adjusted R^2 change = .000) and none of the policy variables were statistically significant. It appears that local economic development policy has no discernable impact on the value added of manufacturing firms in a city.

The **retail sales growth model** is the change in inflation-adjusted sales from 1987 to 1997 for all retailers within a city. Table 12.6 reports that the control variables explain about nine percent of the variance in retail sales growth (adjusted R^2 = .086). Population is significant and positively correlated with retail sales (p < 0.001, β = .178). The percentage of high school graduates variable is also significant and positively correlated with retail sales growth (p < 0.001, β = .248). Larger cities and cities with higher levels of human capital appear to have higher volumes of retail sales. The tax variable is again significant and negatively correlated with the dependent variable (p < 0.05, β = -.163). Apparently retail sales are lower in cities with higher taxes.

Adding the policy variables to the regression explains an additional two percent of the variance in retail sales (adjusted R^2 change = .019). The percent time spent on attraction variable is significant and positively correlated with retail sales (p < 0.05, β = .130), and the number of attraction techniques is significant but negatively correlated with retail sales (p < 0.1, β = -.117). The modest correlations of these policy variables raises doubts about the ability of economic development officials to impact retail sales in their city.

The income growth model was designed to compare the benefits of economic development policy experienced by individuals (per capita income) to the benefits experienced by firms (manufacturing value added, and retail sales growth). But in all three of the regressions, economic development policy had no substantial impact on the income growth of either individuals or firms. The apparent answer to the question, "Who benefits more, individuals or firms?" is "neither." The income growth of individuals and the income growth of firms have no substantial correlation with economic development policy. Local government taxes and expenditures also have no substantial correlation with income growth. Another possible explanation is that the benefits of economic development policy are experienced by only certain individuals or firms, and these benefits are indiscernible in this study's aggregate data.

Table 12.6, Income Growth Model Regression Results

	Per Capita Income Growth				Mfg. Value Added Growth				Retail Sales Growth			
	Block 1		Block 2		Block 1		Block 2		Block 1		Block 2	
	Beta		Beta		Beta		Beta		Beta		Beta	
Control Variables												
population	-.052		-.082		-.254	***	-.239	***	.178	***	.175	**
population growth	.039		.060		.476	***	.490	***	†		†	
mfg. economic base	.082		.072		-.070		-.074		.066		.079	
tech. economic base	.063		.067		.004		-.001		.045		.040	
local taxes (capita)	-.115	**	-.130	**	-.024		-.018		-.163	**	-.053	
mayor form of gov't	-.055		-.055		.010		.009		.003		.014	
crime rate	.129	**	.172	**	-.042		-.034		.044		.089	*
% high school grads	.000		.010		.019		.004		.248	***	.144	**
January temp. avg.	-.049		-.057		-.051		-.067		.069		-.073	
Policy Variables												
ED staff size (capita)			.016				-.069				-.044	
ED budget (capita)			.082				-.001				.059	
% time on attraction			.055				-.051				.130	**
attraction techniques			-.053				.039				-.117	*
% time on retention			.073				.007				.038	
retention techniques			.045				-.006				-.050	
% time on develop.			.055				-.056				-.005	
develop. techniques			.025				-.045				-.010	
loans			.089				-.017				-.010	
incentives			-.027				.037				-.047	
PPP			.087				.080				.043	
"equity" techniques			-.123	*			-.086				.036	
n	412		412		412		412		412		412	
F	1.53		1.27		7.81	***	3.76	***	5.82	***	3.41	***
Adjusted R²	.011		.013		.130		.123		.086		.105	
Adjusted R² change			.002				.000				.019	*

* $p \leq 0.1$ ** $p \leq 0.05$ *** $p \leq 0.01$

Practical Application of the Study

This study discovers only modest evidence that local government economic development programs are correlated with economic growth in American cities. Despite this discouraging news, the results of this study do have certain applications to real-life local economic development policy decisions listed below.

Entrepreneurial Development

The use of business development techniques was statistically significant and positively correlated with overall job growth in this study. Therefore it is recommended that economic development officials commit to the development of new entrepreneurial firms and the expansion of existing firms using techniques such as business incubators, microenterprise programs, revolving loan funds, matching improvement grants, marketing assistance, management training, executive on loan programs, and other similar programs. Many of these business development initiatives provide capital and training, two essential elements needed by any start-up business. Research shows that small businesses and start-up companies are responsible for much of the job creation and economic growth in the U.S (Birch 1987).

Develop High Tech

Economic hardship in U.S. cities is often blamed on a decline in the manufacturing sector. But every city has not experienced a decline in manufacturing. In fact, cities with a technology economic base were more likely to experience growth in the number of manufacturing firms and growth in the overall number of jobs as reported in two of the regressions. Instead of a general decline in manufacturing, what is occurring is a change in the type of manufacturing that is growing. High-tech manufacturing is responsible for "about two-thirds of U.S. economic growth since 1990" (Bee, 2000, p. 15). In the past, economic development activity to promote high-tech development has largely focused on technology zones and tech-focused business incubators that rely on technology transfer from universities to entrepreneurs. These can be effective tools, but it is also essential that all of the resources are in place to support the unique needs of the research, development and commercialization phases and that a collaborative environment exists, as outlined by Bee, 2000.

Human Capital Investment

In this study, the high school graduate variable was statistically significant and positively correlated with economic growth in two of the regressions. Previous studies have shown a link between human capital and economic growth (Becker, 1970; Asefa and Huang, 1994), and an empirical study by Warner notes, "Evidence suggests that a strategy focusing on human capital is more effective at stimulating per capita income growth than one designed to reduce firm costs" (1989, p. 389). In other words, investing in a city's workers may pay better dividends than investing in a city's firms.

Never Pay For Retail

In this study fiscal incentives are negatively correlated with growth in the number of retail firms and jobs. Retail firms make their location decisions primarily based on profit potential and government incentives are unlikely to influence a retail firm's location decisions, although the retail firm certainly will not turn down an incentive if offered. Knowing the futility of offering incentives to retail, certain local governments, such as Buncombe County, North Carolina prohibit such practices outright (Buncombe County Economic Development Incentive Policy, 1998).

Competitive Regionalism

When firms pit cities against each other in a bidding war for their mobile capital investment, such competition is often zero-sum "if it results in oversubsidization where the public incentives merely relocate a company between individual competing areas" (McCarthy, 2000, p. 1). An approach dubbed "competitive regionalism" is a potential solution to the zero-sum game. "Competitive regionalism involves cooperative networks of local public, private, and nonprofit bodies, with higher tiers of the state, that focus their economic development efforts for the benefit of the metropolitan region as a whole" (McCarthy, 2000, p. 1). Local governments within a region essentially call a truce between each other which is enforced at the higher state level.

Accountable Growth

Cities that give financial incentives to companies should hold those companies accountable for the economic growth they have promised. Accountability tools include performance criteria, clawbacks, and greater public disclosure. By agreeing on performance criteria up-front, a local government is able to "claw back" their forgone revenue. A firm that promises 500 new jobs but only creates 250 would be required to pay back half of the value of the received incentives. Some incentive programs only pay after the promised jobs are created such as Indiana's Training 2000 grant program. Greater public disclosure of incentives could also improve accountability, especially for politicians. Since politicians are held accountable in the court of public opinion, greater public disclosure of economic development incentives could perhaps improve accountability. Accountability can also be improved using a comprehensive economic development plan. Ihlanfeldt argues that comprehensive plans make incentives "available to all firms that satisfy eligibility criteria, rather than acting as bait to lure a particular company" (1995, p. 341). Offering incentives more equally can eliminate the unjust practice of forcing existing firms and individuals to bear the tax burden of subsidized firms.

Focus on Individuals, not just Firms

If every city doles out corporate welfare equally, cities can therefore no longer expect an advantage over other cities simply by offering incentives. To cease offering incentives, however, would put a city at a disadvantage. Following the logic of Florida's (2002) argument that the creative class drive economic growth, certain cities are attempting to attract educated, creative individuals by ensuring that the quality of life in their city is attractive. Barry Alberts, an economic development official in Louisville, Kentucky suggests, "Competing for firms is the old way, and competing for people is the new way" of economic development (2004). Cities with more amenities are thought to have an advantage in the competition for new firms and new workers, especially high tech workers. Just as the presence of amenities can help attract individuals, the absence of disamenities is also attractive. In this study crime rates were negatively correlated with growth in three of the regressions in the previous chapter which suggests a link between growth and crime. Focusing solely on developing more urban amenities does not guarantee economic growth, but a higher quality of life can certainly be the tiebreaker between cities competing for high tech workers and firms.

Economic development practice in American cities has increased its fervency in recent years due to political phenomenon such as federal retrenchment and economic phenomenon such as globalization and shifts toward the New Economy. The focus has been on attraction, retention, and development of businesses in the local economy. This study analyzed whether these economic development policies and programs actually impact the local economy. Consistent with previous empirical research, this study finds only modest evidence that economic development policy has positive impacts on economic growth.

Final Thoughts

Cities are not all created equal. Some, like Seattle, Washington with its excellent schools, high-paying jobs, low unemployment, and vibrant arts scene are attractive to individuals. Young workers who are hip, educated, and unattached would much rather live in Seattle than, say, Toledo, Ohio. Their skills are in demand and they have the ability to move around. Other cities, like Boise, Idaho are attractive in the eyes of company owners due to the appealing business climate. Corporate income taxes are low in Boise, as are taxes on commercial property and payroll. Regulations on business activity are lax, especially compared to Los Angeles and other cities in "Taxifornia."

Meanwhile, other American cities are in decline due to a lack of jobs, poor schools and high crime. Detroit, for example has these problems and a declining automotive industry. The harsh winters aren't very appealing either. Many Rust Belt cities are similarly in decline, but cities elsewhere still suffer these same woes. Stockton, California, for example, has high crime, low wages, expensive housing and making matters worse, painfully high taxes. It's no wonder people and firms prefer places like Seattle and Boise over Detroit and Stockton.

How can economic development occur in cities such that a Stockton becomes a Seattle? It has been the aim of this book to offer practical policy strategies for economic development. The early chapters described the history of urban economic development and some economic and political theories that can be applied to a strategy to grow an economy. The following application chapters described nearly a hundred techniques for encouraging economic growth. Throughout the book, numerous anecdotes have illustrated successful ways to improve urban economic life (and a few unsuccessful ways). Many of these anecdotes serve as examples of allowing free market forces to work rather than employing prescriptive government programs, which are often wasteful. And in this final chapter, the empirical analysis confirms that government programs are not as effective in actual economic development as we'd hope. I believe the history, theory, anecdotes and empirical data presented in this book reveal that real economic development is more likely to occur when city leaders follow the Market Cities approach.

REFERENCES

Aberbach, J. D., & Rockman, B. A. (2000). *In the web of politics: three decades of the US federal executive*. Washington, DC: Brookings Institute.

Advisory Commission on Intergovernmental Relations. (1967). *Fiscal imbalance in the American federal system*. (Vol. 2). Washington, DC.

Advisory Commission on Intergovernmental Relations. (1969). *Urban America and the federal system*. Washington, DC.

Affholter, D. P. (1994). Outcome monitoring, in Wholey, J. S., Hatry, H. P., & Newcomer, K. E. eds. *Handbook of practical program evaluation*, San Franscisco: Jossey-Bass.

Ahlbrandt, R. S., & DeAngelis, J. P. (1987). Local options for economic development in a maturing industrial region. *Economic Development Quarterly 1*(February), 41-51.

Ailawadi, Kusum L., Jie Zhang, Aradhna Krishna, and Michael W. Kruger. "When Wal-Mart Enters: How Incumbent Retailers React and How This Affects Their Sales Outcomes." *Journal of Marketing Research* 47.4 (2010): 577-93. Print.

AirBnB Economic Impact. (2014). Retrieved from http://www.airbnb.com/economic-impact.

Alberts, B. (2004, March). *Louisville downtown development plan*. Speech presented at University of Louisville, Louisville, Kentucky.

Ambrosius, M. A. (1988). The effectiveness of state economic development policies: A time-series analysis. *Western Political Quarterly, 42* 283-300.

Ambrosius, M. M. (1989). The effectiveness of state economic development policies: A time-series analysis. *Western Political Quarterly, 42*(3), 283-300.

Anderson, J. E., & Wassmer, R. W. (1995). The decision to bid for business: Municipal behavior in granting property tax abatements. *Regional Science and Urban Economics, 25*, 739-757.

Anderson, J. E., & Wassmer, R. W. (2000). *Bidding for business: The efficacy of local economic development incentives in a metropolitan area.* Kalamazoo, MI: W.E. Upjohn Institute for Employment Research.

Anonymous. (2010, April 17). City of Corona; Gobs of jobs - 1,326 in six months. *Marketing Weekly News.* p. 67.

Appleby, P. (1945) Government is different. In J. M. Shafritz & A. Hyde (Eds.) (1992) *Classics of public administration* (3rd ed.). Bellmont, CA: Wadsworth.

Aron, J. B. (1969). *The quest for regional cooperation: A study of the New York metropolitan regional council.* Berkeley: University of California Press.

Asefa, S., & Huang, W. (Eds.). (1994). *Human capital and economic development.* Kalamazoo, MI: W.E. Upjohn Institute for Employment Research.

Ashtead, J. (2001, November 20). Milton Freidman attacks politicians. *Pravda,* Retrieved September 3, 2003, from http://english.pravda.ru/economics/2001/11/20/ 21390.html.

Aucoin, P. (1990). Administrative reform in public management: Paradigms, principles, paradoxes, and pendulums. *Governance, 3*(2), 115-137.

Audretsch, D. B., Weigand, J., & Weigand, C. (2002). The impact of the SBIR on creating entrepreneurial behavior. *Economic Development Quarterly, 16*(1), 32-38.

Babbie, E. (2001). *The practice of social research* (9th ed.). Belmont, CA: Wadson/Thomson Learning.

Bainbridge, J. (2005). Intel will expand again. *The Gazette.*

Banfield, E. C. (1968). *The unheavenly city.* Little, Brown & Co.: Boston.

Bartik, T. J, & Bingham, R. D. (1997). Can economic development programs be evaluated? In R. D. Bingham & R. Mier (Eds.), *Dilemmas of Urban Economic Development.* Thousand Oaks, CA: Sage.

Bartik, T. J. (1985). Business location decisions in the United States: Estimates of the effects of unionization, taxes, and other characteristics of States. Journal of Business and Economic Statistics, 3, 14-22.

Bartik, T. J. (1991). *Who benefits from state and local economic development policies?* Kalamazoo, MI: W. E. Upjohn Institute for Employment Research.

Bartik, T. J. (1994). Better evaluation is needed for economic development programs to thrive. *Economic Development Quarterly, 8*(2), 99-106.

Bartik, T. J. (1994). Jobs, productivity, and local economic development: What implications does economic research have for the role of government? *National Tax Journal, 47*(4), 847-861.

Bartik, T. J. (2002). *Evaluating the impacts of local economic development policies on local economic outcomes: What has been done and what is doable?* Paper presented at OECD Local Economic and Employment Development Programme, Vienna, Austria.

Bartik, T., & Smith, V. K. (1987). Urban amenities and public policy. In E. S. Mills (Ed.), *Handbook of Regional and Urban Economics* (Vol. II) (pp.1205-1254). St. Louis, MO: Elsevier Science Publishers, B. V.

Barzelay, M. (2001). *The new public management: Improving research and policy dialogue.* Berkeley, CA: University of California Press:.

Basker, E. 2007. The Causes and Consequences of Wal-Mart's Growth. *Journal of Economic Perspectives,* 21(3): 177-198.

Basolo, V. & Huang, C. (2001). Cities and economic development: Does the city limits story still apply? *Economic Development Quarterly,* 15(4), 327-339.

Baum, D. N. (1987). The economic effects of state and local business incentives. *Land Economics, 63*(4), 348-360.

Becker, G. S. (1970). *Human capital: A theoretical and empirical analysis, with special reference to education.* New York: National Bureau of Economic Research.

Bee, E. (2002). Turning community inventions into sustainable technology clusters. *Economic Development Journal,* (Spring), 15-22.

Behn, R. D. (2001). *Rethinking democratic accountability.* Washington, D.C.: The Brookings Institution.

Behrens, Z. (2010, April 5). *City's Internet Business Tax has LegalZoom in a Bind.* Retrieved from http://laist.com/2010/04/05/citys_internet_business_tax_as_lega.php

Belsely, D. A., Kuh, E., & Welsch, R. E. (1980). *Regression diagnostics: Identifying influential data and sources of collinearity.* New York: John Wiley & Sons.

Bennett, E., & Gatz, C. (2008). *Louisville, Kentucky: A restoring prosperity case study.* Washington, D.C.: The Brookings Institution.

Benson, B. L., Johnson, R. N. (1986) The lagged impact of state and local taxes on economic activity and political behavior. *Economic Inquiry, 24,* 389-401.

Benton, J. E., & Gamble, D. (1984). City/county consolidation and economies of scale: Evidence from a time series analysis in Jacksonville, Florida. *Social Science Quarterly, 65,* 190-98.

Bernstein, A. (2000). Backlash: Behind the anxiety over globalization. *Business Week,* April 24, 2000, 38-44.

Bingham, R. D., Bowen, W. M. (1994). The performance of state economic development programs: An impact evaluation. *Policy Studies Journal, 22*(3), 501-513.

Birch, David. (1987). *Job creation in America: How our smallest companies put the most people to work.* Detroit, MI: Free Press.

Birch, Del. (2009). Eyes wide open: A practical guide to business retention. *Public Management 91*(7), 6-8.

Bish, R. (2001). Local government amalgamations: Discredited nineteenth-century ideals alive in the twenty-first century. *C.D. Howe Institute Commentary* 150 (March 2001).

Bish, R. L. (1971). *The public economy of metropolitan areas.* Chicago: Markham Series in Public Policy Analysis.

Bizjak, Tony, & Kasler, Dale, & Lillis, Ryan. (2012, March 1). Officials put public share of Sacramento arena at nearly $265 million. *The Sacramento Bee.* Retrieved from http://www.sacbee.com/2012/03/01/4302313/officials-put-public-share-of.html

Blackwell, M., Cobb, S., Weinberg, D. (2002). The economic impact of educational institutions: issues and methodology. *Economic Development Quarterly, 16* (1), 88-95.

Blair, J. P. (1995). *Local economic development: Analysis and practice.* Thousand Oaks, CA: Sage Publications.

Blair, J. P., & Premus, R. (1987). Major factors in industrial location: A review. *Economic Development Quarterly, 1*(1), 72-85.

Blair, J. P., & Premus, R. (1987). Major features in industrial location: A review. *Urban Affairs Quarterly, 20*(1), 64-77.

Blakely, E. & Bradshaw, T. (2002). *Planning local economic development* (3rd ed.). Thousand Oaks, CA: Sage Publications, Inc.

Blakely, E. J., & Bradshaw, T. K. (1992). State economic development promotions and incentives: A comparison of state efforts and strategies. Sacramento, CA: California Department of Commerce.

Bland, R. (1989) *A revenue guide for local government.* Washington, D.C.: International City/County Management Association.

Blomquist, W., & Parks, R. B. (1995). Fiscal service, and political impacts of Indianapolis-Marion County's Unigov. *Publius: The Journal of Federalism, 25*(4), 37-54.

Boston Consulting Group and The Initiative for a Competitive Inner City. (1998). The business case for pursuing retail opportunities in the inner city. Boston: Author.

Bowman, A. O'M. (1988). Competition for economic development among Southeastern cities. *Urban Affairs Quarterly 4*, 511-527.

Bradbury, K. L., Kodrzycki, K., & Tannenwald, R. (1997). The effects of state and local public policies on economic development: An overview. *New England Economic Review,* (March), 1-12.

Bradbury, K., Downs, A., & Small, K. (1982). *Urban decline and the future of American cities.* Washington, D.C.: The Brookings Institute.

Braddock, D. (1995). The use of regional economic models in conducting net present value analysis of development programs. *International Journal of Public Administration, 18*(1), 59-82.

Bradshaw, T. K., & Blakely, E. (1999). What are 'third wave' economic development efforts? From incentives to industrial policy. *Economic Development Quarterly, 13*(3), 229-244.

Brammer, R., & Tomasik, J. (1995). Retail potential analysis for local economic developers. *Economic Development Review, 13*(2), 32-42.

Browning, E. S. (1993, August 19). Thomson's RCA unit is no TV bonanza–French company narrows losses at U.S. acquisition. *The Wall Street Journal,* p. A7.

Buchanan, P. (2003). Is the neoconservative moment over? *The American Conservative.* June 16, 2003.

Buncombe County, North Carolina (1998). *Economic development incentive policy.*

Burke, E. (1973). *Reflections on the revolution in France,* with Thomas Paine's *The rights of man.* Garden City, NY: Anchor Books.

Burstein, M. L., & Rolnick, A. J. (1995). The economic war among the states: Congress should end the economic war among the states. *The Region.* Retrieved December 31, 2003, from http://news.mpr.org/features/199605/01_wittl_econwar/ ewrolnick.htm

Burstein, M. L., & Rolnick, A. J. (1996). Congress should end the economic war for sports and other businesses. *The Region, 10*(2), 35-36.

Buss, T. F. (2001). The effect of state tax incentives on economic growth and firm location decisions: An overview of the literature. *Economic Development Quarterly, 15*(1), 90-105.

Butler, S. (1981). *Enterprise zones: Greenlining the inner cities.* New York: Universe Books.

Byrns, R. T., & Stone, G. W. (1993). *Microeconomics* (5th ed.), New York, NY: Harper Collins College Publishers.

Cable, G., & Feiock, R. (1998). The adoption of state economic development programs: An event history analysis. *The Journal of Political Science, 26,* 3-15.

Calnan, C. (2003, September 26). Jacksonville, Fla., panel rejects Wal-Mart plan. *Knight Ridder Tribune Business News.* Washington: p. 1.

Calzonetti, F. J., & Walker, R. T. (1991). Factores affecting industrial location decisions: A survey approach. In H. W. Herzog, Jr. and A. M. Schlottmann, (Eds.), *Industry location and public policy.* Knoxville, TN: University of Tennessee Press.

Canada, E. P. (1999). Rocketing Out of the Twilight Zone: Gaining Strategic Insights From Business Retention. *Economic Development Review, 16*(2), 15.

Capps, O., and J.M. Griffin. "Effect of a Mass Merchandiser on Traditional Food Retailers." *Journal of Food Distribution* 29 (1998): 1-7. Print.

Carayannis, E. G., & Alexander, J. (2000). Revisiting SEMATECH: Profiling public- and private-sector cooperation. *Engineering Management Journal, 12*(4), 33-43.

Careley, D. (1977). *City government and urban problems: An introduction to urban politics.* Englewood Cliffs, NJ: Prentice-Hall, Inc.

Carr, J. B., & Feiock, R. C. (1999). Metropolitan government and economic development. *Urban Affairs Review, 34* (January), 476-488.

Charney, A. H. (1983). Intraurban manufacturing location decisions and local tax differentials. *Journal of Urban Economics, 14,* 184-205.

City of Colorado Springs. (2012). Contacts, fast facts, and answers.

City of Richland. (2005). *Business retention and expansion: 2005 survey analysis and report.* Richland, WA.

Clarke, S. E. (1998). Economic development roles in American cities: A contextual analysis of shifting partnership arrangements. In N. Walzer & B. D. Jacobs (Eds.), *Public-private partnerships for local economic development.* Westport, CT: Praeger.

Clarke, S., & Gaile, G. (1992). The next wave: Postfederal local economic development strategies. *Economic Development Quarterly, 6*(2), 187-198.

Clingermayer, J. C., & Feiock, R. C. (1995). Council views toward targeting of development policy benefits. *The Journal of Politics, 57*(2), 508-520.

Cohen, N. (2000). *Business location decision-making and the cities: Bringing companies back.* Washington, D.C.: Center on Urban and Metropolitan Policy, The Brookings Institution.

Colman, W. G. (1989). *State and local government and public-private partnerships: A policy issues handbook.* Westport, CT: Greenwood Press, Inc.

Cooper, M. (2011, December 14). With states desperate to keep jobs, companies have upper hand, report shows. *New York Times.* Page A23.

Corvin, A. (2013, May 27). State, City Foresaw $93M for Nike Deal. *The Columbian.* Retrieved from http://www.columbian.com/news/2013/may/27/state-city-foresaw-93m-for-nike-deal/#.UlcP_2RKl-o

Coughlin, C., & Segev, E. (2000) Location determinants of new foreign-owned manufacturing plants. *Journal of Regional Science, 40*(2), 323-35.

Coughlin, C., Terza, J. V., & Arromdee, V. (1989). State characteristics and the location of foreign direct investment within the United States. *The Review of Economics and Statistics, 73*(4), 675-683.

Coughlin, C., Terza, J. V., & Cartwright, P. A. (1987). An examination of state foreign export promotion and manufacturing exports. *Journal of Regional Science, 27*(3), 439-449.

County and City Data Book: 1994 Edition [Data file]. Washington, DC: U.S. Census Bureau.

County and City Data Book: 2000 Edition [Data file]. Washington, DC: U.S. Census Bureau.

Covel, S. (January 10, 2008). Moving across the country to cut costs: Cheaper wages, expenses in North Carolina help Industrial Motion regain financial footing. *Wall Street Journal,* B4.

Culp, D., Finn, P., Knox, W. J., Miller, T., & Tilney, J. S. (1980). Evaluation of the Community Economic Development Program: Long-term evaluation and final report. Cambridge, MA.: Abt Associates, Inc.

Cummings, S., & Killmer, M. (1997). Urban poverty, public policy, and the underclass. In R. K. Vogel (Ed.), *Handbook of research on urban politics and policy in the United States.* (pp. 306-323). Westport, CT: Greenwood Press.

De Figueiredo, R. J., Meyer-Doyle, P., & Rawley, E. (2013). Inherited agglomeration effects in hedge fund spawns. *Strategic Management Journal, 34*(7), 843-862.

Dewar, M. E. (1998). Why state and local economic development programs cause so little development. *Economic Development Quarterly, 12*(1), 68-87.

Dietz, F. (1998). Technology development drives state economies. *Mechanical Engineering, 120*(4), 36-39.

Digby, M. (1983). Evaluating state industrial development programs. *Public Administration Quarterly, 6*(Winter), 434-449.

Dillan, D. (1999). *Mail and Internet surveys : The tailored design method,* (2nd ed.), New York: John Wiley and Sons.

DiLorenzo, T. J. (1983). Economic competition and political competition: an empirical note. *Public Choice, 40,* 203-209.

Drucker, P. F., Michaels, J. W., & Gall, N. (1983). Schumpeter and Keynes' Wagnerian vision. *Forbes, 131*(11), 124-132.

Dunne, T., Roberts, M. J., & Samuelson, L. (1989). Plant turnover and gross employment flows in the U.S. manufacturing sector. *Journal of Labor Economics, 7*(1), 48-72.

Economic Development 1999 [Data file]. Washington, DC: International City/County Management Association.

Economic Development 2004 [Data file]. Washington, DC: International City/County Management Association.

Economic Development 2009 [Data file]. Washington, DC: International City/County Management Association.

Economic Development Administration. (2002). *Enhancing community success in attracting private capital investment and lucrative job opportunities: Interim investments guide.* Washington, DC: U.S. Government Printing Office.

Ecoparks gaining momentum. (2001, January). *Civil Engineering, 71*(1), 19.

Eisenschitz, A. (1993). Business involvement in the community: Counting the spoons or economic renewal? In D. Fasenfest (Ed.), *Community economic development: Policy formation in the U.S. and U.K.* (pp. 141-156). London: MacMillan.

Eisinger, P. (1988). *The rise of the entrepreneurial state: State and local economic development policy in the United States.* Madison, WI: University of Wisconsin Press.

Eisinger, P. (1990). Do American states do industrial policy? *British Journal of Political Science, 20*(4), 509-535.

Eisinger, P. (1995). State economic development in the 1990s: Politics and policy learning. *Economic Development Quarterly, 9*(2), 146-158.

Enrich, P. D. (1996). Saving the states from themselves: Commerce clause constraints on state tax incentives for business. *Harvard Law Review, 110*(2), p. 377.

Erickson, R. A., & Friedman, S. W. (1989). *Enterprise zones: An evaluation of state government policies.* Washington, D.C.: U.S. Department of Commerce, Economic Development Administration, Technical Assistance and Research Division.

Feiock, R. C. (1985). *Local government policy and urban economic development.* Unpublished doctoral dissertation. University of Kansas, Lawerence.

Feiock, R. C. (1987). Urban economic development: Local government strategies and their effects. In S. S. Nagel (Ed.), *Research in Public Policy Analysis and Management.* London: JAI Press, Ltd.

Feiock, R. C. (1988). Local government economic development incentives and urban economic growth. *Public Administration Quarterly, 12*, 140-150.

Feiock, R. C. (1991). The effects of economic development policy on local economic growth. *American Journal of Political Science, 35*(3), 643-655.

Feiock, R., & Rowland, C. K. (1990). Environmental regulation and economic development: The movement of chemical production among states. *The Western Political Quarterly, 43*(3), 561-576.

Fisher, P. C., & Peters, A. H. (1998). *Industrial incentives: Competition among American states and cities*. Kalamazoo, MI: W. E. Upjohn Institute for Employment Research.

Fisher, R. C. (1997). The effects of state and local public services on economic development. *New England Economic Review, 5,* 53-83.

Fitzgerald, J., & Leigh, N. G. (2009). *Economic revitalization: Cases and strategies for city and suburb*. Thousand Oaks, CA: Sage Publications.

Fitzgerald, J., & McGregor, A. (1993). Labor-community initiatives in worker training in the United States and United Kingdom. *Economic Development Quarterly, 7*(2), 172-182.

Flores, H. (1999). An essay on the state and the state of Latino politics. *Urban News, 13,* 1-7.

Florida, R. (2002). *The rise of the creative class: And how it's transforming work, leisure, community and everyday life*. New York: Basic Books.

Fortune, Inc. (1977). *Facility location decisions*. New York: p. 6.

Fosler, R. S. (1992). State economic development policy: The emerging paradigm. *Economic Development Quarterly, 6*(1), 3-13.

Fox, W., & Murray, M. (1991). The effects of local government public policies on the location of business activity. Chapter 6 in H. Herzog, Jr. and A. Schlottmann, (Eds.), *Industry location and public policy* (pp. 97-119). Knoxville, Tn: University of Tennessee Press.

Franklin, R. S. (2003, March). Domestic migration across regions, divisions, and states: 1995 to 2000. (Census 2000 Special Report CENSR-7). Washington, D.C.: U.S. Census Bureau.

Frieden, B. (1989). The downtown job puzzle. *Public Interest, 97,* 71-86.

Friedman, J. Gerlowski, D. A., & Silberman, J. (1992). What attracts foreign multinational corporations? Evidence from branch plant location in the United States. *Journal of Regional Science, 32,* 403-418.

Friedman, M. (1948). A monetary and fiscal framework for economic stability. *The American Economic Review, 38*(3), 245-264.

Friedman, N. (2013, April 13). Beaverton Hopes Repaired Relationship with Nike Will Help City's Future. *The Oregonian*. Oregon Live. Retrieved from http://www.oregonlive.com/beaverton/index.ssf/2013/04/beaverton_hopes_repaired_relat.html

Frisken, F. (1991). The contributions of metropolitan government to the success of Toronto's public transit system. *Urban Affairs Quarterly, 27*(2), 268-292.

Fry, E. H. (1998). *The expanding role of state and local government in U.S. foreign affairs*. New York: Council of Foreign Relations Press.

Fujita, M., Krugman, P. R., & Venables, A. (1999). Spatial Economy: Cities, Regions and International   Trade. *MIT Press*.

Fusfeld, D. R. (1999). *The age of the economist* (8th ed.). Reading, MA: Addison Wesley.

Gladwell, Malcom. (2011, August 18). 'Psychic Benefits' and the NBA Lockout. *Grantland*. Retrieved from http://www.grantland.com/story/_/id/6874079/ psychic-benefits-nba-lockout

Glaeser, E. L., Kallal, H. D., Scheinkman, J. A., & Shleifer, A. (1992). Growth in Cities. *Journal of Political Economy, 100*(6), 1126-1152.

Goetz, E. G. (1994). Expanding possibilities in local development policy: An examination of U.S. cities. *Political Research Quarterly, 47*(1), 85-109.

Goldsmith, M. (1999). Welfare industry's failure a literal shame. *The Australian Financial Review*, February 2, 1999.

Goldsmith, S. (1999). *The entreprenuerial city: A how-to handbook for urban innovators.* Manhattan Institute for Policy Research: New York, New York.

Goldsmith, W. W., & Blakely, E. J. (1992). *Separate societies: Poverty and inequality in U.S. cities.* Philadelphia: Temple University Press.

Goldstein, M. I. (1985). Choosing the right site. *Industry Week, 15*, 57-60.

Goss, E. P. (1999). Do business tax incentives contribute to a divergence in economic growth? *Economic Development Quarterly, 13*(3), 217-228.

Goss, E. P., & Phillips, J. M. (1997). The effect of state economic development agency spending on state income and employment growth. *Economic Development Quarterly, 11*(1), 88-96.

Gottlieb, P. (1994). Amenities as economic development tools: Is there enough evidence? *Economic Development Quarterly, 8*, 270-285.

Gottlieb, P. (1995). Residential amenities, firm location and economic development. *Urban Studies, 32*(9), 270-285.

Granger, M. D., & Blomquist, G. C. (1999). Evaluating the influence of amenities on the location of manufacturing establishments in urban areas. *Urban Studies, 36*(11), 1859-1874.

Grant, D. S. II, & Wallace, M. (1994). The political economy of manufacturing growth and decline across the American states, 1979-1985. *Social Forces, 73*(1), 33-63.

Green, G. P., Fleischmann, A., & Kwong, T. M. (1996). The effectiveness of local economic development policies in the 1980s. *Social Science Quarterly, 77*(3), 609-625.

Grossman, J., & Andres, C. (2000). Ten Myths of Business Retention: How to Get Your Business Retention and Expansion Budget Approved. *Economic Development Review, 17*(1), 65.

Gruidl, J. & Walzer, N. (1992). Does local economic development policy affect community employment growth? *Journal of the Community Development Society, 23*(2), 53-65.

Hamlin, R. and Lyons, T. (1996). *Economy without walls: Managing local development in a restructuring world.* Westport, CT: Praeger.

Haug, P. (1991). The location decisions and operations of high technology organizations in Washington state. *Regional Studies, 25*, 525-541.

Hawkins, C.V. (2011). Local economic development joint ventures and metropolitan networks. *Public Affairs Quarterly, Spring,* 59-92.

Hays, R. A. (1997). Housing. in R. K. Vogel (Ed.), *Handbook of research on urban politics and policy in the United States,* Westport, CT: Greenwood Press.

Heckman, J. J. (2000, February). *Policies to foster human capital.* JCPR Working Paper No. 154. Chicago, Il: Northwestern University/University of Chicago Joint Center for Poverty Research.

Heilman, W. (2009). Intel completes sale of Colorado Springs manufacturing plant. *The Gazette.*

Heilman, W. (2010). A taxing question: Intel gone, from the Springs expands in Oregon,   Arizona. *The Gazette.*

Hekman, J. S., & Greenstein, R. (1985). Factors affecting manufacturing location in North Carolina and the South Atlantic. In D. Whittington, (Ed.), *High hopes for high tech,* 147-72. Chapel Hill, NC: University of North Carolina Press.

Hicks, M. J. (2006). What is the local: WAL-MART EFFECT?. *Economic Development Journal, 5*(3), 23-31.

Hill, C. W. (2002). *Global Business Today.* New York: McGraw-Hill Irwin.

Hill, L. B. (2002). The ombudsman revisited: Thirty years of Hawaiian experience. *Public Administration Review, 62*(1), 24-41.

Hinkley, S., & Hsu, F. (2000). Minding the candy store: State audits of economic development. Flint, MI: Charles Stewart Mott Foundation.

Holmes, S. 1998, December 9. "College schedules for night workers: Louisville program saves UPS jobs and promotes education, *New York Times*, (December 9, 1998) A26.

Hood, C. (1991) A public management for all seasons? *Public Administration, 69*(1), 3-19.

Hoppes, R. B. (1991). Regional versus industrial shift-share analysis–with help from the Lotus spreadsheet. *Economic Development Quarterly, 5*(3), 258-267.

Hotchkiss, J. L., Sjoquist, D. L., & Zobay, S. M. (1999). Employment impact of inner-city development projects: The case of underground Atlanta. *Urban Studies, 36*(7), 1079-1093.

Humberger, E. (1983). Business location decisions and cities. An information bulletin of the Community and Economic Development Task Force of the Urban Consortium. Washington, DC: U.S. Department of Housing and Urban Development.

Ihlanfeldt, K. R. (1995). Ten principles for state tax incentives. *Economic Development Quarterly, 9*(4), 339-356.

Ihlanfeldt, K. R., & Sjoquist, D. L. (2001). Conducting an analysis of Georgia's economic development tax incentive program. *Economic Development Quarterly, 15*(3), 217-229.

Ihlanfeldt, K. R., Sjoquist, D. L. (1991) The role of space in determining the occupations of black and white workers. *Regional Science and Urban Economics, 21*, 295-316.

Imbroscio, D. L. (1998). Reformulating urban regime theory: The division of labor between state and market reconsidered. *Journal of Urban Affairs, 20*, 233-248.

International Herald Tribune. (2006). Nike and Oregon city hope to get along again. *The New York Times*. Retrieved from http://www.nytimes.com/2006/10/02/business/worldbusiness/02iht-nike.2998782.html?_r=0

Internet Business Tax Ordinance - Economic Summary. (n.d.). Retrieved from http://www.lachamber.com/clientuploads/JBG_committee/030810_InternetBusiness.pdf

Jackson, K. (2012, February 15). Governor approves KOZ extension. *The Times-Tribune*. Page A4.

Jacobs, J. (1961). The Death and Life of Great American Cities. New York: Vintage.

Janoski, D. (2005, December 4). TJ Maxx Story Unhappy One for Township. *The Times Leader.* Page 1A.

Jones, B. D. (1990). Public policies and economic growth in the American states. *The Journal of Politics, 52*(1), 219-233.

Jones, B. D. (1990). Public policies and economic growth in the American states. *The Journal of Politics, 52*(1), 219-233.

Jones, J. 2000, January 22. UPS recruits workers in Eastern Kentucky, *The Louisville Courier Journal*, p.B1.

Jones, S. A., Marshall, A. R., & Weisbrod, G. E. (1985, September). Business impacts of state enterprise zones. Paper presented the U.S. Small Business Administration, Washington, D.C.

Kain, J. (1992). The spatial mismatch hypothesis: Three decades later. *Housing Policy Debate, 3*, 371-460

Kasabach, P. (2011). Price incentives based on proximity to urban areas. *NJBIZ* *24*(17), 17.

Kee, J. E. (1994). Benefit-cost analysis in program evaluation, in J. S. Wholey, H. P. Hatry, & K. E. Newcomer (Eds.), *Handbook of Practical Program Evaluation,* San Franscisco: Jossey-Bass.

Kennedy, M. (1984). The fiscal crisis of the city. In M. Smith (Ed.), *Cities in transformation: Class, capital, and the state.* Newbury Park, CA: Sage Publications.

Kettl, D. F. (2000). *The global public management revolution: a report on the transformation of governance.* Washington, DC: Brookings Institute.

Keynes, J. M. (1936). *The general theory of employment, interest and money.* New York: Harcourt, Brace & Company.

Kirk, R. (1978). *The conservative mind: From Burke to Eliot* (6th ed.). Chicago: Regnery/ Gateway.

Kish, M. (2013, August 9). Nike Readies Last Touches of a Giant Real Estate Play. *Portland Business Journal.* Retrieved from http://www.bizjournals.com/ portland/print-edition/2013/08/09/nike-readies-giant-real-estate-play. html?page=all

Kleinberg, B. (1995). *Urban America in transformation.* Thousand Oaks, CA: Sage Publications, Inc.

Kleniewski, N. (1989). Urban economic development: a new battleground. *Dissent, 36*(1), 15-17.

Klepper, S., & Sleeper, S. (2002). *Entry by spinoffs.* Jena, Germany: Max-Planck-Inst. for Research into Economic Systems, Evolutionary Economics Group.

Klitgaard, R., & Treverton, G. F. (2003). *Assessing partnerships: New forms of collaboration.* Arlington, VA: IBM Endowment for The Business of Government.

Kodrzycki, Y. (1997). Training programs for displaced workers: What do they accomplish? *New England Economic Review,* (May), 39-57.

Koven, S. & Strother, S. (2002). Saving jobs in Louisville, Kentucky. *Economic Development Journal, 1*(1), 19-22.

Koven, S. G. (1988). *Ideological budgeting.* New York: Praeger Publishers.

Koven, S. G., & Lyons, T. S. (2010). *Economic development strategies for state and local practice.* Washington, DC: International City/County Management Association.

Koven, S. G., & Shelley, M. C. (1989). Public policy effects on net urban migration. *Policy Studies Journal, 17*(4), 705-718.

Kristol, I. (1999). *Neo-Conservatism: The autobiography of an idea.* Chicago: Ivan R. Dee, Inc.

Kristol, I. (2003). The neoconservative persuasion. *The Weekly Standard, 8*(47), 23-25.

Ladd, H. F., & Yinger, J. (1991). *America's ailing cities: Fiscal health and the design of urban policy.* Baltimore, MD: Johns Hopkins University Press.

Ladd, J., & Ladd, H. F. (1989). The determinants of state assistance to central cities, *National Tax Journal, 42*(4), 413-428.

Levy, J. M. (1990). What local economic developers actually do: Location quotients versus press releases. *APA Journal, Spring,* 153-160. Linder, S. H. (1999). Coming to terms with the public-private partnership: A grammar of multiple meanings. *The American Behavioral Scientist, 43*(1), 35-51.

Lewis, P. G. (2002). Offering incentives for new development: The role of city social status, politics, and local growth experiences. *Journal of Urban Affairs, 24*(2), 143-157.

Lewis, P. J. (1996). *Shaping suburbia: How political institutions organize urban development.* Pittsburgh: University of Pittsburgh Press.

Lind, D. A., Marchal, W. G., & Wathen, S. A. (2003). *Basic statistics for business and economics* (4th ed.). New York: McGraw-Hill.

Litan, R. E. (2000). The "globalization" challenge: The U.S. role in shaping world trade and investment. *The Brookings Review,* Spring 2000, 35-37.

Locke, J. (1980). *Second treatise of government.* Indianapolis, IN: Hackett Publishing Company.

Logan, J. R. (2002). *Regional divisions dampen '90s prosperity: New Census data show economic gains vary by region.* Albany, NY: Lewis Mumford Center for Comparative Urban and Regional Research.

Lösch, A. (1964). *The economics of location.* New Haven, CN: Yale University Press.

Loudat, T. & Kasturi, P. (2008). Economic Impact of Transient Vacation Rentals (TVRs) on Maui County. Retrieved from http://www.ramaui.com/UserFiles/File/Governent_Affairs/EconomicImpactTVRsJan2008.pdf.

Louisiana Department of Economic Development. (2003). Enterprise zone program: the facts. [brochure]. Baton Rouge, LA: Author.

Lowe, E. A. (2001). *Eco-industrial park handbook for Asian developing countries.* A report to Asian Development Bank, Environment Department. Emeryville, CA: RPP International.

Luger, M. I. (1987). The states and industrial development: Program mix and policy effectiveness. In J. M. Quigley (Ed.), *Perspectives on Local Public Finance and Public Policy,* Vol. 3. Greenwich, CT: JAI Press.

Luger, M. I., & Goldstein, H. A. (1991). *Technology in the garden: Research parks and regional economic development.* Chapel Hill, NC: University of North Carolina Press.

Luke, J., Ventriss, C., Reed, B.J., & Reed, C. (1988). *Managing economic development.* San Francisco: Jossey-Bass Publishers.

Lynch, C. (2004, February 16). Louisville to nurture its businesses. *The Courier-Journal*, pp. F1, F2.

Lynch, R. G. (1995). *Do state and local tax incentives work?* Washington, D.C.: Economic Policy Institute.

Lyon, L., Felice, L., Perryman, M., & Parker, E. (1981). Community power and population increase: An empirical test of the growth machine model. *American Journal of Sociology, 86*, 1387-1400.

Mahtesian, C. (1994, November). Romancing the smokestack. *Governing,* 36-40.

Maki, W. R., & Lichty, R. W. (2000) *Urban regional economics: concepts, tools, applications.* Ames, Iowa: Iowa State University Press.

Malecki, E. J. (1984). High technology and local economic development. *Journal of the American Planning Association, 50*(3), 262-270.

Manufacturing jobs disappearing in economic slowdown. (2001, July 19). *The Oakridger*, p. B1.

Marlin, M. R. (1990). The effectiveness of economic development subsidies. *Economic Development Quarterly, 4*(1), 15-22.

Marshall, A. (1920). *Principles of economics, 8th ed.* London: Macmillan.

Mattare, M., Ashley-Cotleur, C., & Masciocchi, C. M. (2012). A new small city business incubator: A business community's attitudes and desired services. *Journal of Strategic Innovation and Sustainability 8*(1), 46-56.

Matz, D., & Ledebur, L. (1986). The state role in economic development. In N. Walzer & D. Chicoine (Eds.), *Financing economic development in the 1980s: Issues and trends.* (pp. 85-102). New York: Praeger Publishers.

Maumbe, K. (2006). *Application of the conversion and tracking models in measuring the effectiveness of Travel Michigan's 2003 travel advertising campaign.* Unpublished doctoral dissertation.Michigan State University, East Lansing.

Maynard, M. (2012, October 01). Feds slam wisconsin public-private partnership for economic development. *McClatchy-Tribune Business News* Retrieved from http://search.proquest.com/docview/1081663419?accountid=8459

McCarthy, L. (2000). *Competitive regionalism: Beyond individual competition.* (Reviews of Economic Development Literature and Practice: No. 2). Washington, D.C.: U.S. Economic Development Association.

McDonald, J. F. (1983). An economic analysis of local inducements for business. *Journal of Urban Economics, 13,* 322-336.

Metropolitan College. *Opening the door to a brighter future.* (Louisville, KY: Pamphlet. n.d).

Metzger, J. T. (1996). The theory and practice of equity planning: An annotated bibliography. *Journal of Planning Literature, 11*(1), 112-126.

Meyerson, H. (2001). California's progressive mosaic. *The American Prospect, 12*(11), 17-23.

Microenterprise Journal (2003, December 31). About us. Retrieved from: http://www.microenterprisejournal.com/

Mikesell, J. 1995. *Fiscal administration: Analysis and applications for the public sector,* (4th ed.). Belmont, CA: Wadsworth Publishing Company.

Milward, H. B., & Newman, H. H. (1989). State incentive packages and the industrial location decision. *Economic Development Quarterly, 3*(3), 203-222.

Moe, R. C. (1987) Exploring the limits of privatization, in J. M. & Hyde, A. eds. (1992) *Classics of public administration* (3rd ed.). Bellmont, CA: Wadsworth.

Montesquieu, C. S. B. (1914). *The spirit of laws.* London: G. Bell & Sons, Ltd.

Monticello Main Street, Inc. (n.d.) *Facade improvement matching grants available.* Retrieved January 31, 2004, from http://www.monticellomainstreet.org/facade_improvement.htm

Morfessis, I., & Malachuk, D. (2011). Economic development in the post-crisis era. *Economic Development Journal, 10*(3), 19-29.

Morgan, W. E. (1967). *Taxes and the location of industry.* Boulder, CO: University of Colorado Press.

Mueller, D. C. (1989). *Public choice II: A revised edition of public choice.* Cambridge, UK: Cambridge University Press.

Muller T., & Humstone, E. (1996). What happened when Wal-Mart came to town? A report on three Iowa communities with a statistical analysis of seven Iowa counties. Washington: National Trust for Historic Preservation.

Muller, T. (1976). *Assessing the impact of development.* Washington, DC: U.S. Department of Housing and Urban Development.

Mullin, S. P. (2002). *Public-private partnerships and state and local economic development: leveraging private investment.* Washington, DC: Economic Development Administration.

Murray (1984). *Losing ground.* New York: Basic Books.

Nathan, R. P., & Adams, C. (1977). *Revenue sharing: The second round.* Washington, DC: Brookings Institution.

National Performance Review. (1993).

Neumark, David, Junfu Zhang, and Stephen Ciccarella. "The Effects of Wal-Mart on Local Labor Markets." *Journal of Urban Economics* 63.2 (2008): 405-30. Print.

Newman, R. J. (1983). Industry migration and growth in the South. *Review of Economics and Statistics, 65,* 76-86.

Noll, Roger, & Zimbalist, Andrew. (1997). Sports, Jobs, & Taxes: Are New Stadiums Worth the Cost? *Brookings.* Retrieved from http://www.brookings.edu/articles/1997/summer_taxes_noll.aspx

Novak, M. (1982). *The spirit of democratic capitalism.* New York: Simon and Schuster.

O'hUallacháin, B., & Satterthwaite, M. A. (1992). Sectoral growth patterns at the metropolitan level: An evaluation of economic development incentives. *Journal of Urban Economics, 31,* 25-58.

Orfield, B., (1997) *Micropolitics: a regional agenda for community and stability.* Washington, D.C.: Brookings Institute and the Lincoln Land Institute.

Palmer, J. (2003). Data center breaks ground in Cedar Falls, Iowa, industrial park. *Waterloo Courier,* p. B1.

Papageorgiou, N. A., Parwada, J. T., & Tan, K. M. (2012). Where do Hedge Fund Managers Come from? Past Employment Experience and Managerial Performance. In *SSRN Working Paper Series.* Rochester: Social Science Research Network. Retrieved September 11, 2014, from ABI/INFORM Complete; ProQuest Research Library.

Papke, J. A. (1990, August). The role of market-based public policy in economic development and urban revitalization: A retrospective analysis and appraisal of the Indiana Enterprise Zone program. Year Three Report prepared for The Enterprise Zone Board, Indiana Department of Commerce.

Papke, L. E. (1994). Tax policy and urban development: Evidence from the Indiana Enterprise Zone program. *Journal of Public Economics, 54,* 37-49.

Parachuri, Srikanth, Joel A.C. Baum, and David Potere. "The Wal-Mart Effect: Wave of Destruction or Creative Destruction?" *Economic Geography* 85.2 (2009): 209-36. Print.

Parks, R. B. (1985). Metropolitan structure and systematic performance: the case of police service delivery. In K. Hanf & T. A. J. Toonen (Eds.), *Policy Implementation in Federal and Unitary States.* Netherlands: Dordrecht.

Paruchuri, S., Baum, J. C., & Potere, D. (2009). The Wal-Mart Effect: Wave of Destruction or Creative Destruction? *Economic Geography, 85*(2), 209-236.

Pennsylvania House on Appropriations (2012, February 3). Senate Bill 1237, Printers No. 1918.

Pennsylvania Legislative Budget and Finance Committee (2009, July 9). *An Evaluation of The Keystone Opportunity Zone (KOZ) Program.*

Peters, A. H., & Fisher, P. S. (1997). Do high unemployment states offer the biggest business incentives? Results for eight states using the 'Hypothetical Firm' method. *Economic Development Quarterly, 11*(2), 107-122.

Peterson, P. (1981). *City limits.* Chicago: The University of Chicago Press.

Phillips, J. M., & Goss, E. P. (1995). The effects of state and local taxes on economic development: A meta-analysis. *Southern Economic Journal, 62*, 297-316.

Pitcoff, W., & Widrow, R. (1998) The National Congress for Community Economic Development: A voice for CDCs. Retrieved November 5, 2003, from http://www.nhi.org/online/issues/100/ncced.html

Plaut, T., & Pluta, J. (1983). Business climate, taxes and expenditures and state industrial growth in the United States. *Southern Economic Journal, 50*, 99-119.

Political Philosophy. The Internet Encyclopedia of Philosophy. Retrieved on October 20, 2003 from: http://www.utm.edu/research/iep/p/polphil.htm

Porter, M. E. (1998). Clusters and competition: New agendas for companies, governments, and institutions. In M. Porter (Ed.), *On Competition* (pp. 197-287). Boston: Harvard Business School Press.

Porter, M. E. (1998). The microeconomic foundations of economic development [parts I and II]. In *The Global Competitiveness Report 1998* (pp. 38-63). Geneva: World Economic Forum.

Porter, M. E. (2000). Location, competition, and economic development: Local clusters in a global economy. *Economic Development Quarterly 14*(1), 15-34.

PR Newswire. (1998, October 28). *"Crabs mean business: Conectiv launches business attraction campaign in Northeast."* [Press release].

PR Newswire. (2011, December 29). *"California Redevelopment Association and League of California Cities Urge Immediate Legislative Action to Revive Redevelopment in Wake of State Supreme Court's Ruling Abolishing This Vital Job-Creating Tool."* [Press release]. Retrieved from URL http://www.bizjournals.com/prnewswire/press_releases/2011/12/29/SF28329.

Premus, R. (1982, June). *Location of high technology firms and regional economic development.* Washington, D.C.: Subcommittee on Monetary and Fiscal Policy of the Joint Economic Committee, U.S. Congress, G.P.O.

Reed, L. W. (1996). Time to end the economic war between the states. *Regulation 19*(2), 35-44.

Reese, L. A., & Fasenfest, D. (1997). What works best?: Values and the evaluation of local economic development policy. *Economic Development Quarterly 11*, 195-221.

Reese, L. A., & Ohren, J. F. (1999). You get what you pay for: Agency resources and local economic development policies. *Journal of Public Budgeting, Accounting, & Financial Management, 11*(3), 431-469.

Reese, L. A., & Rosenfeld, R. A. (2002). *The Civic Culture of Local Economic Development,* Thousand Oaks, CA: Sage Publications.

Reich, R. (1983). *The next American frontier.* New York: Penguin Books.

Reich, R. (1991). *The work of nations.* New York: First Vintage Books.

Reich, R. (1998). *Locked in the cabinet.* New York: First Vintage Books.

Reynolds, P., & White, S. B. (1997). *The entrepreneurial process: Economic growth, men, women, and minorities.* Westport, CT: Quorum Books.

Rigby, D. L., & Essletzbichler, J. (2002). Agglomeration economies and productivity differences in U.S. cities. *Journal of Economic Geography.* 2(4), 407-432.

Riper, T. V. (2008, January 17). Why Wal-Mart may just be good for the U.S. *Forbes.* Retrieved April 17, 2012, from http://www.msnbc.msn.com/id/22719054/ns/business-forbes_com/t/why-wal-mart-may-just-be-good-us/#.T43CnbNSRWw

Rondinelli, D. A., Burpitt, W. J. (2000). Do government incentives attract and retain international investment? A study of foreign-owned firms in North Carolina. *Policy Sciences, 33,* 181-205.

Rosenau, P. V. (1999). Introduction: The strengths and weaknesses of public-private policy partnerships. *The American Behavioral Scientist, 43*(1), 10-35.

Rosenbloom, D. H., & Kravchuk, R. S. (2002). *Public administration: Understanding management, politics, and law in the public sector* (5th ed.), New York: McGraw-Hill.

Ross, D., & Friedman, R. E. (1990). The emerging third wave: new economic development strategies. *Entrepreneurial Economy Review, 90,* 3-10.

Rubin, B. M., & Wilder, M. G. (1989). Urban enterprise zones: Employment impacts and fiscal incentives. *Journal of the American Planning Association, 55*(4), 418-431.

Rubin, H. (1986). Local economic development organizations and the activities of small cities in encouraging economic growth. *Policy Studies Journal, 14,* 363-388.

Rubin, H. J. (1988) Shoot anything that flies; Claim anything that falls: Conversations with economic development practitioners. *Economic Development Quarterly, 2*(3), 236-251.

Rubin, I. S. & Rubin, H. J. (1987). Economic development incentives: The poor (cities) pay more. *Urban Affairs Quarterly, 23*(1), 37-62.

Ruigrok, W., & van Tulder, R., (1995). *The logic of international restructuring.* London: Routledge.

Rulon, M. (2004, February 23). Sweet deal won uranium plant from Kentucky: Bottom-line cost advantage aided Ohio's courtship. *The Courier-Journal,* p. F1.

Rusk, D. (1995). *Cities without suburbs* (2nd ed.). Washington, D.C.: The Woodrow Wilson Center Press.

Salinas, P. W. (1986). Urban growth, subemployment, and mobility. In E. Bergman (Ed.), *Local economies in transition.* Durham, N.C.: Duke University Press.

Salvesen, D., & Renski, H. (2003, January). *The importance of quality of life in the location decisions of new economy firms.* Chapel Hill, NC: Center for Urban and Regional Studies, The University of North Carolina at Chapel Hill.

Savas, E. (2000). *Privatization and public-private partnerships.* New York: Seven Bridges Press, LLC.

Savitch, H. V., & Kantor, P. (2002). *Cities in the international marketplace: The political economy of urban development in North America and Western Europe.* Princeton, N.J.: Princeton University Press.

Savitch, H. V., & Vogel, R. K. (2000). Paths to new regionalism. *State and local government review. 32*(3), 158-168.

Savitch, H. V., & Vogel, R. K. (Eds.). (1996). *Regional politics: America in a post-city age.* Thousand Oaks, CA: Sage Publications, Inc.

Sbragia, A. (1996). *Debt wish: Entrepreneurial cities, U.S. federalism, and economic development.* Pittsburgh: University of Pittsburgh Press.

Schmenner, R. W. (1982). *Making business location decisions.* Englewood Cliffs, N.J.: Prentice-Hall.Siegel, B., & Waxman, A. (2001, June). *Third-tier cities: Adjusting to the New Economy.* Somerville, MA: Mt. Auburn Associates, Inc.

Schmenner, R. W. (1994). Service firm location decisions: Some Midwestern evidence. *International Journal of Service Industry Management, 5*(3), 35-56.

Schmitter, P. (1974). Still the century of corporatism? *Review of Politics, 36*, 85-131.

Schneider, M. (1986). Fragmentation and the growth of local government. *Public Choice, 48*, 255-263.

Schneider, M. (1992). Undermining the growth machine: The missing link between local economic development and fiscal payoffs. *Journal of Politics, 54*, 214-230.

Schumpeter, J. A. (1934). *Theory of economic development: An inquiry into profits, capital, credit, interest and the business cycle.* Cambridge: Harvard University Press, Cambridge. Translated by R. Opie.

Schwarz, J. E., & Volgy, T. J. (1992, September). *The impacts of economic development strategies on wages: Exploring the effect on public policy at the local level.* Paper presented at the annual meeting of the American Political Science Association, Chicago, IL.

Seley, J. E. (1981). Targeting economic development: An examination of the needs of small business. *Economic Geography, 57*(1), 34-51.

Semiconductor Industry Association (2012). Retrieved from http://www.siaonline. org/galleries/gsrfiles/GSR_0812.pdf

Sharp, E. B. (1991). Institutional manifestations of accessibility and urban economic development polity. *The Western Political Quarterly, 44*(1), 129-147.

Siegel, B., & Waxman, A. (2001). *Third tier cities: Adjusting to the new economy.* Washington, D.C.: U.S. Economic Development Administration.

Siegel, F. (1997). *The future once happened here: New York, D.C., L.A., and the fate of America's big cities.* New York: The Free Press.

Sierra Madre Community Redevelopment Agency. (2012). Required Obligation Payment Schedule (Per AB 26- 34167 and 34169). Sierra Madre, CA.

Sievert, D. M., & Dodge, J. W., Jr. (2001). *Introduction to economics.* Waukesha, WI: Glengarry Publishing.

Simon H. (1957) *Models of man, social and rational: Mathematical essays on rational human behavior in a social setting.* New York: John Wiley.

Singh, Vishal P., Karsten T. Hansen, and Robert C. Blattberg. "Impact of a Wal-Mart Supercenter on a Traditional Supermarket: An Empirical Investigation." *Chicagobooth.edu.* University of Chicago, Booth School of Business, Feb. 2004. Web. 2 May 2012.

Sjoquist, D. L. (1982). The effect of the number of local governments on central city expenditures. *National Tax Journal, 35*(1), 79-88.

Smith, A. (1776). *An inquiry into the nature and causes of the wealth of nations.* London: W. Strahan and T. Cadell.

Spindler, C. J. (1994). Winners and losers in industrial recruitment: Mercedes-Benz and Alabama. *State and Local Government Review, 26*(3), 192-204.

Stiglitz, J. E., & Wallsten, S. J. (1999). Public-private technology partnerships: Promises and pitfalls. *The American Behavioral Scientist, 43*(1), 52-73.

Stansel, D. (2011). Why some cities are growing and others shrinking. *Cato Journal, 31*(1), 285-303.

Stone, C. N. (1989). *Regime politics: Governing Atlanta, 1946-1988.* Lawrence, KS: University Press of Kansas.

Stone, Kenneth E., Georgeanne Artz, and Albery Myles. "The Economic Impact of Wal-Mart Supercenters on Existing Businesses in Mississippi." *Mississippi University Extension Service* (2002). Print.

Stutzer, M. J. (1985). The statewide economic impact of small-issue industrial revenue bonds. *Federal Reserve Bank of Minneapolis Quarterly Review, Spring,* 2-13.

Sullivan, D. M. (2002). Local governments as risk-takers and risk-reducers: An examination of business subsidies and subsidy controls. *Economic Development Quarterly, 16*(2), 115-126.

Tabachnick, B. G., & Fidell, L. S. (2001). *Using multivariate statistics* (4th ed.). Needham Heights, MA: Allyn and Bacon.

Tannenwald, R. (1997). State regulatory policy and economic development. *New England Economic Review,* (March), 83-99.

Thompson, J. R. (1989). The Toyota decision. *Economic Development Review,* 7(4), 21-23.

Thomson will cut 820 jobs at Indiana plant. (2003, June 14). *The Courier-Journal,* p. B7.

Thottam, J. (2003). Where the good jobs are going. *Time.* August 4, 2003, 36-39.

Tiebout, C. M. (1956). A pure theory of local expenditures. In P. C. Cheshire & A. W. Evans (Eds.), *Urban and Regional Economics* (pp. 416-424). Brookfield, VT: Edward Elgar Publishing Company.

Tiebout, C. M. (1956). Regional and interregional input-output models: An appraisal. In P. C. Cheshire & A. W. Evans (Eds.), *Urban and regional economics* (pp. 140-147). Brookfield, VT: Edward Elgar Publishing Company.

Tolbert, C. M., Lyson, T. A., & Irwin, M. D. (1998). Local capitalism, civic engagement, and socioeconomic well-being. *Social Forces, 77*(2), 401-427.

Tompkins, W. (2004, March 4). 'It's great to have a win': New call center will bring 1,600 jobs to Louisville. *The Courier-Journal,* pp. F1-2.

U.S. Department of Commerce. (2003). What is economic development? Retrieved February 27, 2003, from http://www.osec.doc.gov/eda/html/2a1_whatised.htm userobject15ai1729735.html

U.S. General Accounting Office. (1988, December). Enterprise zones, lessons from the Maryland experience. (Report to Congressional Requesters). Washington, D.C.: Author.

Ullman, J. B. (2002). Structural equation modeling. In. B. G. Tabachnick and L. S. Fidell (Eds.), *Using multivariate statistics* (4th ed) (pp. 653-771). Needham Heights, MA: Allyn & Bacon.

United Parcel Service. 2001a. United Parcel Service Fact Sheet, Retrieved September 24, 2001 from http://pressroom.ups.com/about/facts/view/1,1415,267,00.html

United Parcel Service. 2001c. Welcome to UPSjobs.com, Retrieved October 31, 2001 from www.ups.jobs.com/.

University of Kentucky New Economy Committee (2001, October). *New Economy regional plan for the greater Lexington area.* Retrieved March 24, 2004, from http://www.rgs.uky.edu/neweconomyoverview.pdf

Urata, S., & Kawai, H. (2000). The determinants of the location of foreign direct investment by Japanese small and medium-sized enterprises. *Small Business Economics, 15*(2), 79-90.

Van Dusen Wishard, W. (1999). What the future holds: Three themes that affect America and the world. In F. Maidment (Ed.), *Annual editions: International Business* (pp. 91-94). Guilford, CT: McGraw-Hill/Dushkin.

Vaughn, R. J. (1980). State tax incentives: How effective are they? *Commentary, 4*(1), 3-5.

Vernon, R. (1966). *The myth of urban problems.* Boston: Harvard University Press.

Vogel, R. K. (1997). National urban policy. In R. K. Vogel (Ed.), *Handbook of research on urban politics and policy in the United States,* Greenwood Press: Westport, CT.

Wade, S. (1999, August 2). "New Neighbors; Linking immigrants with employers: Cuban refugees begin UPS jobs," *The Louisville Courier Journal.*

Walker, R. T., & Greenstreet, D. (1991). The effect of government incentives and assistance on location and job growth in manufacturing. *Regional Studies, 25*(1), 13-30.

Walzer, N., & Jacobs, B. D. (Eds.). (1998). *Public-private partnerships for local economic development.* Westport, CT: Praeger.

Wassmer, R. W., & Anderson, J. E. (2001). Bidding for business: new evidence on the effect of locally offered economic development incentives in a metropolitan area. *Economic Development Quarterly, 15*(2), 132-148.

Wasylenko, M. (1987). Fiscal decentralization and economic development. *Public Budgeting and Finance,* (Winter), 57-71.

Wasylenko, M. (1997). Taxation and economic development: The state of the economic literature. *New England Economic Review,* (March), 37-52.

Wasylenko, M., & McGuire, T. (1985). Jobs and taxes: The effect of business climate on states' employment growth rates. *National Tax Journal, 38*(4), 497-512.

Weinberger, J. (2001). Conservatism. In S. M. Lipset (Ed.) *Political philosophy: theories, thinkers, and concepts.* (pp.37-45). Washington, D.C.: CQ Press.

Weinberger, J. (2001). Liberalism. In S. M. Lipset (Ed.) *Political philosophy: theories, thinkers, and concepts.* (pp.37-45). Washington, D.C.: CQ Press.

Weiss, C. (1998) *Evaluation* (2nd ed.) Upper Saddle River, NJ: Prentice Hall.

Wells, S. (2013, April 18). Beaverton All Smiles about Nike's Washington County Expansion Plans. *Beaverton Valley Times.* Retrieved from http://portlandtribune.com/bvt/15-news/150729-beaverton-all-smiles-about-nikes-washington-county-expansion-plans

West Virginia Development Office (n.d.) Workforce development for employers. Retrieved December 31, 2003 from: http://www.wvdo.org/workforce / employers.html.

Wherry, R. J. Sr. (1931). A new formula for predicting the shrinkage of the coefficient of multiple correlation. *Annals of Mathematical Statistics, 2,* 440-457.

Whitney, M. (2003). Manufacturing survivors: Capital investment is their lifeline. *Tooling and Production, 69*(6), 44.

Williams, T. P. (2003). *Moving to public-private partnerships: Learning from experience around the world.* Arlington, VA: IBM Endowment for The Business of Government.

Willon, P. (2010, March 6). L.A. council votes to cut taxes for Internet-based firms . *Los Angeles Times.*

Wilson, W. (1887) The study of administration, in J. M. Shafritz & A. Hyde (Eds.) (1992), *Classics of Public Administration,* (3rd ed.) Bellmont, CA: Wadsworth.

Wilson, W. J. (1987). *The truly disadvantaged: The inner city, the underclass, and public policy.* Chicago: The University of Chicago Press.

Wood, R. (1961). *1400 governments.* Cambridge, MA: Harvard University Press.

Woodward, D. P. (1992). Locational determinants of the Japanese manufacturing start-ups in the United States. *The Southern Economic Journal, 58*(3), 699-708.

Wu, A., & Wu, R. (2003). A trip to the construction site of dreams. *Zhejiang Online,* Retrieved September 20, 2003, from http://www.zjol.com.cn/gb/node2/node138665/node139012/node149968/node162419/node162422/

Wyly, E. K., Glickman, N. J., & Lahr, M. L. (1998). A top ten list of things to know about American cities. *Cityscape 3*(3), 7-32.

Younas, J., & Nandwa, B. (2010). Financial openness and capital mobility: A dynamic panel analysis. *International Review of Applied Economics, 24,* 239-246.

Zinger, J. T., Blanco, H., Zanibbi, L., & Mount, J. (1996). An empirical study of the small business support network–the entrepreneur's perspective. *Canadian Journal of Administrative Sciences, 13*(4), 347-357.

Zodrow, G. (2010). Capital mobility and capital tax competition. *National Tax Journal, 63,* 865-902.